WESTMAR COLLEGE

W9-AFB-719

READING AND STUDY SKILLS
IN THE SECONDARY SCHOOL

GARLAND REFERENCE LIBRARY
OF SOCIAL SCIENCE
(VOL. 309)

READING AND STUDY SKILLS IN THE SECONDARY SCHOOL
A Sourcebook

Joyce N. French

89-1200

GARLAND PUBLISHING, INC. • NEW YORK & LONDON
1986

© 1986 Joyce N. French
All rights reserved

Library of Congress Cataloging-in-Publication Data

French, Joyce N., 1929–
  Reading and study skills in the secondary school.

  (Garland reference library of social science ; vol.
309)
  Includes indexes.
  1. Reading (Secondary education) 2. Study, Method of.
I. Title. II. Series: Garland reference library of
social science ; v. 309.
LB1632.F74 1986   428.4′07′12   85-45144
ISBN 0-8240-8724-0 (alk. paper)

Printed on acid-free, 250-year-life paper
Manufactured in the United States of America

TO DON

CONTENTS

PART A   THE PROCESS, THE TEXT, THE TASKS

Taking Tests

Underlining, Notetaking and Summarizing

SQ3R

Writing

PART B   STRATEGIES FOR INSTRUCTING

PREFACE

This book examines the various reading and study skills and
strategies students need to function in the secondary school of
today as well as in the later world of work or further schooling.
However, in order to accomplish this goal we need to consider more
than just a hierarchy of skills and a list of strategies. We must
address the issue of not just what to teach, but how to teach, how
to involve students in the process, how to involve professionals in
the process. The realities of schooling demand that it is not
sufficient to identify what should be taught. We must also identify
the vehicles for making it happen.

This sounds wonderful. You will surely know just what to do
after reading the text and researching the bibliography. Actually,
we have some bad news and some good news for you. The bad news is
that we do not have one model of reading, one theory of how to teach
reading, one set of recipes that we know will work with every
student. There are many uncertainties here: uncertainties in terms
of conflicting research results or lack of research results;
uncertainties in terms of which strategy may be best for a
particular student in meeting the demands of a particular school or
teacher. The good news is that these very uncertainties can make us
better teachers. MacGinitie has written of "The Power of
Uncertainty," asserting that not only is uncertainty part of the
very process of reading, but that "in a very real way, the good
teacher is uncertain, seeking" (p. 682). This book is designed to
help you in your process of examining these uncertainties and
seeking ways to assist students in becoming willing, effective
readers. "Only an uncertain person can learn; only an uncertain
person can show how learning is done. That is the power of
uncertainty" (p. 679).

The topics chosen have been organized into two categories.
Part A includes those items dealing with what needs to be taught,
what students need to learn. A theoretical framework is provided
identifying reading models and reading processes. We look at
secondary schools, the problems, realities, and potentials they
provide for reading instruction. We agree with Guthrie that "we
must move beyond debates of reading to more specific discussions of
word recognition, sentence processing, text comprehension, critical
evaluation and communicative functions" (p. 751). Those specific
areas are addressed. The remainder of Part A looks at the specifics
of the tasks of thinking and studying with various reading units and
with a wide variety of strategies.

Part B is concerned with the question of how to make this happen: how to motivate students, how to assess their reading competencies, how to utilize the potential of computers, how to provide for a variety of student needs, and how to involve content teachers in this process.

Each chapter contains an overview of the particular topic and an annotated bibliography. The text examines issues, highlights research, and provides practical suggestions for the content and/or reading classroom. In doing this, it draws on the items in the bibliography. When appropriate we point out contradictions or disagreements among the authors. When possible, the bibliography has been subdivided according to topic. This has not been feasible in every chapter because authors often tend to write about overlapping topics or focus on one topic but relate it to others. This tendency makes for interesting, productive reading but not always for a neat categorization of citations.

The bibliographies were developed using RESOURCES IN EDUCATION and CURRENT INDEX TO JOURNALS IN EDUCATION as the primary sources. In addition, EDUCATION INDEX was consulted. BOOKS IN PRINT was a valuable tool in identifying current books on the topic. Finally, journals and publishers, brochures were scanned thoroughly and periodically to insure that a broad group of books and periodicals was surveyed. Each item was examined in depth by the author.

Items included in the bibliography were chosen because of their impact on our knowledge of the field, their relevance to the secondary classroom, and the ease with which they could be obtained. With only a very few exceptions, all citations date from 1980 to 1984. This was done to insure that the citations were current and that the bibliographies would contain fresh material and would not duplicate older sources. We recommend that the reader review the many excellent bibliographies provided in the books and periodicals cited to obtain older citations. The citations provide information on both theoretical, research based topics and on classroom applications. In the case of research, we have frequently cited articles that summarize a body of research studies. Occasionally, we have cited the primary source, usually because it provides an example of something particularly pertinent to the secondary teacher.

The book is designed with the content teacher and with the reading teacher as the intended audience. The aim is to have these two groups of professionals achieve a working relationship that results in more effective reading/study skill instruction for students. It is also designed for both the preservice and the inservice teacher. The preservice or inexperienced teacher may want to read the text and the bibliography, sampling relevant items in

the bibliography in the library. The student can use the book,
particularly the bibliography, as a research tool. The inservice
teacher may want to use this book differently.   Decide on your
purpose in reading and evaluate how much you already know about the
topics. Then, either read the whole book or choose relevant topics
to meet your particular needs. The book is designed to be used in a
variety of ways. We hope you take advantage of this.

    One of the features of this book is that it requires active
information processing on the part of the reader.   A multitude of
suggestions are made to the reader, but detailed examples are not
provided. Rather, the reader is directed to a variety of sources
for those examples.   We are asking you to be active readers,
processing the information on a variety of levels and adapting it to
your unique situation in order to make the information your own.
You are independent learners and you are in control. The task that
remains is for you to enable your students to achieve this state.

    Finally, a special thank you to Anne McKillop for her
thoughtful reading of the manuscript and for her very useful
comments.

REFERENCES

Guthrie, John T. "Meaning of 'Reading.'"   JOURNAL OF READING 26
    (May 1983): 750-751.

MacGinitie, Walter H.   "The Power of Uncertainty." JOURNAL OF
    READING 26 (May 1983): 677-683.

READING AND STUDY SKILLS
IN THE SECONDARY SCHOOL

CHAPTER 1

THE PROCESS OF READING

The need for teachers to live with uncertainty probably starts with the literature on reading theory, particularly that relating to comprehension. Because of the lack of one generally accepted theory or model of reading, supported by empirical data, we must examine a variety of reading theories. However, as teachers, we need to be concerned not only with theoretical constructs of the reading process and of comprehension but also with notions of how learners learn, how readers develop and mature, and how this relates to characteristics of skilled and unskilled readers. By putting these pieces together we can assemble a framework for viewing current school programs as well as for formulating guidelines for effective reading programs and strategies for secondary school students and teachers.

Looking at Theory

Effective Learners

To determine how to teach reading to secondary students we must begin with a look at the larger process of how children learn and remember. This is the first piece of our framework. A great deal has been written about this topic. Since the focus of this book is on reading we can only summarize some of this theory. Your courses on educational psychology are relevant here in fleshing out a brief quote.

Brown, Bransford, Ferrara and Campione (12) after summarizing relevant research have proposed that:

> To be an effective learner, she (the learner) will need to know something about her own characteristics, her available learning activities, the demand characteristics of various learning tasks, and the inherent structure of materials (Flavell & Wellman, 1977). She must tailor her activities finely to the competing demands of all these forces in order to be a flexible and effective learner. In other words, she must learn how to learn. (p. 85)

Now, consider how reading theory relates to this model of the effective learner.

Reading Theory

The second piece of the framework is concerned with reading theory.   All theories of reading, in some fashion, must deal with the two variables of the reader and the text as well as how each contributes to the reader's comprehension of the text (19). It may seem an over-simplification to reduce the complexities involved in reading comprehension to these two basic variables; however, this strategy will give the practitioner a useful place to start.   The difference between theories seems to arise from the emphasis each theorist places on each variable and how the variables are seen to interact (if they do).   See Figure 1 for some possible characteristics of each variable, as suggested by the various theorists. This graphic overview provides a road map for the reader in analyzing the different theories.

Figure 1

THE READER

Cognitive Factors   Linguistic Factors

Age related characteristics   Language background
Interest/motivation   Competence with
Prior knowledge of content   graphemic,
  and text structure   syntactic and
Strategies for: semantic cues
  information processing   Strategies for
  problem solving   processing
  remembering   linguistic cues
  self-monitoring

THE TEXT

Semantic Features   Linguistic Features

Hierarchical   Clarity of Expression
  organization of ideas   Syntactic complexity
Text structure   Linguistic complexity
Complexity of ideas
Redundancy of ideas

Again, at the risk of over-simplification, let's look at some general categories of reading theory and at some of the major ideas associated with reading. Keep in mind the two variables and their characteristics. Consider how comprehension occurs.   Theoretical approaches to reading include:

Bottom-up. The reader moves from individual word and sentence units to meaning. The demands of the text are critical, with the reader reacting to them. The process is "text" or "data" driven. (7, 9, 10)

Top-down. The reading process starts with the reader and with meaning.   The reader uses his prior knowledge to predict words and content and uses available content to predict future meaning. The process is viewed as "concept" driven. (9, 10)

Interactive. The reader and the text interact, with both variables influencing the efficiency and effectiveness of reading comprehension. (6, 9, 10, 14, 19)

Constructive. The reader integrates the information presented, its context and his background knowledge, using these to construct meaning that may go beyond what is actually written. (5, 8, 17)

Levels of processing and attention. Reading requires more than appropriate background knowledge and linguistic and cognitive skills. Information is processed at a hierarchy of levels, from the physical and sensory to the semantic. At the semantic level, associations are made with prior knowledge. The "depth of processing" influences both comprehension and recall of information. Reading involves attending and the self-monitoring of comprehension and memory. (3)

What does all of this imply about reading and the secondary school student? The problem of which theory or approach is "correct" is for us, as teachers, probably unsolvable. We can recognize elements of all these theories in our students and in ourselves as readers. The poor reader, with no background in chemistry, who is struggling with decoding words, identifying vocabulary and understanding concepts often appears to be "text driven." He must deal with each unit of the text. He reads and may not even know that he has not understood. He may understand but only partially. Some of the author's message is lost. Unfortunately, he does not recognize this. He may not be able to monitor his comprehension and/or take steps to improve it. However, when the same reader is reading about soccer, video games or automobiles, he predicts some content, vocabulary and meaning based on what he knows. He isn't stumped by difficult words. He knows what a carburetor is and can read the word. He has prior knowledge and uses it.

It is difficult for us as practitioners to view reading as either/or, as one theory or another. Crismore's (14) notion that readers operate on a continuum of focusing on getting the message to predicting the message is appealing. He suggests that the reader's place on the continuum is determined by his purpose in reading, his familiarity with the message, his interest and motivation; and the discourse type and complexity. We will see these factors interacting in different ways when our reader is reading a chemistry text and an account of a soccer game.

What does the literature say about our reader? Prior knowledge, or schema, is important. Schema for both content and process affect comprehension and recall. For the content factors Crismore (14) cites the need for knowledge of content or topic (topical or content schemata) and knowledge of the text structure or text genre which is used to present the content (text structure or organization schemata). Process factors refer to <u>how</u> information is processed. This process schemata includes "attending, encoding, generating, inferencing, retrieving and the self-monitoring of these procedures" (p. 8). Anderson and Pearson (1), in addition to supporting the critical relationship between schema and comprehension, stress that "the reader's schema is a structure that facilitates planful retrieval of text information from memory and permits reconstruction of elements that were not learned or have been forgotten" (p. 285).

Interest in the material and motivation to accomplish the task are critical elements in successful reading according to Tonjes and Zintz (11). Little or, at best, limited progress, particularly with secondary students, can be made without considering the affective dimension of reading.

Readers need to be able to monitor their comprehension by being aware of what skills and strategies they should be using and by being able to check the success themselves and make changes if needed (2).

The goal of reading must be to learn. Brown (3) states it clearly and succinctly. Students "must learn how to learn from reading" (p. 50). Many of them do not do this automatically. There appear to be a number of variables involved in learning from text. Brown, Campione and Day (13) advocate that often students need to be trained to learn from texts. They state:

> The essential aim of training is to make the trainee more aware of the active nature of learning and the importance of employing problem-solving, trouble-shooting routines to enhance understanding. If learners can be made aware of (1) basic strategies for reading and remembering, (2) simple rules of text construction, (3) differing demands of a variety of texts to which their information can be put, and (4) the importance of activating any background knowledge which they may have, they cannot help but become more effective learners. Such self-awareness is a prerequisite for self-regulation, the ability to orchestrate, monitor, and check one's own cognitive activities. (p. 20)

These notions of the reader are all reinforced when we think of our student reading the chemistry text and the newspaper report of the soccer game. Pezdek's (8) focus in comprehension and memory on the "interaction of the information presented with the context in which it is presented and the existing knowledge schemata of the subject" (p. 68) also gives us a very useful way of looking at our student. The unskilled reader who is also a soccer player may successfully read about the report of a local soccer game in the newspaper but he may have enormous difficulty reading a detailed chapter in a sports text on the history and theory of soccer in Argentina. His knowledge about the game and the particular players allows him to comprehend literally and draw inferences in the first situation, while the same knowledge is insufficient in the second situation.

The language, sentence structure and text structure in the newspaper are fairly simple and familiar. The information is limited and deals with one aspect of soccer presented in a simple, obvious text structure probably organized chronologically. Much more and more varied information is presented in the sports text undoubtedly using a complex text structure.

Another area which appears obvious to secondary teachers is that of the connection between reading and writing. We expect students to read and to write about their reading. The question theorists and researchers have been grappling with is the effect that one has on the other. Crismore (14) raises a number of issues here. Are the processes similar? Is one an outgrowth of the other or are they mutually reinforcing? His tentative conclusion is that "reading and writing are reciprocal and mutually reinforcing processes because both involve the structuring of meaning" (p. 15). This emphasis on common cognitive processes is echoed by others. Easton (15), for example, stresses the common elements of the two processes, also emphasizing the cognitive and linguistic similarities.

Both Crismore (14) and Easton (15) discuss the idea that writing gives the reader insights into the role of the author and the strategies he uses to convey ideas and information. Sanacore (18) is explicit in stressing that "by encouraging students to identify and write various types of discourse (and discourse forces), teachers can help them understand different processes and constructs. This awareness can improve reading comprehension, since students gain insights and reinforce behaviors that are similar in both writing and reading" (p. 717).

The question still remains though, does writing improve reading comprehension? Gebhard (16) says yes, asserting that it has been demonstrated that "reading and writing are not only complementary language processes but that acquiring encoding and composing skills assists students in developing decoding and comprehending skills" (p. 207). Although not everyone is willing to go this far, there is substantial agreement that both reading and writing require thinking (including abstracting, categorizing, generalizing, etc.) and a knowledge of text structure as well as content. Although the research here is not conclusive, there is certainly a beginning base to support the premise that writing can improve reading. The notion seems logical and is appealing to us as teachers.

In understanding the impact of theory, think about your students. How many times have you said to the reader "pay attention to what you're reading!" Unfortunately, there seems to be more involved than merely attending to the words. How deeply we attend, how much we are involved with what the writer says, what we do with the writer's words and ideas are aspects of attention that seem to have a role in our comprehension.

The unskilled reader with little knowledge of chemistry is likely to skim the chemistry text. Simply reading to the end of the chapter is sufficient activity for him. At best, he may underline

items that seem important. Sometimes everything seems important.
The account of the soccer game is another matter. The reader jots
down the three plays that seem particularly useful. He makes a
diagram of the plays and the players. He thinks about the strengths
and weaknesses of the other players on his team. He puts the names
of the players into his diagram to propose these other possibilities
to the coach and the team. It becomes clear to him if he has
misunderstood the soccer text because during and after reading he is
actively involved with comprehending and applying the information.
This may not be the case with the chemistry text. He may or may not
realize when he has misunderstood the chemistry material. You have
seen him monitor his own comprehension when he says "No, that's
wrong. I don't think that could be right." He may go back and
reread some or all of the text. However think of the circumstances
in which that reaction occurs.

Reading is unquestionably a complex activity. We need to
examine all aspects of it in order to work effectively with
students.

Skilled Readers

We have looked at characteristics of effective learners and
critical elements of reading. We now need to put the two together
and look at skilled readers. What can we expect of them? Reading
theory, combined with empirical research has provided some
definitions of a "good" or "skilled" reader. Using your prior
knowledge and experience, you can probably make some predictions
about what will be on that list. Use the following summary, adapted
from Brown (3, p. 49), as a guidepost in your reading. Test the
characteristics of a "skilled" reader against those of your students
or against yourself as a reader.

Skilled readers:

know how to learn from reading.

are actively engaged in the process of gathering information,
hypothesizing content and concepts, and evaluating the
sufficiency and reliability of information.

monitor their own comprehension, recall and purpose.

In order to appreciate the skilled reader, consider briefly
some differences between unskilled and skilled readers.

Focus. Skilled readers focus on meaning. Unskilled readers
tend to focus more on decoding skills. Whether this is a
function of their capabilities or of how they have been taught
is still open to question.

Materials. Skilled readers use reading materials as a source
of information. Unskilled readers use materials as a way of
gaining reading skills as well as information. Think of the
problem this causes high school students when everyone in the

class has the same biology text.

Instruction. Skilled readers have control over their own acquisition of information and can use instruction as a way of integrating ideas and concepts concerning content. Unskilled readers must rely on instruction for much information. The locus of control is in the hands of the teacher. Instruction for these students must have a dual purpose of acquiring content information and concepts as well as reading and learning skills.

Summary

In building a framework for looking at schools, we have highlighted some requirements for effective learning, various approaches to the reading process, and characteristics of readers, both skilled and unskilled. Now we will look at how this relates to the current status of reading in secondary schools.

Reading in Secondary Schools

Reading Achievement

First, let us look at the status of the reading achievement in secondary schools. Are high school students skilled readers? Are they comprehending written information in a way that will enable them to be successful in jobs or in post-secondary schools? The current popular dissatisfaction with the reading achievement of our high school grades is evident from the fact that over half of the states have instituted minimum competency requirements for high school graduation. Colleges and universities have begun skill centers. A growing field for teachers is developmental and remedial college instruction. Professional organizations concerned with basic skills on the college level have been founded. Business and industry have started programs in skill instruction because workers come to them unable to read on-the-job materials. There is a growing outcry and concern over problems of adult literacy. These developments highlight perceived and real problems with reading achievement in secondary schools.

Next, consider some data developed by the National Assessment of Educational Progress (34). This group studied three skill areas: reference skills, literal comprehension and inferential comprehension comparing 9-, 13- and 17-year-olds on three different occasions—1970-71, 1974-75 and 1979-80. Between 1971 and 1980 9-year-olds showed a significant gain in all three skill areas. Overall scores for 13- and 17-year-olds did not show any significant gain over the ten-year period. Overall it appears that the youngest age group is improving and the older two are holding their own. However, literal comprehension increased significantly for 13-year-olds and inferential comprehension declined significantly for 17-year-olds. This decline was the highest for the highest achievers. The decline in inferential comprehension for 17-year-olds is worrisome because that is the heart of adult reading. It is even more worrisome because the decline was the most serious for the best readers.

In addition, according to Petrosky's (25) analysis of the data, "students seem not to have learned the problem-solving strategies and critical thinking skills by which to look for evidence to support their interpretations and judgments...almost none of the seventeen year olds demonstrated any knowledge or use of techniques for analyzing a passage" (p. 16). In evaluating written materials, students demonstrated a superficial approach to the task. Evaluation criteria were vague and general, with little supporting evidence for the conclusion presented.

Two other interesting items emerged from the study. All groups thought it was important to read but the percentage who enjoyed reading and who read almost daily declined with age. For 13- and 17-year-olds, time spent on homework tended to be associated positively with performance on the reading comprehension tests.

How can we explain these results? Chall (29) looks back to the instruction students received in elementary school. She hypothesizes that the gains for 9-year-olds "may be attributed, at least partly, to the stronger reading instruction in school and to the stronger home reading environment of the 1980 cohort as compared to the 1971" (p. 8). Secondary school students of today did not always receive the instruction they needed. This has a cumulative effect.

Another factor here might be the difficulty of the material read by secondary students. Chall identifies the increased demands made on the reader by more "complicated, literary, abstract, and technical" (p. 11) texts as well as increased world knowledge, cognitive abilities, and language skills as contributing to the "deceleration in reading achievement" (ibid.) as students get older. This is echoed by Calfee and Curley (4).

> By the time students reach junior high school, they are expected to handle texts comparable to those encountered by adults--the vocabulary is determined by the topic rather than by word counts; the sentences are longer and more complex; the pictures are gone; both content and structures may be unfamiliar. We believe that many youngsters fail to make the step from the primer to the textbook. (p. 162)

The problems of inappropriate elementary instruction and difficult texts and concepts may be compounded by instruction or the lack of it offered in the secondary school. Nelson and Herber (23) suggest that "secondary school reading programs rarely provide instruction in the skills most needed for successful performance in secondary schools. The NAEP results should not be surprising to anyone. Students cannot be held responsible for what schools do not teach" (p. 147). Secondary school reading requires emphasis on word knowledge and meaning, not simply decoding. It requires a holistic approach to text, with an emphasis on meaning and on constructing meaning from text. "This process involves reasoning, reasoning from what is known to what is new, reasoning in, around, and beyond the text material" (24, p. 238).

Petrosky (25) concurs. The performance of secondary students is a "direct reflection of current practices in testing and instruction" (p. 16). We are not teaching or requiring that students develop problem-solving, critical thinking skills.

It appears that in working in secondary schools we are often faced with:

the need to improve overall reading achievement, both maintaining basic skill instruction and improving higher levels of comprehension. (22, 23, 24, 34)

the challenge of working with a wide variety of reading levels in one grade level. (20, 26)

a variety of reading needs, both for skilled and unskilled readers. (20, 22)

Effective Teaching

Second, we need to consider some of the attributes of effective teaching. Since teaching occurs within a school setting, first let's look at the research on effective schools. Much of this has been conducted in elementary schools, with fewer studies in secondary schools. The June 1983 issue of PHI DELTA KAPPAN clearly documents the problems with this body of research, so it may behoove us not to dwell on the findings. However, we certainly have some indications that schools need to be structured to allow learning to take place (28). Stallings, Needels and Stayrook (36), in examining how to teach basic skills in secondary schools, identified the need to provide an orderly atmosphere, an expectation of achievement, access to student information by teachers, and administrative support for teachers' efforts in the classroom and for their professional growth.

Within this setting let's look at the effective teacher. Much of the literature on teacher effectiveness documents the importance of activities such as direct instruction in academic tasks with clearly stated goals and objectives, classroom management that allows learning to take place and provides time-on-task, as well as a classroom atmosphere that encourages learning (21, 28). Pike (33) would consider these as representing teaching as "behaving." She adds another dimension to effective teaching—teaching as "thinking." This is an "inner aspect" of effective teaching that we often overlook. It requires a sophisticated form of planning which is more than sequencing activities. It is selecting a course of action from a variety of alternatives and making decisions and judgments. Teaching based on this kind of planning is "thinking."

Reading teachers expect to teach students a particular sequence of reading skills, probably based on a list provided by the school district or a publisher. This is teaching as "behaving." Teaching as "thinking" is modifying the list and/or the sequence, adding and deleting items, always based on how the student performs, what the classroom and text demands are, and what skills the student identifies as important. It is, in fact, this second aspect that can contribute significantly to the development of skilled readers. The complexity of the task of reading demands "teaching as thinking."

In examining the negative side of the picture Houck (32) has identified specific "barriers" to success. These include:

> (1) the scars from a history of previous unsuccessful attempts to develop reading skills; (2) the student's current attitude toward reading and perhaps school itself; (3) failure to collect instructionally meaningful base-line data needed to guide intervention efforts; (4) failure to commit sufficient time needed to produce improvement; (5) surface behaviors which may be incompatible with remedial efforts; (6) use of remedial techniques and materials that do not respond to the student's age, interests, and sensitivities; and (7) failure to employ a systematic monitoring scheme necessary for ongoing data-based instructional decisions. (p. 30)

Consider how many of these barriers are related to the lack of effective teaching.

School Personnel: Staff and Function

Finally, in looking at schools, we need to define personnel and the programs offered. The staff member traditionally identified to teach reading skills has been the reading specialist. Content teachers have been resistant to teaching reading skills. Frequently they have generally not been trained to teach reading, as Farrell and Cirrincione (31) found in their study of state certification requirements for content teachers. The primary responsibility of content teachers, in fact, is to teach content. "I don't teach reading, I teach literature." Unfortunately, many students can't read the material in the English curriculum. Reading, as Smith and Feathers (35) found in their study of social studies classrooms, is not always "an essential or even central activity in the classes studied" (p. 266). However, because of the widespread nature of the reading problem in secondary schools and in spite of resistance, it has often been suggested that content teachers assume this responsibility (23, 24, 25, 31, 35).

The situation may be changing, albeit slowly and unevenly. Part of the change may come from insuring that content teachers obtain the necessary background in teaching reading and part may come from presenting the need in a reasonable and acceptable manner to content teachers. Farrell and Cirrincione (31) found that an increasing number of states (currently 73%) now have a reading requirement for certification as a content teacher. However, as they point out, we do not have the data to determine the effectiveness of this reading requirement. Singer and Donlan (27) found that content teachers demonstrated less resistance when approached from the perspective of teaching students how to learn from the text.

Perhaps the role of the content teacher is evolving, not as a teacher of reading but as a teacher of thinking, with reading of content material a part of the larger process of thinking.

The role of the reading specialist traditionally has been to help students acquire mastery of reading skills and develop a positive attitude toward reading as well as to assist in choosing text books. However, with our increased knowledge about the learning process as well as the reading process, reading specialists must now also be concerned with learning how to learn, with developing strategies for problem solving and comprehension monitoring which can be transferred to all content areas. The emphasis is on "processing skills" with the teacher as a model (30). We cannot settle for basic skills instruction. As Valmont (37) suggests "Minimum Competency Doesn't Mean Minimum Teaching."

In addition, we cannot work solely with low functioning students in secondary school reading programs. We also need to develop all levels of reading skills for all levels of students (20, 23, 24). The result is that reading programs should include a variety of developmental as well as remedial levels. At all levels reading needs to be taught as a complex, cognitive, linguistic process with content teachers and reading specialists working together to foster the development of skilled readers (22, 26). Reading programs must be geared to the demands of secondary, not elementary, school with a staff development program geared to involve all the professional staff (23).

Summary

The challenge is clear. We have acquired a substantial body of information about the reading process and characteristics of the reader and the text. We have a good sense of what constitutes effective teaching and indications of how to organize and structure programs in secondary schools. There are some uncertainties in all of this. The final research project has not been completed. The final, definitive theory has not been formulated. In spite of this, we know enough to move ahead in our planning for secondary students.

READING AND STUDY SKILLS IN THE SECONDARY SCHOOL

BIBLIOGRAPHY

Looking at Theory

Books

1. Anderson, Richard C., and P. David Pearson. "A Schema-Theoretic View of Basic Processes in Reading Comprehension." HANDBOOK OF READING RESEARCH. Edited by P. David Pearson, Rebecca Barr, Michael L. Kamil and Peter Mosenthal. New York: Longman, 1984, pp. 255-291.

Anderson and Pearson present a clear detailed review of schema theory which is particularly useful to those unfamiliar with the ideas because it includes explanations of the various steps taken in applying schema to a concrete situation. They also examine the relationships among schema and inferences, allocation of attention, and memory. The focus of the chapter on theory and research provides an invaluable framework for other authors' discussions of instructional strategies.

2. Baker, Linda, and Ann L. Brown. "Cognitive Monitoring in Reading." UNDERSTANDING READING COMPREHENSION. Edited by James Flood. Newark, Delaware: International Reading Assn., 1984, pp. 21-44.

Based on the assumption that cognitive monitoring is an essential strategy for readers, Baker and Brown review and critique research methods in the area of cognitive monitoring for comprehension. They also review specific research on cognitive monitoring in nine activities that are important to comprehension, including establishing purpose, modifying rate and strategies, identifying important elements, using structure, using prior knowledge, recognizing contextual constraints, evaluating text, dealing with comprehension failure and establishing standards for assessing your own comprehension level. They conclude that less mature, less competent readers are not as likely as experienced successful readers to use these strategies or to monitor their success in them when they do use them. The authors point out that the causal relationship here is not clear.

3. Brown, Ann L. "Learning How to Learn From Reading." READER MEETS AUTHOR/BRIDGING THE GAP. Edited by Judith A. Langer and M. Trika Smith-Burke. Newark, Delaware: International Reading Assn., 1982, pp. 26-54.

Brown examines learning theory, relating it to the tasks and competencies of skilled readers. The review of theory and research provides a useful framework for understanding both the tasks of reading and the significance of the structure of the instructional situation. While the emphasis is on theory, many practical implications are suggested.

4. Calfee, Robert C., and Robert Curley. "Structures of Prose in the Content Areas." UNDERSTANDING READING COMPREHENSION. Edited by James Flood. Newark, Delaware: International Reading Assn., 1984, pp. 161-180.

   The authors view text structure as a critical element in the comprehension of reading materials for secondary students. They present a detailed and useful discussion of the structures of narrative and expository text.

5. Goodman, Kenneth S. "The Process and Practice of Reading." BECOMING READERS IN A COMPLEX SOCIETY. Eighty-third Yearbook of the National Society for the Study of Education. Edited by Alan C. Purves and Olive Niles. Chicago, Illinois: The University of Chicago Press, 1984, pp. 79-114.

   Goodman views reading as a "meaning-seeking, tentative, selective and constructive" (p. 97) act which uses the writer's control of language and form and the characteristics of the text in the process of the constructing meaning. He examines the cue systems and the cognitive strategies the reader uses in comprehending. Clear examples make this chapter on reading theory useful for the beginning student.

6. Mason, Jana M., and the Staff of the Center for the Study of Reading, University of Illinois. "A Schema-Theoretic View of the Reading Process as a Basis for Comprehension Instruction." COMPREHENSION INSTRUCTION: PERSPECTIVES AND SUGGESTIONS. Edited by Gerald G. Duffy, Laura R. Roehler, and Jana Mason. New York: Longman, 1984, pp. 26-38.

   A brief review of the history of theories of comprehension sets the stage for a thoughtful discussion of the interactive nature of reading comprehension. The interaction between information from the text and from the reader's mind takes place at "many different levels of analysis: lexical, syntactic, semantic, planning and interpretive" (p. 29) and involves the construction of hypotheses about the reading. The refinement of the constructed hypotheses is seen as a process similar to problem solving, requiring interaction between top-down and bottom-up processes. The discussion of "interpretive knowledge" illustrates the importance of knowledge about the form and intent of different kinds of writing.

7. Pearson, P. David, and Kaybeth Camperell. "Comprehension of Text Structures." COMPREHENSION AND TEACHING: RESEARCH REVIEWS. Edited by John T. Guthrie. Newark, Delaware: International Reading Assn., 1981, pp. 27-55.

   Pearson and Camperell have made a complex topic understandable! The examples given make clear the various complex relationships between text structure and comprehension. The review of research on the structure of both sentences and the entire text gives a useful framework for viewing the reading process and provides some suggestions for helping students utilize the various text structures.

8. Pezdek, Kathy. "Arguments for a Constructive Approach to Comprehension and Memory." READING AND UNDERSTANDING. Edited by Frank B. Murray. Newark, Delaware: International Reading Assn., 1980, pp. 40-73.

    Pezdek has identified five characteristics of the constructive processes of comprehension and memory in relation to word meaning, prior knowledge, integration of items in memory, storage in memory of original material, and inferences. She has reviewed research and theory relating the discussion to reading. The focus on memory is particularly useful for the secondary teacher.

9. Readence, John E., Thomas W. Bean, and R. Scott Baldwin. "The Process of Reading to Understand." CONTENT AREA READING: AN INTEGRATED APPROACH. Dubuque, Iowa: Kendall/Hunt, 1981, pp. 10-29.

    The authors have made the complex theory and research relating to reading comprehension understandable and relevant to the secondary classroom. The chapter focuses on the cognitive and linguistic aspects of fluent reading and on their interaction. Illustrative activities give the reader an opportunity to participate in a dialogue with the authors and to experience the complexities of the reading process. Because of this the chapter is particularly useful for the student beginning the study of reading.

10. Samuels, S. Jay, and Michael L. Kamil. "Models of the Reading Process." HANDBOOK OF READING RESEARCH. Edited by P. David Pearson, Rebecca Barr, Michael L. Kamil and Peter Mosenthal. New York: Longman, 1984, pp. 185-224.

    Samuels and Kamil present a detailed history and description of model building in reading, examining bottom-up and interactive models in particular. The material focuses on theory and research and is especially useful for indicating problems with models and directions for future research.

11. Tonjes, Marion J., and Miles V. Zintz. "The Mature Reader: A Self-Assessment." "Promoting Affective Dimensions in Content Reading." TEACHING READING/THINKING/STUDY SKILLS IN CONTENT CLASSROOMS. Dubuque, Iowa: Wm. C. Brown, 1981, pp. 5-52.

    Tonjes and Zintz propose that reading, thinking and studying are interrelated. They present a series of self-assessments for the mature reader to highlight the variety and scope of skills involved and to allow the adult reader to assess individual areas of strengths and weaknesses. In addition, the authors provide a wealth of practical guidelines, self-assessments and activities for teachers in the areas of motivation, attitudes, interests and values. Related theory emphasizing the affective dimensions of motivation is clearly presented. Of particular interest to the secondary teacher is the discussion of nonverbal communication.

Periodicals

12. Brown, Ann L., John D. Bransford, Roberta A. Ferrara, and Joseph C. Campoine. LEARNING, REMEMBERING, AND UNDERSTANDING. (Technical Report No. 244) Urbana: University of Illinois, Center for the Study of Reading, June 1982. 264pp. (ED 217 401)

The authors present a comprehensive review of the literature in these three areas as they relate to academics. The descriptions and analyses of learners, learning variables and the interactions between them, while theoretical, have much relevance for teachers. The discussion of study skills and summarizing as well as metacognition is of particular interest to secondary teachers. The emphasis is on the use of strategies in learning with a recognition of the importance of cognitive, emotional and social variables over a wide age range.

13. Brown, Ann L., Joseph C. Campione, and Jeanne D. Day. "Learning to Learn: On Training Students to Learn from Texts." EDUCATIONAL RESEARCHER 10 (February 1981): 14-21.

The authors have taken their general notions about learning how to learn and transferred them to learning from text. Learning activities, the characteristics of the learner, the nature of materials and critical tasks are all made relevant to reading. If students understand these variables and their relationships, they can become active learners, monitoring their own learning. While the discussion focuses on theory and research, it provides an extremely useful framework for the teacher.

14. Crismore, Avon. COMPOSITION, COMPREHENSION AND TEXT TYPE SCHEMATA. 1982. 61pp. (ED 218 580)

Crismore views reading and writing as related cognitive acts because both are based on similar schemata: content or prior knowledge; text structure (microstructure and macrostructure); and process. In discussing process schemata, the role of metacognition is emphasized. He provides a thorough review of the literature relating to these three areas in order to show that reading and writing should be taught together.

15. Easton, Lois Brown. "Strengthening The Reader As Writer And The Writer As Reader." Paper presented at the Annual Meeting of the National Council of Teachers of English, Washington, D.C., November 19-24, 1982. 24pp. (ED 227 446)

Easton examines various models of the connections between reading and writing and concludes that they are both part of the communication process and should be taught together. She advocates direct teaching of the connections by instructing in areas such as common terminology, organizational plans and relationships, cohesive ties, and visual, verbal and structural cues. The author includes a wide variety of specific instructional techniques, from the sentence level to the novel level, for achieving the aim of growth in both areas.

16. Gebhard, Ann O. "Teaching Writing in Reading and the Content Areas." JOURNAL OF READING 27 (December 1983): 207-211.

Because of the "healthy effect on reading comprehension and general learning" (p. 211), Gebhard proposes that reading teachers take a leadership role in organizing and implementing school-wide writing programs. In order to involve a wide number of students, she advocates designing writing projects that are intended to communicate to a larger audience than just teachers and insuring that the projects and the topics are of consequence. Assignments should be varied moving from the simple and concrete to the complex and abstract. Finally, assignments need to help the student integrate new information into prior knowledge as well as encourage use of imagination.

17. McNeil, John D. "A Janus Look At Reading Comprehension." Paper presented at the Annual Meeting of the Claremont Reading Conference, Claremont, California, January 21-22, 1983. 11pp. (ED 225 131)

The author supports and explains a constructivist view of reading comprehension and places it within the mainstream of the history of reading theory. He gives examples of instructional and learning strategies for reading both narrative and exposition.

18. Sanacore, Joseph. "Improving Reading Through Prior Knowledge and Writing." JOURNAL OF READING 26 (May 1983): 714-720.

Activating prior knowledge and developing writing skills can improve reading comprehension in the content areas. Sanacore presents a review of strategies designed to accomplish this task. To activate prior knowledge he looks at Langer's prereading plan, PReP; Thelen's structured overview; and Thomas and Robinson's PQ4R. To develop writing skills, Sanacore reviews Brewer's discourse types and forces; Petrosky's similarities in reading, response to literature and composition; and Robinson's writing patterns in the content areas. This article provides an excellent place to start the investigation of these critical areas. The text and the references provide a number of alternatives for the teacher.

19. Stansell, John C., and Diane E. DeFord. "When Is a Reading Problem Not a Reading Problem?" JOURNAL OF READING 25 (October 1981): 14-20.

The reader and the text are the focus used by Stansell and

DeFord for analyzing the reading process of high school and college readers. The article is based on the assumption that a student can be a good reader and still not comprehend. The content of the material can provide a bridge between the reader and the text. Practical implications for the content teacher are highlighted.

Reading in Secondary Schools

Books

20. Early, Margaret, and Diane J. Sawyer. "Many Kinds of Readers and Learners." READING TO LEARN IN GRADES 5 TO 12. New York: Harcourt Brace Jovanovich, 1984, pp. 78-100.

The authors describe the varieties of readers in both middle and high schools, presenting a clear picture of their problems and their strengths as well as the various pressures and demands they face. A particularly interesting section deals with future job prospects and skills. The skills identified for 1990 include many of the cognitive strategies required for effective reading such as critical thinking, problem solving, organization, and application.

21. Heilman, Arthur W., Timothy Blair, and William H. Rupley. "Teacher Effectiveness and Reading." PRINCIPLES AND PRACTICES OF TEACHING READING. Columbus, Ohio: Charles E. Merrill, 1981, pp. 20-43.

This chapter draws together much of the research on teacher effectiveness and proposes that the teacher diagnose needs, provide students with structure and direct instruction, as well as an opportunity to learn and apply skills, and promote student involvement in learning.

22. Lamberg, Walter J., and Charles E. Lamb. "Reading Programs and the Secondary Curriculum." READING INSTRUCTION IN THE CONTENT AREAS. Chicago: Rand McNally, 1980, pp. 15-30.

The authors present a detailed overview of four levels of secondary reading (content area, developmental, remedial and recreational reading) emphasizing problems and programs for each level. The diversity in secondary schools of student needs and instructional strategies is evident in this chapter.

23. Nelson, Joan, and Harold L. Herber. "Organization and Management of Programs." SECONDARY SCHOOL READING: WHAT RESEARCH REVEALS FOR CLASSROOM PRACTICE. Edited by Allen Berger and H. Alan Robinson. Urbana, Illinois: ERIC Clearinghouse on Reading and Communication Skills and the National Conference on Research in English, 1982, pp. 143-157.

Nelson and Herber examine the assumptions underlying remedial and corrective classes in secondary schools and conclude that these assumptions do not support the currently prevailing model. Rather, the authors propose a reading program firmly rooted in the content areas. All secondary school students need reading programs designed to meet their particular needs; all teachers need to be involved in teaching students to learn from reading. Staff development is crucial and general guidelines are provided.

24. Nelson-Herber, Joan, and Harold L. Herber. "A Positive Approach to Assessment and Correction of Reading Difficulties in Middle and Secondary Schools." PROMOTING READING COMPREHENSION. Edited by James Flood. Newark, Delaware: International Reading Assn., 1984, pp. 232-244.

Nelson-Herber and Herber present a persuasive case for reading instruction in secondary schools within the content classroom. They propose to address strengths, not weaknesses, and to emphasize reading-reasoning processes, not isolated basic skills. Any corrective reading instruction should be related to content instruction and should be limited to a few students who are demonstrably weak in basic skills. They suggest that because we have not recognized the differences between elementary and secondary reading, we are providing corrective reading to more students than really need it. What these students need is not instruction in basic skills but instruction in secondary reading skills within the content classrooms.

25. Petrosky, Anthony R. "Reading Achievement." SECONDARY SCHOOL READING: WHAT RESEARCH REVEALS FOR CLASSROOM PRACTICE. Edited by Allen Berger and H. Alan Robinson. Urbana, Illinois: ERIC Clearinghouse on Reading and Communication Skills and the National Conference on Research in English, 1982, pp.7-20.

The author reviews findings from the 1979-80 assessment of reading and literature by the National Assessment of Educational Progress and concludes that students have acquired basic reading skills but have not demonstrated abilities in critical reading. Much of this can be traced to the reading instruction they have received. Some general suggestions are made for improving secondary programs including testing with open-ended questions; involvement of all teachers; integration of speaking, reading and writing; inservice training; and careful examination of textbooks.

26. Roe, Betty D., Barbara D. Stoodt, and Paul C. Burns. "Reading in the Secondary School." SECONDARY SCHOOL READING INSTRUCTION: THE CONTENT AREAS. Boston: Houghton Mifflin, 1983, pp. 1-13.

The authors put much responsibility on content teachers for the development of and involvement in a secondary reading program. The chapter outlines the phases of a reading program, the range and significance of reading achievement levels, the implications of minimum reading competency, and content teacher preparation in reading.

27. Singer, Harry, and Dan Donlan. "Reading in the High School." "Teacher Attitudes." "Individual Differences Among Students." READING AND LEARNING FROM TEXT. Boston: Little, Brown, 1980, pp. 1-47.

The beginning chapters of this text look briefly at the history of reading in high school, focusing mainly on the content teacher. They include guidelines for a high school reading program and inventories to determine the attitude of content teachers toward reading. The authors review ranges of high school reading abilities and their implications.

Periodicals

28. Baumann, James V. "Implications for Reading Instruction from the Research on Teacher and School Effectiveness." JOURNAL OF READING 28 (November 1984): 109-115.

Baumann discusses those areas which are identified with effective teaching. They include: instructional leadership, assumptions about teaching and learning, goals and objectives, time allocations, time-on-task, success rates, management, teacher monitoring of students' learning, direct instruction, instructional organization and classroom atmosphere. Although, as the author points out, many of the suggestions are common sense, it is difficult to tell from the article whether the author is referring to studies with elementary students or secondary students.

29. Chall, Jeanne S. "Literacy: Trends and Explanations." Award Address presented at the Annual Meeting of the American Educational Research Association, Montreal, Canada, April 11-15, 1983. 22pp. (ED 232 135)

Chall reviews the findings from a variety of sources on the reading levels and abilities of a wide age range of readers. She concludes that younger students appear to be doing better than older students. She speculates on possible reasons for this concluding that we need more research and knowledge in the area of "literacy practices...and on the growth of literacy in individuals over time" (p. 14).

30. Collins, Allan, and Edward E. Smith. TEACHING THE PROCESS OF READING COMPREHENSION. Urbana: University of Illinois, Center for the Study of Reading, September 1980. 43pp. (ED 193 616)

Collins and Smith stress that teaching the processes of comprehension monitoring and hypothesis formulation and evaluation are critical skills for reading for depth and detail. They specify the kinds of failures that can occur and make suggestions for remedies. They advocate a teaching strategy based on teacher modeling and active student participation.

31. Farrell, Richard T., and Joseph M. Cirrincione. "State Certification Requirements in Reading for Content Area Teachers." JOURNAL OF READING 28 (November 1984): 152-158.

The authors examined the certification requirements in relation to instruction in reading for content teachers in the 52 states and the District of Columbia. They found that an increasing number of states (37) now had some requirement. They raise an important issue--that of implementation of reading instruction in the classroom. Does the training make a difference? Further evaluation is needed to answer this critical question.

32. Houck, Cherry. "The Reading Disabled Adolescent: An Examination of Significant Factors Influencing Program Success." READING IMPROVEMENT 20 (Spring 1983): pp. 28-36.

Houck presents a detailed, useful analysis of seven barriers to success in programs dealing with adolescent reading problems. She examines the factors of attitudinal scars from previous programs, current attitude toward reading and school, needed information, time required for instruction, surface behaviors, relevance of techniques and materials, and a systematic monitoring scheme.

33. Pike, Kathy. "Have You Disabled A Student Today? A Look At Teacher Effectiveness." Paper presented at the Annual Meeting of the International Reading Association, Chicago, Illinois, April 26-30, 1982. 33pp. (ED 216 311)

Pike presents a comprehensive and thorough review of research in the areas generally associated with teacher effectiveness: direct instruction, classroom management and classroom climate and expectations. The discussion of "teaching as behaving" is useful to any secondary teacher. In addition, the author examines other critical aspects of teacher effectiveness: planning, decision making, judging, i.e., "teaching as thinking."

34. READING COMPREHENSION OF AMERICAN YOUTH: DO THEY UNDERSTAND WHAT THEY READ? RESULTS FROM THE 1979-80 NATIONAL ASSESSMENT OF READING AND LITERATURE. Education Commission of the States. Denver, Colorado: National Assessment of Educational Progress, July 1982. 89pp. (ED 217 396)

This report focuses on the data relating to reading and study skills resulting from the 1979-80 assessment of reading and literature. Of particular interest to secondary school teachers is the information comparing elementary and secondary students on literal and interpretive comprehension, attitudes toward reading and homework, and reading habits.

35. Smith, Frederick R., and Karen M. Feathers. "The Role of Reading in Content Classroom: Assumption vs. Reality." JOURNAL OF READING 27 (December 1983): 262-267.

Smith and Feathers report on a study they conducted in two middle school social studies classes and two high school history classes to determine the role of reading in those rooms. The results were certainly discouraging for those who support the need to include this kind of instruction. In fact, they found that "reading was not an essential or even central activity in the classes studied" (p. 266). The discussion provides useful insights into looking at the role of reading in content classrooms.

36. Stallings, Jane, Margaret Needels, and Nicholas Stayrook. HOW TO CHANGE THE PROCESS OF TEACHING BASIC SKILLS IN SECONDARY SCHOOLS. PHASE II AND PHASE III. FINAL REPORT. Menlo Park, California: SRI International, May 1979. 279 pp. (ED 210 670)

The authors studied 43 teachers and 905 students in 6 locations. They concluded that time-on-task, feedback, probing questions and a positive, structured, supportive atmosphere were important in improving reading scores. A critical element was the teacher's ability to stay involved with the students the entire period. The problem of obtaining sufficient qualified teachers was raised.

37. Valmont, William J. "Minimum Competency Doesn't Mean Minimum Teaching." Paper presented at the Annual Meeting of the International Reading Association, New Orleans, Louisiana, April 27-May 1, 1981. 8pp. (Ed 214 104)

Valmont cautions against the tendency to lowering standards and expectations by teaching toward the minimum competency tests. He stresses: avoid teaching skills in isolation; encourage reading in a wide variety of materials; expect more than minimum reading competency.

CHAPTER II

WORDS AND SENTENCES

Text structure occurs on a number of levels. Words and sentences are frequently called the microstructure while paragraphs and longer units of text are referred to as the macrostructure. In examining aspects of text structure we will begin with words and sentences.

When a student cannot read a particular word or a number of words in a selection, it is easy to place the responsibility on the elementary school for not teaching and on the student for not learning. When a student can read a word successfully and fluently, it is easy to make the assumption that he knows what the word means. By avoiding these problems and placing the responsibility on others we not only do students a disservice, but we undermine the entire secondary school program. Success in all academic areas is related to a student's ability to read words, to understand and use them as well as to comprehend sentences.

Reading Words

Theory

If you're concerned about a secondary school student's general inability to "read" words you are probably dealing with an unskilled reader. Remember the characteristics of skilled and unskilled readers. Now see how these apply to "reading" words (Figure 1).

Figure 1

READING WORDS

Secondary School Students

Unskilled readers	Skilled Readers
Utilize one strategy to "read" words	Utilize more than one strategy/switch strategies
Engage in serial letter-by-letter processing	Recognize most words as a single unit or as part of a larger unit
Use attention for decoding	Use attention for comprehension
Seek meaning by decoding	Seek meaning directly

23

The question for both content and reading teachers is how to help secondary students decode and make the transition to becoming skilled, active readers.

Tierney, Readence and Dishner (43) point out that "no aspect of reading instruction has been the subject of more debate than that dealing with word identification instruction" (p. 142). Another area of uncertainty!

"Reading" words will be broadly defined to include two major approaches to reading unknown or not mastered words. In the first approach the emphasis is placed on decoding words. Decoding can be broadly defined as the use of phonic and structural analysis to read unknown words. Notice the similarity here to the bottom-up approach to reading. The reader reads individual words and puts them together to read sentences, paragraphs, etc. Stress is placed on mastering phonics, morphemes and word lists. Reading and understanding depend on skill mastery, which is achieved through "the word."

Think of beginners and unskilled readers you have known. They come to unknown words, lack the skills needed to read the word, stumble, move on, repeat the sequence (or give up!), lose the meaning of the passage, and fail to comprehend the writer's message. Much of our remedial instruction in reading has centered on the mastery of decoding skills in order to overcome these problems. Why do we do this?   Otto and Smith (47) cite LaBerge and Samuels in asserting that when decoding of individual words is automatic, the reader is able to devote full attention to larger units of text and thus obtain and maintain meaning, although automatic decoding "is not sufficient to guarantee good comprehension" (p. 24).

The common features of most skill-oriented programs include: sequential instruction of specific skills, mastery learning, study of words in isolation and practice in context once mastery has been achieved. The major differences among programs arise from how the authors deal with questions of whether to teach all phonics generalizations and whether to incorporate meaning into decoding instruction, and if so, how (48, 49, 50).

Some problems have been associated with this approach to teaching decoding. Unfortunately, many of the phonic rules we have taught students often have limited applicability (39, 45). The problem is compounded for students with different linguistic backgrounds. Also, secondary students have often had many years of decoding instruction with countless practice sheets. Something didn't work! In addition, decoding instruction in secondary schools has served to isolate the reading specialist from the content teacher, and leave the latter with no alternative when the student cannot decode a word. Content teachers are not trained to teach phonics, are often not receptive to the idea and, in fact, it is not their primary responsibility.

Almost inadvertently many content teachers have tended to use the second major approach to reading unrecognized words. This is a "meaning" approach, or a top-down approach to reading words. Since content teachers tend to focus on the content and the context of the material, they may suggest the student reread the sentence and figure out what the word means. If he reads for meaning he may identify or read the word because of his prior knowledge of the general or specific meaning. Teachers may verify the student's informed guess as to what the word is or may send the student to the dictionary for verification. Cunningham, Cunningham and Arthur (38) caution against telling the student before he has made an informed guess in order to avoid excessive dependence on the teacher. Unfortunately, this meaning approach may not occur frequently enough to be helpful. In fact, the content teacher often may not even be aware that the student cannot read the word.

Meaning-oriented approaches have been developed which begin with use of context as the cue for decoding an unknown word. Often these programs are discussed in the context of teaching reading in content areas. The emphasis is firmly on meaning. If context doesn't help the student decode the word, then he is commonly directed to look at morphemes (roots and affixes) or ask for help from the teacher and/or dictionary. The most common difference between meaning-oriented approaches involves whether and how to provide direct instruction in phonics and structural analysis (39, 42, 44, 45).

In determining how to teach decoding to remedial students, Otto and Smith (47) state:

At certain times and for certain purposes, a skill-centered approach is appropriate; at other times and for other purposes a meaning-centered approach will be more fruitful. The critical need is not for another model, but for teachers to know that they can and should use both. (p. 26)

But, how do you balance both? J. Otto (46), after reviewing research dealing with adolescents, concluded that:

A whole language approach to remedial instruction is beneficial. Instruction which optimizes student use of grammar and focuses on meaning appears to facilitate student achievement more consistently than isolated phonics instruction. (p. 249)

Would she ever use a strictly skills-centered phonic approach with adolescents? Probably not. She states that "intense instruction in sight words, vocabulary and phonics instruction by a variety of methods does not seem appropriate for these older students" (p. 246).

Nelson-Herber and Herber (24), looking specifically at secondary students, assert that:

Further intensive phonics instruction does not appear to be as beneficial as the use of a whole language approach that places emphasis on the use of syntactic and semantic cues as well as on graphic cues. (p. 242)

Generally, as you can see by reading the more detailed program descriptions, most suggestions in the literature contain elements of both approaches.   The differences in the approaches of various programs seem to lie in where the major emphasis is put.

Teaching adolescents to read words doesn't need to be either/or. The traditional, narrow focus on teaching all phonic and syllabication rules ignores the larger picture of meaning and context, to say nothing of motivation.   The other alternative of focusing solely on meaning is equally difficult. A skilled reader can often "read a word" using context, but the unskilled reader may well have difficulty working only with meaning, particularly if he has limited background knowledge and vocabulary as well as difficulties decoding a number of the words.

Reading words through a dual approach has a number of significant advantages over using one or the other. First, not all words respond to one strategy and second, not all readers seem to become equally facile with any one strategy. Finally this provides a way for both the content and the reading teachers to work successfully with students and to work with each other.

Practice

The implementation of theory into practice involves both reading and content teachers. We need to teach students to use a variety of strategies for successful word reading: decoding (phonics and structural analysis) and context.   Reading teachers can use all of them; content teachers can concentrate on the use of context but can also utilize relevant and easily transferred phonic rules, sound/symbol correspondences and morphemes.

1. In teaching phonics, identify useful, frequently occurring, transferable generalizations and letter-sound correspondence which you have determined that the student does not know. Don't teach what he already knows. Reading specialists can provide content teachers with a basic list of ones that the student can be expected to use. (38, 39, 45, 49)

2. In teaching structural analysis, generate a list of common, useful morphemes, and their meanings. These can be taught and reinforced by both reading and content teachers. The advantage of this approach is that meaning can be directly related to reading the word. (39, 40, 42, 44)

3. Teach the use of context as a strategy for "reading" words. Use a variety of contextual cues, both syntactic and semantic. (38, 39, 40, 42, 44)

4. Relate "reading" words to "understanding" words. Stress word meaning as well as reading and using words in sentences. (50)

5. Develop dictionary skills as a reinforcement for pronounciation

and meaning and also as a means of verification of the student's original prediction. (39, 42)

6. Develop flexibility in using strategies as well as a "set for diversity." Readers can combine strategies and can try alternate strategies if one strategy doesn't work. (39)

7. Teach strategies in a functional setting. Use a textbook the student needs to read. Concentrate on real material for practice and transfer. This is critical for motivation. Cooperation here between reading teachers and content teachers can make the reading useful and motivating to the student. (38)

One final caution. Teach only skills identified as needed. "Needed" means that content texts used require the skill and/or the student has been found not to know and have mastered it. Even more important for motivation, the skill should be identified by the student as "needed."

Suggestions for Implementation

Because of the nature of instruction at the secondary level, it is probably inevitable that the reading teacher will assume the major responsibility for teaching the skills discussed in this section to students who are experiencing difficulty in reading. However, there are a number of areas where the reading teacher and the content teacher can cooperate. One area might be jointly choosing appropriate content materials to be used for reinforcement and transfer. The content teacher can also reinforce the application of particular phonic and structural analysis skills taught by the reading teacher. In all of this, though, the content teacher can play a primary role in developing a list of useful roots and prefixes for the subject area, in emphasizing the use of context as a strategy for reading words, and in motivating students to want to read words.

Understanding and Using Words

Theory

Research has consistently, over a period of time and with a variety of language groups, demonstrated that word knowledge is a significant component in comprehension. Agreement on why this is so is not universal. Anderson and Freebody (51) have summarized three different positions which have been developed to explain the high correlation between word knowledge and reading comprehension.

1. The instrumentalist hypothesis states that "knowing words enables text comprehension" (p. 81). Because the reader knows the words he can comprehend the text. "While, like everyone else, the advocate of the instrumental hypothesis favors lots of reading and varied language experience, the distinctive feature of this view is that it invites direct vocabulary building exercises" (p. 86). Consider the parallels between this

hypothesis and the "bottom-up" theory of reading.   Both stress
the   word   as   the   important   unit   leading   to   meaning   and
comprehension.

2. The verbal aptitude hypothesis   suggests   that   vocabulary
    knowledge   is   "a   reflection of verbal ability and it is verbal
    ability   that   mainly   determines   whether   a   text   will   be
    understood" (p. 81).   Implications of this hypothesis range from
    recommending   "family   planning"   (ibid.)   to   maintaining   that
    "verbal ability grows in proportion to the volume of experience
    with   language"   (ibid.).   Educational recommendations include
    maximizing the amount of reading and   providing   for   drill   and
    practice   in   "fundamental"   reading   skills   (i.e.,   word
    vocalization,   speeded   word   recognition,   and   memory   of   the
    literal   content   of the text).   The emphasis here, again, is on
    the "word."

3. The   knowledge   hypothesis   stresses   that   prior   knowledge   is
    essential   for   comprehending   text.   Knowledge of appropriate
    words is simply a signal that   the   reader   has   the   conceptual
    framework   needed   for   comprehension.   "Individual word meanings
    are merely the exposed   tip of the conceptual iceberg" (p.   82).
    Educational   recommendations   of   this hypothesis, of necessity,
    stress teaching words as part of and as reflections of   concepts
    as   well   as   developing   categories   and   relationships   while
    developing word meaning.   "The significant aspect of   vocabulary
    is   in   the learning of concepts not just words....concepts come
    in clusters that are systematically interrelated" (p. 87).   The
    parallels   here   between   the knowledge hypothesis and the "top-
    down" theory of reading are evident.   Prior   knowledge   and   the
    overall   concept   provide   the   framework   for   vocabulary
    development.

         Remember the uncertainties facing reading teachers?   You can
    add   another   uncertainty   to   your   list.   Anderson and Freebody in
    evaluating the three hypotheses conclude that we   do   not   have   the
    theoretical   tools   or   the   data   to   determine   which is the "most
    tenable" (p. 82).   In fact, probably none of them will turn   out   to
    be   all   right   or   all   wrong.   "No serious scholar in reading or
    related   fields rigidly adheres to any one of   these   positions"   (p.
    89).   On the other hand, Johnson, Toms-Bronowski and Pittleman (66)
    after   reviewing   research   on   word   knowledge   conclude   that
    "information   based   on   both   the   list-learning   and   information
    processing studies lend support to the general knowledge   hypothesis
    regarding word acquisition and word knowledge" (p. 20).

         So   far, we have skirted the issue of defining "word" and "word
    knowledge."   Let's look at a sampling of   definitions   from   current
    texts, keeping these three hypotheses in mind.

         Vacca (59):   "Every   subject   matter   field   creates   a   unique
    language to represent its important concepts.   Words   are   just
    labels--nothing more or less--for these concepts" (p. 59).

         Friedman and Rowls (52): "To have meaning, words must refer to objects and events" (p.109). These references include: concrete events, abstraction categories, (concrete events grouped according to common character), hierarchical categories (classes of hierarchically arranged categories), and programmatic references (chronological and cause/effect relationships) between classes and categories.

Readence, Bean and Baldwin (57): "Words are defined by the ways and the extent to which they are related to all other words" (p. 108). They have denotations (broad meanings) and connotations (subtle shades of meaning) and are in a state of flux as concepts are redefined and expanded and as experience changes and broadens.

Roe, Stoodt and Burns (58): "Words are labels for thoughts, ideas, concepts and for the relationships among them; thus, words permit manipulation of ideas....Concept development and vocabulary are interrelated....Words also function to organize the world of experience" (p. 34).

Johnson, Toms-Bronowski and Pittleman (66): "Vocabulary knowledge or word concept knowledge is viewed, then, as an integration of the many possible associated links for any word with the situational constraints that together construct a word's meaning" (p. 7). They suggest (p. 20) four factors in word knowledge: "clustering" words into categories to remember them; utilizing semantic relations to understand words in sentences; arranging word concepts into hierarchical categories; and using links or "networks" to connect word concepts structures.

These authors clearly imply that a student's ability to understand and use words goes beyond the traditional list learning and involves words as part of concept development. It may be as Anderson and Freebody hold. The understanding of words may come from more than one source. This is certainly reminiscent of the interactive approach to reading.

Now we need to move from theory into practice. Think of the texts secondary students read. They contain many words that are unfamiliar, technical or are used in unusual ways. In fact, Chall (29) as well as Calfee and Curley (4) identified vocabulary as one of the features that makes secondary reading difficult. Yet, as Graves (53) points out, we rarely have systematic, rigorous, thorough programs of vocabulary instruction in secondary schools.

In reviewing suggestions, consider how they could be implemented in a secondary school as well as their relation to the three hypotheses. Although many of the current suggestions in the literature reflect the knowledge hypothesis, there are others that are based on either or both of the other two hypotheses or combine all three approaches.

Practice

Based on theory, vocabulary instruction in the secondary school can take a wide variety of forms. Unfortunately, in practice, the kinds of instructional strategies actually used are often quite limited: looking the word up in a dictionary, using it in a sentence, and memorizing lists of words and their meanings for the weekly quiz. Direct instruction, for vocabulary development should include a variety of approaches, not be limited to one strategy. It is also possible to teach vocabulary indirectly through modeling. Let's consider some options for developing word meaning.

1. Use structural analysis as a key to the meaning of a word. The identification of the meaning of useful affixes and roots in a content area and the application of this knowledge to reading the content text can give the student a direct and motivating way to increase word knowledge. You are also connecting word meaning to word knowledge. (40, 42, 44, 58, 59, 69)

2. Provide direct instruction in context analysis. The reader can identify word meaning through the use of the syntactic and semantic cues in a particular context and can refine word meaning through the use of a variety of contexts. This strategy requires the use of inference in order to understand the relationship between the word and its context. Commonly, these include at least definition, description, comparison/contrast and cause/effect. (41, 58, 59, 66)

3. Involve students in the prediction/confirmation of meaning through context. Before reading, students predict possible meaning based on prior knowledge. During reading they confirm or change the prediction depending on information received from the context. (56, 67)

4. Teach students to combine the use of structural analysis and context. This is a powerful combination, providing the student with a way of checking and refining the meaning of the morphemes in a particular context. (44, 59)

5. Stress the use of categories and word associations. Provide instruction and practice in conceptualizing words, possibly using mapping or networking. (52, 54, 55, 56, 57, 58, 59, 60, 63, 64)

6. Use graphic organizers. These are teacher- or student-generated visual diagrams which define the hierarchical relationships of categories and concepts. They can also relate new concepts to background knowledge. (52, 54, 55, 57, 58, 59, 63, 64, 66)

7. Introduce the technique of feature analysis to compare and contrast the significant distinguishing semantic features of similar or related words. (54, 55, 61, 66, 68)

8. Use analogies as a way of reinforcing and extending vocabulary categories and concepts. (54, 62, 63)

9. Provide opportunities for growth in word knowledge at all stages
   of the reading process: before reading in order to preteach
   vocabulary and activate prior knowledge; during reading in order
   to reinforce vocabulary and comprehension; and after reading in
   order to reinforce meaning and to insure use of the words. The
   aim is to have the student manipulate words and word meanings
   and to become the activating, generating agent in the process.
   (56, 60, 65, 68)

10. Insure that words and concepts are useful and needed. This is
    particularly important with secondary students. They must
    perceive the reasons and usefulness of the words they are
    learning. (53, 65)

11. Model your own interest in vocabulary and ways of acquiring it
    as appropriate situations arise. This might include identifying
    an interesting word and discussing examples, similar words,
    images or experiences that come to mind. (64)

12. Be eclectic in your approach to vocabulary instruction. When
    planning vocabulary lessons, consider the students' needs, the
    characteristics of the material to be read and the particular
    words to be understood. This is "teaching as thinking." (56)

All of these strategies go beyond memorizing 15 words for a
test on Friday. They put word knowledge squarely into a larger
context, that of relating words to concepts, other words, and
sentences. Even in the case of structural analysis, those who
advocate relating morphemes to subject vocabulary or to context are
looking for links between words. Words cannot be taught, learned or
used effectively in isolation.

The challenge for both content teachers and reading teachers is
to make vocabulary building interesting and useful for the student,
while also insuring that transfer to content materials occurs. The
suggestions given are based on an eclectic approach, one strongly
stressing the top-down, knowledge view of vocabulary but also
incorporating some of the bottom-up, instrumental, strategies. The
stress put by the verbal aptitude hypothesis on extensive reading to
increase word knowledge is also advocated by the other two
hypotheses. It certainly forms the foundation of a vocabulary
building program along with other strategies.

Suggestions for Implementation

Because of the critical importance of understanding and using
words in the comprehension of content texts, the content teacher
must play a central role in the development of vocabulary strategies
and activities. The reading teacher may introduce these strategies
to individuals or to the whole science class and may serve as a
resource to the content teacher in planning lessons. Nevertheless,
the content teacher must take a leadership role in implementing a
program of vocabulary development by instructing students in a
variety of strategies throughout the year and by encouraging
students to use them as they read and study.

Understanding Sentences

Theory

So far, we have dealt with individual words. Students, however, rarely read individual words. They read sentences. Even when readers decode and know the meaning of each word, they may not comprehend the sentence because of its syntactic and/or semantic features. The problem, of course, is compounded for students when they are not certain how to decode every word efficiently and successfully and when the meaning of all the words is not already known. At that point the sentence becomes the primary unit of meaning. The syntactic and semantic features of the sentence may be the means for decoding and assigning meaning to individual words, as well as for comprehending the sentence.

We will consider two aspects of theory: first, why readers have difficulties comprehending written sentences and, second, how we can help readers to overcome them.

It has been suggested that the difficulties readers have with written sentences may be due to a variety of factors. Snow and Coots (78) cite the absence of prosody in written language as a possible variable. What is prosody? Think about spoken language. Consider how much meaning you get by listening to the stress or loudness the speaker puts on certain words or phrases. "I really dislike THAT." "I REALLY dislike that." The written words are the same. The spoken words convey a difference in meaning and attitude. "I can come home" spoken without a rising inflection at the end is very different from the same sentence with a rising inflection at the end. The speaker's timing of the words, the pauses given between syntactically related words, enables the listener to identify intrasentence units. "The loss of prosodic information in text may be a major source of difficulty for poor readers" (ibid., p. 42).

Another source of difficulty is the complexity of written language as contrasted to oral language. Seidenberg (77) discusses "form-schema" or "the syntactic expectations people make use of in reading or text-processing" (p. 352) as a prerequisite for reading comprehension and concludes that "because written language is not simply speech written down, it is more difficult to comprehend" (p. 353).

What are some of the syntactic features that make written sentences difficult to comprehend? Harris and Sipay (70) cite Fry's concept of "kernel distance" as an important feature. "The number of words separating subject from verb and verb from object depends mainly on the presence or absence of embedded phrases or clauses and therefore seems a reasonable indicator of one cause of sentence difficulty" (pp. 469-470). In fact, think about the preceding sentence. Look at the distance between "number" and "depends" and "seems." The subject is certainly separated from the two verbs. You probably had to think about the sentence before you understood it fully.

Also within the sentence itself, McNeil, Donant and Alkin (72) suggest that problems occur with word order, the passive voice, clauses and antecedents for pronouns. Both Weaver (74) and McNeil (71) substantiate these problem areas and provide numerous examples.

All of these problems relate to syntactic complexity. However, semantic complexity may also be a source of useful information as well as a source of difficulty. First, consider these sentences:

The boys went to the store. The girls went to the store.

The boys went to the store because the girls went to the store.

The second example, although longer and more complex, certainly gives you more information. What happens to the meaning of the example if you insert a different word for the underlined word? Try: nevertheless, therefore, before, when, after. Look what happens to the meaning! The information load in complex and compound sentences is heavier than in the simple sentences, but the author's meaning may be clearer and more explicit (7).

On the other hand, the semantic relationships between items in the sentence may be implied, not explicitly stated. There may also be multiple, not singular relationships. For example, Cronnell (75) has illustrated a variety of these complexities in cause-effect sentences and concludes that "we should not be surprised if students have difficulty understanding cause-effect relations when they read. And we should consider that students may need explicit instruction on how to identify and infer such relations" (p. 166).

The question is, do we rewrite texts in order to avoid these problems or do we teach students how to read complex sentences? Stevens (79) responds emphatically that "rather than 'water down' all children's reading material, educators must help their charges deal with the complexities of written language so that children can read and appreciate the richness of our written heritage" (p. 185). We agree with Stevens, although at times you may have to make some compromises. You may be faced with the choice of two texts: one filled with complex sentences, with many long embedded clauses, with much use of the passive voice and with frequent examples of "kernel distance"; the other written in a simpler, more direct manner. All other things being equal, you may choose the more immediately expedient route by electing the simpler text. This in no way, however, negates our responsibility to teach sentence comprehension.

But how? What strategies?

Practice

The literature suggests two basic strategies. The first one we will consider is the analysis of sentences into syntactic units, focusing on the grammar. Proponents of this strategy cite the difficulties caused by sentence complexities and the need for direct instruction in the surface structure of the sentence (79).

The second group of strategies involves the manipulation or synthesis of the syntactic and semantic units into new or different grammatical units. The focus here is on ideas and meaning. Crismore (14) reviews some of the research in this area and suggests that "manipulations of sentence structure, (immersing students in the intricacies of the sentences), in the internal workings of sentences, is a fundamental to comprehension" (p.20) particularly for the poor to average reader. Pearson and Camperell (7) are more cautious, but nevertheless positive, about the benefits of manipulation of sentence parts, suggesting "that attention to microstructure, specifically allowing students to actively manipulate it, pays at least short range dividends in comprehension growth" (p.37).

1. Provide direct instruction in the analysis of sentence structure. This refers to items such as: multiple subjects, verbs, passive voice, anaphora, markers signaling types of elements within sentences and connectives indicating coordination and subordination. (41, 73, 74, 79)

2. Insure that students have practice actively manipulating parts of sentences. This can include sentence anagrams, the combining of single words into sentences. (71, 81)

3. Teach sentence combining as a syntactic and semantic strategy for the active manipulation of sentences into longer, more complex units. This strategy also allows the student to use writing in combination with the reading. (7, 14, 15, 76, 77, 80)

4. Introduce sentence patterning as a way to understand the structure of sentences and as a way to express ideas in expanded and transformed sentences. (77, 80)

5. Emphasize the meaning relationships between parts of the sentence, for example, causal relations, time, and sequence. Use questions to highlight these and instruct in the use of signal words to help in indentifying them. (73)

6. Allow time for "guided practice" and verbal interaction among students and between students and teachers. Don't limit activities to worksheets. (74)

Again, as in the case of word reading and vocabulary building, an eclectic approach in strategies to instruction is recommended. The need to use the student's own reading materials to the fullest possible extent for instruction and application must be repeated here.

Suggestions for Implementation

Many of the items included in this section have traditionally been in the domain of the English teacher, and will certainly continue to reside there. However, for students who are experiencing difficulty, more instruction, practice and reinforcement may be needed. This is where the reading teacher can contribute.   The problems of comprehending sentences can be knotty. The student may well need individual help and instruction that includes both reading and writing of sentences. The reading teacher can make these connections and can provide the individual instruction needed.

Summary

In this chapter, we have begun to look at the problem of reading comprehension, because comprehension cannot occur efficiently and completely if the reader has difficulty reading the words, doesn't know what the words mean or doesn't comprehend the sentences. These are all parts of the surface structure of the text that must be considered when we view the problem of comprehension.

BIBLIOGRAPHY

Reading Words

Books

38. Cunningham, James, W., Patricia M. Cunningham, and Sharon V. Arthur. "Remedial Reading." MIDDLE AND SECONDARY SCHOOL READING. New York: Longman, 1981, pp. 245-281.

This chapter presents an overview of issues of concern to the remedial reading teacher including: selecting and scheduling students, organizing materials and programs, and diagnosing and remediating students. The section on techniques for improving phonics is particularly useful. The focus is on strategies for decoding polysyllabic words using a compare/contrast decoding strategy in which known one-syllable words are used as a cue for decoding two-and three-syllable words. Stress is also placed on words in context as well as on words in the student's own textbooks.

39. Friedman, Myles J., and Michael D. Rowls. "Word Identification and Prediction Skills." TEACHING READING AND THINKING SKILLS. New York: Longman, 1980, pp. 65-109.

Friedman and Rowls put word identification skills squarely into the category of predicting and thinking, not into a category of rote learning. Skills in using sight identification, phonics identification, word structure and context are all appropriate in different situations and in various combinations. Numerous examples and suggestions are helpful to the novice and to the expert alike in understanding combinations and in implementing instruction. The discussion of context is particularly useful for secondary teachers.

40. Johnson, Dale D., and P. David Pearson. "Developing Word Identification Processes." TEACHING READING VOCABULARY. New York: Holt, Rinehart and Winston, 1984, pp. 111-149.

This chapter provides an invaluable and comprehensive framework for understanding the use of phonics, structural analysis and context in word identification. The discussion is detailed, replete with lists, guidelines and examples. The sections on structural analysis and context are particularly useful for secondary teachers. The recurring emphasis is on the role of meaning in word identification. Although many of the examples are for elementary age students, they can be adapted to secondary. The material is probably more appropriate for reading teachers than content teachers.

41. McNeil, John D., Lisbeth Donant, and Marvin C. Alkin. "Word Attack Skills." HOW TO TEACH READING SUCCESSFULLY. Boston: Little, Brown, 1980, pp. 89-127.

The authors present a sequence of word attack skills from prereading to upper grades. This sequence including phonics, structural analysis and context is particularly useful for the secondary teacher. Some benchmarks for evaluating students and for determining needed instruction are included. Behavioral objectives are given for each skill, making the skill clear and concrete for the teacher unfamiliar with the topic. The discussion of upper level contextual analysis skills is particularly helpful in identifying some syntactical problems.

42. Readence, John E., Thomas W. Bean, and R. Scott Baldwin. "Essential Processes of Content Reading." CONTENT AREA READING: AN INTEGRATED APPROACH. Dubuque, Iowa: Kendall/Hunt, 1981, pp. 30-54.

The authors, in writing for the content teacher, stress the importance of "meaning-oriented" strategies to help students "make sense of print." The result is a useful and clearly articulated sequence of decoding strategies combining the use of context and morphemes. The emphasis for the teacher is on meaning. The task analysis and examples given make this a useful resource for the teacher.

43. Tierney, Robert J., John E. Readence, and Ernest K. Dishner. "Strategies for Improving Word Identification." READING STRATEGIES AND PRACTICES: GUIDE FOR IMPROVING INSTRUCTION. Boston: Allyn and Bacon, 1980, pp. 142-167.

The authors present four major approaches to word identification: the analytic method, synthetic word families, syllabaries, and Goodman's Reading Strategy lessons. Although the emphasis is mainly on elementary school readers, the discussion of the theory and procedures gives both the reading and the content teachers a useful overview of alternatives.

44. Tonjes, Marion J., and Miles V. Zintz. "Enhancing Vocabulary Development." TEACHING READING/THINKING/STUDY SKILLS IN CONTENT CLASSROOMS. Dubuque, Iowa: Wm. C. Brown, 1981, pp. 133-169.

Understanding words and reading text are linked both conceptually and in practice because mature readers use more than one strategy to read unknown words. The authors advocate a sequence of steps based on: context, structural analysis (morphemes), sounds (phonics) and dictionary. Examples are given for each step which can be applicable in any teaching situation. The discussion of vocabulary development includes a useful section on word origins and denotations and connotations. A number of activities have been included which are useful for a variety of content areas.

45. Weaver, Constance. "How Are Words Perceived?" "How Does Context Aid in Word Identification?" PSYCHOLINGUISTICS AND READING: FROM PROCESS TO PRACTICE. Boston: Little, Brown, 1980, pp. 34-95.

Through a series of sequential activities, in which the reader actively participates, Weaver questions the need for "overteaching" phonics. Instead she suggests limiting phonics instruction to seven rules and to the identification of patterns in words. The activities demonstrating the role of context in word identification are particularly useful as an introduction to the topic. The stress on three kinds of context: context within a sentence, within a selection and the reader's personal context of knowledge and experience is useful for the secondary content teacher.

Periodicals

46. Otto, Jean. "A Critical Review of Approaches to Remedial Reading for Adolescents." JOURNAL OF READING 23 (December 1979): 244-250.

Otto reviews remedial reading for adolescents and concludes that approaches which stress syntactic and semantic cues appear to be more useful that those which stress isolated phonics.

47. Otto, Wayne, and Richard J. Smith. "Skill-Centered and Meaning-Centered Conceptions of Remedial Reading Instruction: Striking a Balance." TOPICS IN LEARNING AND LEARNING DISABILITIES 2 (January 1983): 20-26.

Otto and Smith discuss the implications of theory for instruction and assessment. A skill-centered approach and a meaning-centered approach both have value for teaching decoding and comprehension. The contribution of the LaBerge-Samuels Reading Model, with its emphasis on achieving automaticity in decoding, is that while we stress meaning, we also need to give some instruction in decoding skills.

48. PROJECT SCORE: A TUTORIAL READING SYSTEM FOR THE LEARNING HANDICAPPED STUDENT. South San Francisco: South San Francisco Unified School District, November 1980. 31pp. (ED 201 958)

SCORE (Success Controlled Optimal Reading Experience) is a sequential phonics program based on a mastery teaching model incorporating principles of operant conditioning and systematic reinforcement. The program uses a word-list format to introduce and teach a sequence of decoding or phonic skills. It has been used successfully with students of varied ages and various reading problems. SCORE is designed to be monitored by a reading specialist and taught by an aide. The description gives an overview, not detailed specifics.

49. Ryder, Randall James. "Phonics: Considerations for Secondary Students." READING WORLD 21 (October 1981): 23-28.

Ryder suggests two constraints in phonics instruction for secondary students. First, teachers should restructure their phonics instruction to focus primarily on selected patterns of letter-to-sound correspondence rather than general rules. Stress variant-predictable patterns (c before a,o,u or a consonant = /k/) or invariant patterns. Only common variant-unpredictable patterns (such as ea) should be taught. This should be done through the use of "an associate group of words." Second, teachers need to determine what the student has not mastered and teach only that. Don't teach everything! In addition to direct instruction in phonics, Ryder recognizes the usefulness of reading as a means of learning the letter-sound correspondences.

50. Trembley, Philip W. "Vertical Word Processing: A New Approach for Teaching Written Language to the Learning Disabled Adolescent." JOURNAL OF LEARNING DISABILITIES 15 (December 1982): 587-593.

Although the article is written for the "learning disabled" population there is much here that can be applied to any adolescent with decoding difficulties. Structured, nonassumptive teaching is advocated as a way of preventing failure with its concomitant frustration and anxiety. Words are categorized into phonic processing or structural processing levels. The emphasis is on sequence of skills, mastery of words in isolation, development of meaning and context, and both the reading and writing of words. This article is more useful to the reading specialist who has a primary responsibility for teaching decoding skills to secondary students than to the content teacher.

Understanding and Using Words

Books

51. Anderson, Richard C., and Peter Freebody. "Vocabulary Knowledge." COMPREHENSION AND TEACHING: RESEARCH REVIEWS. Edited by John T. Guthrie. Newark, Delaware: International Reading Assn., 1981, pp. 77-117.

The aim of this chapter is ambitious: "to summarize what is known about the role of vocabulary knowledge in reading comprehension" (p. 77). In fact, the authors do review much theory and research, ranging from establishing that there is a relationship between word knowledge and reading comprehension, to examining the possible hypotheses as to why it exists and the instructional implications of these hypotheses. The discussion has particular relevance for secondary school teachers, providing them with a framework for examining vocabulary programs and activities. The difficulties in "knowing" a word and in measuring this knowledge are not as directly transferable to the classroom. However, this discussion is extremely useful in providing cautions and raising questions for teachers who are concerned with students' vocabulary knowledge.

52. Friedman, Myles I., and Michael D. Rowls. "Vocabulary Building." TEACHING READING AND THINKING SKILLS. New York: Longman, 1980, pp. 109-139.

Certain words appear and reappear in this chapter. They include: abstractions, categories, hierarchies, relationships, inductive reasoning, deductive reasoning. These words certainly give the flavor of the chapter and a sense of the authors' message. Words are related in hierarchies of categories. Acquiring word knowledge is a reasoning, not a rote memory task. Emphasis is placed on developing teaching aids and strategies.

53. Graves, Michael F. "Selecting Vocabulary to Teach in the Intermediate and Secondary Grades." PROMOTING READING COMPREHENSION. Edited by James Flood. Newark, Delaware: International Reading Assn., 1984, pp. 245-260.

Graves classifies words according to the student's knowledge of the word or concept. He identifies four categories: words in the student's oral vocabulary; words with more than one meaning, only one of which is already known; words in neither the oral or written vocabulary; and words representing new and difficult concepts. For each category the author examines the kinds of words, their relevance for secondary students, and the teacher's role in identifying them.

54. Johnson, Dale D., and P. David Pearson. "Developing a Meaning Vocabulary: Part II." TEACHING READING VOCABULARY. New York: Holt, Rinehart and Winston, 1984, pp. 33-50.

This is a very useful chapter with a strong orientation toward instructional activities but one soundly based in reading theory. Johnson and Pearson provide detailed examples and instructions on relating vocabulary to concept development through semantic networking, mapping and feature analysis and analogies. The examples seem to be drawn more from elementary than secondary teaching situations, but many of the activities can be adapted to secondary areas. The authors also present a later chapter on content reading including these vocabulary strategies.

55. McNeil, John D. "Teaching Vocabulary from an Interactive View of Reading Comprehension." READING COMPREHENSION: NEW DIRECTIONS FOR CLASSROOM PRACTICE. Glenview, Illinois: Scott, Foresman, 1984, pp. 96-113.

McNeil is strongly in the camp of those who support the knowledge hypothesis: knowledge of a word involves its meaning as well as the meaning of other words, ideas and concepts related to it. He gives explicit instructions and examples for teaching vocabulary as a network of ideas including mapping, refocused mapping, semantic feature analysis and the Frayer model.

56. Moore, David W., John E. Readence, and Robert J. Rickelman.
    "Preteaching Vocabulary." PREREADING ACTIVITIES FOR CONTENT
    AREA READING AND LEARNING. Newark, Delaware: International
    Reading Assn., 1982, pp. 35-49.

    The authors make a persuasive case for preteaching
    vocabulary, citing the relation of vocabulary to comprehension,
    the change in the meanings of words depending on concepts and
    contexts, and the need to activate a student's schemata. In
    the activities presented, emphasis is placed on the active
    participation of the student in the process of predicting,
    inferring, and confirming word meaning from context as well as
    in categorizing words to develop word meaning and related
    concepts. The examples given are specific, useful and easily
    replicated in a classroom or lab setting.

57. Readence, John E., Thomas W. Bean, and R. Scott Baldwin.
    "Content Area Vocabulary Development." CONTENT AREA READING:
    AN INTEGRATED APPROACH. Dubuque, Iowa: Kendall/Hunt, 1981,
    pp. 104-126.

    According to the authors, direct instruction is essential for
    vocabulary development. A wide variety of strategies and
    activities are clearly presented, all based on the need to
    preteach vocabulary, model its use, make it meaningful,
    reinforce it and be eclectic in the methods used. The
    underlying assumption is that words symbolize concepts. The
    strategies proposed, for the most part, reflect this
    assumption.

58. Roe, Betty, D., Barbara D. Stoodt, and Paul C. Burns.
    "Concepts and Word Meanings." SECONDARY SCHOOL READING
    INSTRUCTION: THE CONTENT AREAS. Boston: Houghton Mifflin,
    1983, pp.33-67.

    The title of the chapter expresses the authors' assumption
    that concept development and word meaning are related and that
    developing students' word knowledge in this way can increase
    comprehension. They suggest the strategies of word
    association, conceptual development, context and structural
    analysis. A particularly useful feature of this material is
    the fact that examples ar systematically given for the various
    content areas.

59. Vacca, Richard T. "Laying the Groundwork for Vocabulary and
    Concepts." CONTENT AREA READING. Boston: Little, Brown,
    1981, pp. 57-87.

    Vocabulary development requires planned instruction and
    should lead to independence in vocabulary building. In doing
    this, Vacca stresses the relationships between concepts and
    words. He does not neglect the need to interest students in
    words. Based on these premises, the strategies suggested cover

a wide range of approaches from concept and context to
morphemes and dictionaries. The numerous examples are clear
and will suggest classroom and reading lab applications.

60. Vacca, Richard T. "Reinforcing and Extending Technical
     Vocabulary." CONTENT AREA READING. Boston: Little, Brown,
     1981, pp. 223-253.

Vacca recommends that numerous activities be planned to
provide for essential reinforcement of content vocabulary. The
activities are not aimed primarily at developing definitions,
but at developing concepts and relationships. Definitions are
the first step toward understanding concepts. Detailed
instructions are given for planning these activities, involving
categories, analogies, word sorts and structured overviews,
with examples from various content areas. The focus is always
on active student involvement in manipulating words. The
author suggests that reinforcement exercises be done
individually and discussed in small groups or even in a whole
class.

Periodicals

61. Baldwin, R. Scott, Jeff C. Ford, and John E. Readence.
     "Teaching Word Connotations: An Alternative Strategy."
     READING WORLD 21 (December 1981): 103-108.

This discussion of the use of feature analysis to teach word
connotations is particularly explicit, presenting a sequence of
steps easily adaptable to many situations. Feature analysis
begins with the teacher supplying the "features which can be
used to clarify the connotations of the words" (p. 106), the
words to be studied from the text and a context for the words.
Students fill in a matrix comparing the various words for each
of the features. The use of questioning strategies and student
developed context are useful for clarification and
reinforcement.

62. Bellows, Barbara Plotkin. "Running Shoes Are to Jogging as
     Analogies are to Creative/Critical Thinking." JOURNAL OF
     READING 23 (March 1980): 507-511.

Bellows presents an easily duplicated sequence for teaching
analogies and illustrates applications to many content areas.
Her reasons for teaching analogies are many, ranging from
teaching details, word meaning and context to preparing for
advanced aptitude tests. Probably one of the most significant
reasons is the stress on creative, logical thinking. In
addition she emphasizes that the student become an active
participant by requiring that he discuss reasons and create and
defend original analogies.

63. Dupuis, Mary M., and Sandra L. Snyder. "Develop Concepts
     Through Vocabulary: A Strategy for Reading Specialists to Use

with Content Teachers." JOURNAL OF READING 26 (January 1983): 297-305.

Vocabulary and concepts can and should be taught together. This will help the student with reading problems and will draw on the strengths of both the content teacher and the reading specialists. The authors define concepts, using Hafner's definition, as a "class of things or ideas with common elements or characteristics" (p. 298) and suggest using Henry's four basic operations for concept development (joining, excluding, selecting and implying) as the basis for vocabulary development. Specific examples are given for each operation relating vocabulary to concept. Much emphasis is put on making choices and explaining the reasons for the choices.

64. Frager, Alan M. "An 'Intelligence' Approach to Vocabulary Teaching." JOURNAL OF READING 28 (November 1984): 160-164.

Frager advocates two approaches to vocabulary teaching: direct instruction and modeling. In the first approach he suggests using structured overviews, categorization and vocabulary cards. In the second approach he advocates using impromptu techniques such as "talk-through" and Manzo's Subjective Approach to Vocabulary. By interrupting instruction to develop vocabulary we model its importance for our students.

65. Haggard, Martha Rapp. "The Vocabulary Self-Collection Strategies: An Active Approach to Word Learning." JOURNAL OF READING 26 (December 1982): 203-207.

This classroom strategy is designed to satisfy two requirements: first that words studied are useful to students and second that students be taught skills for continued independent vocabulary growth. Students supply and define words. Group discussion clarifies, refines or extends the definitions. Assignments using the words reinforce the definitions. Haggard suggests that this strategy is easily adapted to content areas although she cautions that it requires "sustained, consistent use in order to be effective" (p. 206).

66. Johnson, Dale D., Susan Toms-Bronowski, and Susan D. Pittleman. AN INVESTIGATION OF THE TRENDS IN VOCABULARY RESEARCH AND THE EFFECTS OF PRIOR KNOWLEDGE IN INSTRUCTIONAL STRATEGIES FOR VOCABULARY ACQUISITION. Madison, Wisconsin: Wisconsin Center for Educational Research, The University of Wisconsin, November 1981. 63pp. (ED 214 118)

This theoretical paper presents a thorough review of historical research on the relationship between word knowledge and reading comprehension. After examining the instrumentalist hypothesis, the verbal hypothesis and the knowledge hypothesis to explain the relationship, the authors conclude that the last appears to be the most convincingly supported by current research. The review of the literature is clear and useful.

The authors have taken an additional step which makes this document particularly useful by including a discussion of teaching strategies that are related to the knowledge hypothesis. They define and illustrate contextual analysis, key-words, semantic mapping, and semantic feature analysis.

67. Kaplan, Elaine M., and Anita Tuchman. "Vocabulary Strategies Belong in the Hands of Learners." JOURNAL OF READING 24 (October 1980): 32-34.

Student commitment and active involvement are the keys to developing independence in determining the meanings of unknown words. Five easily replicated strategies are discussed, all designed to accomplish this. The focus in the strategies is on using relevant words, predicting meaning, building networks of meaning and utilizing context.

68. Stieglitz, Ezra L., and Varda S. Stieglitz. "SAVOR the Word to Reinforce Vocabulary in the Content Areas." JOURNAL OF READING 25 (October 1981): 46-50.

The authors have applied the strategy of feature analysis to the problem of reinforcing and using vocabulary after the student has had some experience with the topic. The activity is recommended for small groups, within a content area, with the group members eventually generating the words, the semantic features and filling in the matrix. Instructions are provided for introducing the strategy and developing the group's ability to reinforce content vocabulary actively and independently.

69. Templeton, Shane. "Using the Spelling/Meaning Connection to Develop Word Knowledge in Older Students." JOURNAL OF READING 27 (October 1983): 8-14.

Five sequential levels of instruction are proposed, based on the spelling similarities between words of related meanings. By understanding and exploring these connections, Templeton suggests that both word knowledge and spelling abilities will be improved. The discussion gives specific guidance on patterns of relationships between meaning and spelling, from silent/sounded consonants (sign/signal) to alternation patterns in related words (consume/consumption, assume/assumption). No specific suggestions for developing lessons are given. The lessons would certainly need to be made interesting, motivating and relevant for most high school students. Serious teachers of reading and of English will, however, gain some useful information from the article.

Understanding Sentences

Books

70. Harris, Albert J., and Edward R. Sipay.   "Improving Reading

Comprehension, I." HOW TO INCREASE READING ABILITY. New York: Longman, 1980, pp. 447-478.

Harris and Sipay discuss problems and methodologies associated with understanding words and sentences. The section on vocabulary development emphasizes the direct study of words, rather than words as part of concepts. The section on understanding thought units presents a clear, useful discussion on the difficulties readers encounter in sentence and phrase comprehension and possible remedial activities.

71. McNeil, John D. "Improving Comprehension of Sentences." READING COMPREHENSION: NEW DIRECTIONS FOR CLASSROOM PRACTICE. Glenview, Illinois: Scott, Foresman, 1984, pp. 114-131.

The author presents sentence patterns that can cause difficulty in comprehension as well as specific techniques for overcoming these difficulties. The stress is on the active comprehension of sentences, using strategies such as anagrams and sentence combining.

72. McNeil, John D., Lisbeth Donant, and Marvin C. Alkin. "Skills for Comprehension in Reading." HOW TO TEACH READING SUCCESSFULLY. Boston: Little, Brown, 1980, pp. 129-152.

The authors examine a variety of specific comprehension skills that can contribute to literal and inferential comprehension. The reviews of sequence, syntactical structures, punctuation, affixes, main ideas, logical conclusions and context clues are very specific with examples and behavioral objectives. The range of objectives within each skill, while not complete, is very useful in helping the secondary teacher see how a skill might develop. In addition, "newer ideas" including language constraints, self-mediated learning strategies, elaboration, and schema theory are discussed. This chapter can serve as an introduction to these topics.

73. Pearson, P. David, and Dale D. Johnson. "Understanding Longer Discourse: Part II." TEACHING READING COMPREHENSION. New York: Holt, Rinehart and Winston, 1978, pp. 108-132.

Pearson and Johnson explore the meaning relationships between words in sentences and among sentences in paragraphs. They provide many examples for causal, temporal, sequential, anaphoric, and main idea relations. A variety of instructional suggestions are made which can be easily adapted.

74. Weaver, Constance. "How Can We Help Readers Develop Good Reading Strategies?" PSYCHOLINGUISTICS AND READING: FROM PROCESS TO PRACTICE. Boston: Little, Brown, 1980, pp. 204-248.

Weaver states that good reading strategies involve predicting, sampling, confirming or correcting in order to

comprehend text. These are done both in light of the reader's
prior knowledge and the information stated and implied in the
text. The author includes a wealth of examples and activities
for using graphic/phonic, syntactic and semantic context to
teach students reading strategies. The discussion of syntactic
cues is particularly useful for revealing problems students may
have in processing text.

Periodicals

75. Cronnell, Bruce. "Cause and Effect: An Overview." READING
    WORLD 21 (December 1981): 155-166.

    Cronnell believes that understanding cause-effect relations
    is essential to reading comprehension, both on a sentence level
    and in connected discourse. Unfortunately, this is also a
    source of difficulty for readers, both young and old. He
    examines cause and effect relations in all their complexities:
    true statements of cause and effect as compared to conditional
    statements of purpose, condition and concession; single and
    multiple causes and effects; and literal and implied cause and
    effect relations. The numerous examples and the detailed lists
    of markers as well as various possible sentence constructions
    make this article particularly useful as a resource.

76. Klein, Marvin. "The Development and Use of Sentence Combining
    in the Reading Program." Paper presented at the Annual
    Meeting of the International Reading Association, St. Louis,
    Missouri, May 1980. 32pp. (ED 186 845)

    Klein presents a complex topic with clarity and conciseness
    and includes many useful examples. Sentence combining is viewed
    as "one of the most promising single recent developments which
    can contribute directly to both written composition skills and
    reading comprehension improvement" (p. 2). He explains "open"
    and "closed" approaches to sentence combining and illustrates
    how they can be used to teach the various grammatical
    functions. Even more useful are his suggestions on how to
    design activities and use sentence combining in the reading
    program.

77. Seidenberg, Pearl L. "Implications of Schemata Theory for
    Learning Disabled Readers." JOURNAL OF LEARNING DISABILITIES
    15 (June/July 1982): 352-354.

    While Seidenberg recognizes content-schema (the reader's
    semantic expectations) as important in comprehension, she
    focuses on form-schema (the reader's syntactic expectations)
    in this article. The author explores differences between
    spoken and written language, such as the significance of
    function words, the role of prosodic clues, and the kinds of
    cognitive strategies used to remember, comprehend and self-
    correct. The discussion of instructional techniques will serve
    as an introduction to the possibilities in patterning, sentence

combining, sentence decombining and cloze.

78. Snow, David P., and James H. Coots.   SENTENCE PERCEPTION IN
    LISTENING AND READING.   Los Alamitos, California: Southwest
    Regional Laboratory for Educational Research and Development,
    September 1981. 48pp. (ED 208-388)

    The authors present an in-depth review of research concerned
    with the syntactic organization and the information-processing
    organization of sentences. The particular focus is on the
    differences between oral and written sentences and on ways of
    aiding the reader to move from one to the other.   The main
    suggestion to teachers, to segment sentences into meaningful
    phrases in text, seems less than practical in most situations.
    The theoretical discussions are clear and useful in
    understanding some of the problems in sentence comprehension.

79. Stevens, Katherine C.   "Helping Students Understand Complicated
    Sentences." READING HORIZONS 22 (Spring 1982): 184-190.

    Stevens proposes that rather than make text simple with
    uncomplicated sentences we teach students to "deal with the
    complexities of written language" (p. 185).   She provides a
    sequence of activities to accomplish this. The discussion of
    coordination and subordination seems particularly useful both
    to reading and content teachers.

80. Stotsky, Sandra.   "The Role of Writing in Developmental
    Reading." JOURNAL OF READING 25 (January 1982): 330-340.

    Writing as a response to written language is viewed as a
    means of insuring that the reader is actively engaged in the
    comprehension process. Stotsky suggests a number of specific
    writing assignments designed to involve the student in
    analyzing, selecting, organizing and reorganizing information.
    She discusses, in some detail, dictation, reproduction,
    paraphrase writing, precise writing, sentence combining,
    sentence pattern practice and copying.

81. White, Carrie V., Ernest T. Pascarella, and Susanna W. Pflaum.
    "Effects of Training in Sentence Construction on the
    Comprehension of Learning Disabled Children." JOURNAL OF
    EDUCATIONAL PSYCHOLOGY 73 (1981): 697-704.

    The authors, using learning disabled, inner-city students
    (mean age 11.73 years), compared the effects on comprehension
    of anagram/word grouping to analyzing sentences and their
    components. The gains made by the anagram treatment group were
    significantly higher than the sentences study treatment group,
    particularly for those students with higher initial reading
    achievement.   The discussion suggests this may be due to
    focusing on verbs, synthesizing of single words and phrases,
    and determining reasonableness of the sentence.   "The
    manipulation of words and phrases" (p. 703) may be responsible
    for the comprehension gains in this and a prior study.

CHAPTER III

CONNECTED DISCOURSE

This chapter deals with connected discourse, paragraphs, chapters, books or the macrostructure of the text. Most of the material that secondary students must comprehend is connected discourse whether in a content classroom or a reading center. There are two areas we will examine here. Writers observe certain conventions in organizing their thoughts that readers can use in understanding the material. This is the element of text construction and text demand that Brown, Campione and Day (13) identified as critical in learning from text. This is the text structure or organization schemata that Crismore (14) identified as a significant factor in comprehension. Thus, the question of text structure is the first area we will examine. The second area is the level of comprehension on the part of the reader. Much secondary reading demands that readers not only understand what is actually stated but also what is implied. Readers need to be critical of what they read, and they need to apply the information and concepts in a larger context. This second area is one, as we have seen, where secondary students often seem to encounter problems.

Using the Structure of Written Materials

Theory

The importance of schema or background knowledge has already been discussed. So far, schema has referred to knowledge regarding content or subject. There is, however, another kind of schema that has relevance for reading comprehension. This is form schema or an individual's knowledge of the forms or structures used in text to organize information and ideas in expository or narrative text. Readers may have difficulty when they are unaware of these text structures or don't use them as a source of information while reading. The problem is compounded, of course, when authors fail to utilize these forms in their writing.

The questions we need to examine are: what are the structures and how are they defined; what impact do they appear to have on the act of reading; and what are some of the concerns that have been raised about them.

Definitions. The literature refers to three kinds of text structures or ways of organizing information. The first two are commonly associated with expository writing and the third with narratives.

First, there are ways of representing patterns of thought. Armbruster (82) calls these patterns "basic text structures" (p. 203) and identifies: listing, comparison/contrast, temporal sequence, cause/effect and problem/solution. Cheek and Cheek (84) call these structures "organizational patterns" and assert that they are "essential in content learning" (p. 202). We, too, shall refer to them as "organizational patterns" since their function is to represent the organization of the patterns of thought used by an author.

This concept of organizational patterns has its basis in classical rhetoric (4, 90). There is general, but not complete, agreement as to what to include in an inventory of these patterns. Most lists include the ones identified by Armbruster (82). Cook and Mayer (85), however, reviewed a number of these lists and suggested the complexities that have been identified. For example, they cite Kirszner and Mandell's list: "description, exemplification, process, cause and effect, comparison and contrast, division and classification, definition, and argumentation" (p. 101). Vacca (94) strikes what will appear to teachers to be a very practical note. "While the many elaborate classifications and close distinctions have value, particularly in the experimental study of text structure per se, I believe they can be counterproductive to content area reading instruction" (p. 141). He proposes that four patterns be taught: enumeration, time order, comparison/contrast, and cause/effect.

Think of the student reading the report of the soccer game. He can predict with a fair degree of certainty what the organizational pattern or patterns will be and the circumstances in which they will be used. Probably the writer will use time order to show the development of the game and comparison/contrast to highlight differences between the teams. The writer might possibly use a cause/effect pattern if something unusual happened to influence the outcome of the game. The chances are much slimmer that he can make the same hypotheses about the chemistry text. Yet, the organizational pattern is equally important there.

The second text structure to be considered in connection with expository writing is that of a hierarchy of ideas. Ideas and information generally require more than a listing, they require a hierarchy. Some thought unites and orders all the information or ideas presented. It is superior, the rest is subordinate. Thus, the second structure is one that has long been of concern to teachers: main idea and details.

Our reader can anticipate that there is certainly a hierarchy of ideas in the soccer article. One team won and one team lost. A particular player demonstrated outstanding expertise. He not only knows that there is going to be a main idea in the article, but he has the background knowledge needed to help him identify it. Think of the material likely to be included in a chemistry text. The hierarchy is there but may be more difficult for him to identify.

The third text structure, story grammar, is specific to the genre of narratives and includes, in some way, the setting, the characters, the action and the outcome of a story. Definitions of story grammar may differ, but they all account for at least these variables. For example, according to Sadow (110) Rummelhart, in 1975, developed a grammar for simple stories which included:

Setting	Episode
characters	initiating event
time	reaction of main character
place	action
other significant	consequence of action
information	

Impact. What difference will it make to the reader if he is taught to recognize, understand and use these text structures? It has been suggested that:

1. comprehension improves. (82, 84, 87, 114)

2. bottom-up and top-down processing can both occur. (96, 110)

3. recall improves. Text structures seem to provide a framework for enabling recall of text. (14, 82, 83, 85, 89, 90, 98, 114)

4. poorly organized text can be comprehended because the reader can impose a structure on it. (98)

5. text structures can provide a source of information when prior knowledge of content is missing. "The lack of appropriate knowledge may be overcome somewhat by relying on the manner in which the text is structured" (85, p. 102). (85, 89)

6. metacognition may occur. The reader can monitor comprehension by using these structures to predict areas to be comprehended and to fill in the missing ones. (83, 98)

There appear to be a number of substantial reasons for teaching students to use these text structures. We must also, however, examine the concerns that have been raised here.

Concerns. Underlying the three areas of concern we will examine is Kintsch's (87) belief that we need more research evidence as well as a processing model of comprehension that includes the characteristics of expository text. Then, questions of when and how readers use text structures can finally be answered. In the meantime, what are some of the questions being raised regarding text structure?

First, the difficulty in defining, identifying and comprehending the complexity of human thought solely by relying on

knowledge of text structure is certainly of concern. "The meaning
of a text...depends as much on the reader's background and goals as
on the characteristics of the text itself" (87, p. 88). Form schema
are not sufficient. We also need, to use Crismore's (14) term,
content schema. For example, in order to understand a narrative,
the reader needs more than a sense of story grammar. He needs some
understanding of human nature and the human condition. In addition,
as Kintsch (87) and Vacca (94) point out, writers, because of the
complexity of their ideas, do not always use only one type of
organizational pattern. They combine patterns.

Second, the relationship of main idea/details to organizational
patterns might be further clarified through additional research.
While many might agree with Arnold's (97, p. 374) formula: topic +
unifying idea = main idea, there is a difference of opinion about
how main idea and details relate to organizational patterns. Main
idea/details may be an additional pattern of organization that
"subsumes" the other patterns and appear in every pattern of
organization (94 p. 152). On the other hand, they may be "subsumed"
by the other organizational patterns. Readers who have trouble with
main idea/detail will have trouble with the other patterns of
organization (91). A third possibility is that main idea/details is
part of the enumeration or listing pattern (84).

An additional question here is, which do you teach first, main
idea or organizational pattern? While Santeusanio (91) points out
that there is some evidence "that it may be preferable to introduce
the concept of main idea after the major organizational patterns
have been introduced" (p. 76), this is certainly not a settled
issue.

A third area of concern relates to story grammars. Kintsch
(87), among others, has identified problems in generating new
stories and distinguishing between stories and nonstories. Story
grammars have also been criticized as being too narrow and too rigid
to meet the needs of complex narratives. Tierney and Mosenthal (93)
suggest an event chain formulation which focuses on the
interconnections between the elements of the narrative as a means of
dealing with complex narratives.

In spite of these problems, as Cook and Mayer (85) point out,
"research has generally been supportive of the notions of story
grammars" (p. 99). It is interesting to note, however, that
textbooks and journals on secondary reading seldom deal with this
topic. This may be because the bulk of secondary reading is in
expository text and/or because there is no substantial body of
research relating story grammars to adolescent/adult literature.

It appears that we are again examining an area with some
uncertainties; however, for teachers, there may not be as many as in
some of the other areas we have investigated. There appears to be
much support in the literature for the hypothesis that identifying
and using text structure aids the reader in a variety of ways.

Practice

Consider the following statements:

"The ability to differentiate between the significant and the nonsignificant in text tends to separate proficient readers from ineffective readers" (102, p. 135).

"The majority of studies in this area report that less skilled (or younger) readers fail to recognize and/or to consider text structure" (104 p. 403).

"You can guide maturing readers by helping them perceive relationships and distinguish important from less important ideas" (94, p. 139).

"When such strategies are not activated spontaneously, it is possible to teach students how to use them and to expect that these strategies would transfer to other reading tasks" (104 p. 403).

Geva (104) contends that although "there is substantial evidence that implicit knowledge of text structure discriminates good readers from poor readers....typically, knowledge of text structure and text structure markers is not taught explicitly in schools" (p. 385). Secondary reading demands that students understand and use the structure of expository text, but they generally have had little experience with it. As Stotsky (111) points out "a large majority of the selections at each grade level, 1-8, are narrative" (p. 5). Both reading specialists and content teachers need to address the problem of instructing and guiding students in using text structures, particularly expository text. In order to teach text structure strategies effectively, Kent's (105) caution that teachers must recognize and understand the differences between narrative and expository text is well taken.

Let's look at suggestions that can apply to the three types of text structure, with the understanding that the emphasis or the focus may differ depending on the form of the text.

1. Use a direct teaching model. Define the structure, explain the process to be used, and then lead students through it. Consider carefully whether to use a subskills approach (This is the main idea. It is usually at the beginning of the paragraph) or a meaning approach (What does this paragraph mean? What does the author want to convey?). If students have had difficulty in the past with the structure, then they probably need direct instruction. (91, 92, 106, 109)

2. Use a diagnostic/prescriptive approach when the student has some understanding of the structure. Identify the student's ability to use a sequence of strategies and instruct in the area of difficulty. (98, 103)

3. Emphasize that understanding and using text structures require the use of thinking skills. (86, 102)

4. Stress the author's purpose in using a particular pattern. Why is he using it? What does he want the reader to gain because of his use of this specific pattern? (86)

5. Instruct in the meaning and use of key words (also called signals or markers) as a means of identifying the author's pattern or for organizing students' writing. (84, 86, 91, 94, 107)

6. Emphasize the interrelatedness of the structures. For example, use organizational patterns as a basis for identifying the main idea. (89, 95, 96, 98)

7. Encourage students to restructure text, particularly if a simple listing pattern is used. (88, 95)

8. Use instructional techniques that are specific, clear and provide structure for the students. These might, for example, include paragraph frames and cloze procedures to highlight organizational patterns or pictures to introduce the concept of main idea. Start with the concrete and move to the abstract. (15, 91, 97, 106, 112)

9. Develop questions that will highlight the particular structure. (91, 92, 99, 110)

10. Provide a graphic aid before, during or after the reading. This might be a pattern guide, which stresses the predominant organizational pattern in the text (84, 88, 94, 107). The graphic aid might be a diagram designed to represent the text structure such as an idea-map, a flowchart, web, or pyramid (96, 100, 104). Provide opportunities for students to complete partially prepared graphic aides or to create their own based on their reading (113).

11. Insure that students move from recognizing text structures to using them to infer the writer's ideas, to generate their own structures and to write using a variety of structures. The goal must be independence, not reliance on the teacher. (14, 15, 16, 18, 89, 94, 96, 97, 101, 106, 108, 112)

12. Teach for transfer to all content areas. Examine the demand of particular subjects in terms of text structure and teach to those demands. (18, 84, 85, 86, 91, 92, 94, 97)

13. Identify potential problem areas for students in specific materials used in the classroom. This is particularly needed in the area of cause/effect but is also important in the other text structures. (91, 92)

14. Use text structure as a variable in choosing textbooks. (82, 89)

Suggestions for Implementation

For the most part, the structures we have been discussing are concrete, can be perceived by teachers and students, and can be identified and diagrammed. These are motivating reasons to incorporate instruction in these strategies in a secondary school reading program. This is an area where the reading teacher and the content teacher can work together very productively and where the student can see the payoff.

The reading specialist can work with the content teacher by:

1. identifying common and important structural elements in the materials used in the particular content area.

2. preparing a list of frequently occurring key words.

3. presenting a demonstration lesson to a whole class based on the materials.

4. providing practice for individual students as needed.

The content teacher can reinforce this instruction by:

1. incorporating instructional strategies such as questions and graphic organizers into lessons.

2. reinforcing techniques through practice in reading and writing.

Comprehending at Various Levels

Theory

So far, the implication has been that everything the author intends to convey to the reader is stated literally. Unfortunately for the reader, this is not always true. In an expository text the author may state that the war was precipitated by the peasant uprising, but may leave it to the reader to figure out that the peasants rebelled because of a shortage of food and because their daughters were being molested. A few cruel landlords were responsible for both of these problems. Did the two problems cause the war? Which one was more important? Were the landlords the cause? Was the war justified? This may all be left to the reader.

In narrative text the author seldom says to the reader "Now, pay attention. This is the setting. Here's the main character. Here's the problem and this is how it's resolved. I don't want you to miss anything, so here's how everything is related."

Finally, in any text, does the author ever indicate "I want you to be critical of the things I'm saying, so be sure to evaluate my language, my statements and my qualifications"? No, that is left up to the discretion of the reader.

Remember the findings of the National Assessment of Educational Progress (34)? These are the very areas that have been highlighted in the literature as problem areas for secondary school students. They deserve careful inspection. First we need to consider some general definitions of levels of comprehension and then look at specific definitions of inferential and critical reading. In addition, we will consider their impact on comprehension as well as concerns that have been raised.

Definitions. Vacca (120), in identifying the levels of comprehension, uses the common description: reading the lines (literal), reading between the lines (inferential) and reading beyond the lines (applied). Ringler and Weber (117) add a critical level in which the reader reacts to and evaluates the text.

There appear to be two kinds of inferencing. Readers:

1. make connections among information, events, and concepts which are stated in the text but which the author has not connected or related. Trabasso (119) calls this "text connecting" (p. 56) while Pearson and Johnson (116) refer to these connections as "textually implicit" (p. 144).

2. fill in missing information in order to make needed connections. Trabasso (119) calls this "slot filling." Pearson and Johnson (116) use the label "scriptually implicit" because the reader needs to use his own script or schema to make this kind of inference. To do this, the reader must know what schema to use and how to use the schema to fill the slot.

Next, Trabasso (119) identifies six varieties of inference: "those which are logical (causal), those which are informational, those which are spatial or temporal, those which are related to script knowledge, those which depend on world knowledge in some general sense and those which are primarily evaluative in nature" (p. 64).

What seems to be required in order to infer? Trabasso (ibid.) includes:

1. background knowledge and vocabulary because without understanding the basic concepts, the reader can't make the necessary connections. Does this sound familiar? Think of some of the discussion in chapters I and II. Also, keep this in mind as you read Chapter IV.

2. knowledge about text structure. This may aid the reader in a "top-down fashion" by providing a set of expectations which enable him to predict content and identify missing areas. Again, a familiar topic! Also, to be repeated in Chapter IV!

3. knowledge about "social interaction and human intentionality" (p. 63). Knowing something about the social status of butlers and about why people act the way they do, will help you identify the butler as the culprit or, maybe in a larger sense, the

victim. Remember the discussion of story grammar?

4. knowledge of "causal relations between events" (ibid.).   By
    having a script available about common causal chains, the reader
    is able, again, to predict and assimilate new information, as
    well as to identify missing information. You probably had a
    script available for the "war" example.

We can add two other items to this list. Holmes (125) suggests
that readers need to be successful problem solvers. Wilson and
Hammill (132) advocate that students need to understand the process
of inferencing.

The definition and description of inferences and inferencing
are certainly more complex than we may have anticipated. This very
complexity may, in fact, account for many of the difficulties
students experience in "reading between the lines."

Now, let's consider a definition of critical reading. Ross
(128) holds that it is "a complex skill essential for reacting
thoughtfully to printed material" (p. 311). What does critical
reading include? The reader is actively engaged in:

1. evaluating the source of the information, including the author's
    qualifications, the author's bias, and the type of publication
    and the date. (128)

2. identifying fact and opinion and evaluating the support given.
    (83, 116)

3. recognizing the style of language. Does it reflect a bias? Is
    it vague or precise? (83, 116)

4. spotting logical inconsistencies and important omissions. (83,
    116)

According to Shirley (129) critical reading, like critical
thinking, involves "the accurate assessment of statements based on
the knowledge of methods of inquiry and logical reasoning" (p. 3).
It is, in fact, critical thinking (131) and includes interpretation,
insight and problem solving (129).

In addition, there may be another factor involved in critical
reading, that of reader predisposition. Santeusanio (118) proposes
that "the difficulties that both adolescents and adults have with
critical reading may be related more to their attitudes and
characteristics than to the complexity of the process of critical
reading itself" (p. 202). We believe what we want to believe.

To say that critical reading is important sounds almost trite.
Pearson and Johnson (116) state the case very strongly. "One may
legitimately question the virtue of preparing students who can read
correctly but cannot evaluate the accuracy of what they read" (p.
134).

Vacca's (120, pp. 121-122) description of applied reading completes our definitions of the levels of comprehension. In applied reading, readers "seek significance," "express opinions," and "draw additional insights." Applied reading is "constructing knowledge," taking the text as the basis for "new insights" and "fresh ideas" by combining and recombining prior and new information.

Why do secondary students come to us with difficulties in these areas? Partly, it may be the kind of instruction students have had in earlier grades. We tend to emphasize decoding skills in the primary grades and do not always stress higher level comprehension skills. Also, materials used in primary grades don't lend themselves easily to inferential and critical comprehension.

Perhaps, in addition, it is as Escoe (103) suggests. There is a lack of a universal text structure that the reader can depend on in making inferences. There are no key words to indicate that the author expects an inference to be made and what information is to be used in making that inference. In addition, there are also no universal expectations on the part of the text, the teacher, or, in some instances, the culture, that the reader will be critical in his reading.

Impact.   There is evidence that instruction in inferential, critical and applied reading:

1. increases comprehension. (115, 121, 125)

2. allows the reader to connect the known with the unknown. (125, 132)

3. requires active participation on the part of the reader. (121)

4. allows for both bottom-up and top-down processing to occur, the former in processing the information to begin construction of an inference, for example, and the latter in using the inference to predict, interpret and integrate new information into the overall framework. (119)

5. allows the reader to move beyond the text, to integrate texts in a thoughtful and meaningful manner and to create unique texts. (120)

Concerns.   There are three concerns which we will examine. First, we have tended to view these levels as separate, discrete and sequential. Lindquist (126), in examining critical reading, states that "the highest level is evaluation" (p. 770) and in order to answer questions on a critical level a reader must be able to answer lower-level questions. Hillocks (123) and Hillocks and Ludlow (124) take much the same posture. In order to answer inferential questions, the reader must first deal with literal level questions.

Vacca (120), on the other hand, believes that "the levels are probably interactive and inseparable" (p. 125). For example, a

reader may first read to find out how the information applies to him
and then read to identify the important literal details. In another
scenario a reader may miss a literal detail until he begins to put
information together to make an inference. At that point he
realizes the significance of the detail and can fit it into the
inference, using the detail to confirm or reject his hypothesis
about the inference. Suddenly, once you begin to suspect that the
"butler did it" you are aware of more of the butler's actions. They
begin to make sense. Now you attend to the man's glove lying on the
hall table!

A second interesting and potentially useful question for
teachers is that of the relationship between inferencing, critical
reading and using story grammar to comprehend narratives. Lindquist
(126) and Hillocks (123) illustrate two points of view. They both
agree that higher level skills are part of a hierarchy of
comprehension levels. In addition, they both relate comprehension
skills to the text characteristics of narratives. However, they
differ in how they relate skills and text characteristics.

Lindquist begins with text structure, providing a specific
guide to the student of the elements of story grammar and asking a
series of specific questions designed to elicit the structure of the
narrative. The questions themselves are based on the hierarchy in
Bloom's Taxonomy and are designed to enhance comprehension of the
content. Hillocks, on the other hand, believes that "before
students can deal with the abstractions which structural analysis
involves, they must be able to deal with the literal and inferential
content of the work" (p. 55). Exactly how to proceed in instruction
is certainly not settled, but we may be able to use the variables of
story grammar and levels of comprehension to improve comprehension
of narratives.

A third concern is the role of questions in developing
comprehension on various levels. Much of the literature assumes
and/or asserts that questions, if worded and sequenced properly,
will improve comprehension on the inferential, critical and applied
levels. Trabasso (119), however, cautions that this is an area
where we need more research evidence.

While these concerns certainly raise important issues, they do
not allow us to forego instruction until all the issues are settled.
Pearson (115) reassures us that "The data are encouraging. It looks
as though we can teach comprehension skills after all" (p. 231).

Practice

Some students demonstrate "developmental improvement" (ibid.,
p. 224); they become more adept at comprehending on various levels
as they mature. However, there are certainly students who need some
help along the way. We need to consider a variety of instructional
strategies if they get to secondary school and are still having
difficulties with anything but literal level comprehension tasks.
Consider these suggestions.

1. Review materials to determine general suitability for the class and for particular students. (117, 125)

2. Assess the student's background knowledge and ability to read on differing levels. (103, 119)

3. Provide a model the student can follow covering the various steps in the process. (125, 129)

4. Instruct in the various components. (115, 122, 128)

5. Model the process of higher level thinking for students. (115, 130, 132)

6. Design graphic organizers to guide in comprehending on various levels. These can be used to introduce the text in class in order to activate and organize background information and to allow individual students to monitor the process on their own. (91, 120, 121)

7. Prepare questions to elicit inferences and critical/applied observations. (117, 118, 123, 126, 129)

8. Consider using statements rather than questions. (127)

9. Integrate the two concepts of text structure and levels of comprehension. (118, 123, 126)

10. Teach a series of steps that will allow the student to self-monitor success in higher level comprehension skills. (121, 122, 125)

11. Aim at having the student become independent in this area. One strategy is to provide opportunities for student-generated observations and questions. Another strategy is to enable students to develop their own set of standards for judging text. A self-monitoring checklist can also foster independence. (115, 117, 121, 122)

12. Insure that a diversity of materials is available and that there are opportunities for group discussion. It is particularly important to provide an opportunity to compare and contrast the elements of critical reading. (115, 128, 131)

13. Provide opportunities to practice in various content areas. (115, 118)

<u>Suggestions for Implementation</u>

This is another area where reading teachers and content teachers can work together profitably--to make the work load easier for each of them and to make the reading instruction more productive for the student. The ultimate payoff, of course, is that the student's comprehension and recall of the content may improve! The same general suggestions for implementation made in the first part of this chapter can also apply here.

Summary

Think back on the items Brown, Campione and Day (13) included in their list of training needs if students are to learn from text. We have identified some very basic, important strategies for learning and remembering on all levels of comprehension and for a variety of text structures. Suggestions have been made for activating prior knowledge and for developing problem-solving, metacognitive strategies. More on these latter topics in Chapter IV. The process is certainly an active one. We are on the way to developing readers who comprehend, recall and "learn from text."

BIBLIOGRAPHY

Using the Structure of Written Materials

Books

82. Armbruster, Bonnie B. "The Problem of 'Inconsiderate Text.'"
     COMPREHENSION INSTRUCTION: PERSPECTIVES AND SUGGESTIONS.
     Edited by Gerald G. Duffy, Laura R. Roehler, and Jana Mason.
     New York: Longman, 1984, pp. 202-217.

     Armbruster documents the importance of coherence or structure
     in comprehension and recall by examining recent research in the
     significance of structure in narratives and expository text.
     She defines coherence in two ways: local and global.   Local
     coherence comes from the links within and between sentences and
     includes linguistic forms and connectives as well as the
     explicit statement of relationships within paragraphs. "Global
     coherence is achieved by text characteristics that facilitate
     the integration of high level, important ideas across the
     entire section, chapter, or book" (p. 203).   The structures
     that reflect fundamental patterns of human thought (listing,
     comparison/contrast, temporal   sequence,   cause/effect   and
     problem/solution) are one text characteristic. Another one is
     the structure of the textbook (titles, subtitles, introduction,
     topic sentences). The author stresses that structure alone is
     not sufficient; the interaction between content and structure
     is significant in achieving coherence.

     The discussion focuses on the theoretical but the inclusion
     of a number of well-chosen quotes from student texts makes the
     points very clear. The argument for using the ideas presented
     as a basis for textbook selection is convincing. Mention is
     made of the need to instruct students in using text
     characteristics as a comprehension strategy.

83. Beach, Richard, and Deborah Appleman. "Reading Strategies for
     Expository and Literary Text Types." BECOMING READERS IN A
     COMPLEX SOCIETY.   Eighty-third Yearbook of the National
     Society for the Study of Education. Edited by Alan C. Purves
     and Olive Niles.   Chicago, Illinois: The University of
     Chicago Press, 1984, pp. 115-143.

     Beach and Appleman provide a clear and useful description and
     analysis of the characteristics of both expository and
     narrative texts and the strategies readers use to comprehend
     them.   In addition, they examine the process of making
     judgments and reading critically in both genres.

84. Cheek, Earl H., and Martha Collins Cheek.   "Organizational
     Patterns for Content Learning." READING INSTRUCTION THROUGH
     CONTENT TEACHING. Columbus, Ohio: Charles E. Merrill, 1983,
     pp. 200-227.

The authors present clear illustrations of organizational patterns in text with suggestions for using signal words and developing concept guides and pattern guides for the various patterns. Examples from the various content areas are particularly helpful.

85. Cook, Linda K., and Richard E. Mayer. "Reading Strategies Training for Meaningful Learning from Prose." COGNITIVE STRATEGY RESEARCH: EDUCATIONAL APPLICATIONS. Edited by Michael Pressley and Joel R. Levin. New York: Springer-Verlag, 1983, pp. 87-131.

Cook and Mayer provide a theoretical framework for examining observable reading, studying and test-taking strategies as well as internal cognitive strategies used to process information. The framework includes three aspects of cognitive learning: knowledge of content, text structure and process. The authors integrate much current research into this framework and finally, examine reading strategies in light of theory and research findings. These strategies include: notetaking, summarizing, underlining, and answering adjunct questions. A final section examines instructional strategies for improving reading skills. These instructional strategies include: SQ3R, REAP, structured overview, DRTA and ReQuest. The focus is on research, with a view to examining what has been done and what needs to be done. However, the secondary teacher will find a wealth of background information here.

86. Friedman, Myles I., and Michael D. Rowls. "Writing Patterns in the Content Areas." TEACHING READING AND THINKING SKILLS. New York: Longman, 1980, pp. 429-451.

Friedman and Rowls identify reading and thinking skills in specific content areas, since not all reading materials in every area demand the same kinds of skills. These are related to writing patterns (listing, sequence, comparison/contrast, cause/effect) with examples and suggestions for teaching. The emphasis on thinking skills is important but the suggestions are not always explicit enough to be applied with ease.

87. Kintsch, Walter. "Text Representations." READING EXPOSITORY MATERIAL. Edited by Wayne Otto and Sandra White. New York: Academic Press, 1982, pp. 87-101.

Kintsch proposes that the meaning of a text depends on the reader's background and goals as well as on the characteristics of the text. In this chapter, he focuses on three major aspects of text representation that highlight various text characteristics. The discussion of sentence-level representations is theoretical and not easily applied by school-based professionals. The discussion of stories reviews story grammars as a means of representing text characteristics of stories and as a basis for comprehending them. The short-comings of story grammars are clearly identified but their usefulness as a basis of predicting sources of information and relationships is also stressed. The discussion of expository texts outlines strategies for nine types of expository texts. Kintsch points out the need for more experimental evidence to support the usefulness of these strategies and predicts that it will be forthcoming.

In both stories and expository prose, text-type characteristics are only part of the representation. Comprehension strategies must also be concerned with content. Text strategies and comprehension strategies work together to guide and enable comprehension. This chapter is theoretical in its orientation. It refers to but does not discuss in detail current research. Kintsch provides an important framework for reading other authors in this field.

88. McNeil, John D. "Comprehending Different Types of Discourse." READING COMPREHENSION: NEW DIRECTIONS FOR CLASSROOM PRACTICE. Glenview, Illinois: Scott, Foresman, 1984, pp. 132 -155.

McNeil examines the features of both narrative and expository text and relates them to strategies readers may use for comprehension. These cover a considerable range and include, for example, self-generated questions based on story grammar, pattern guides constructed by the teacher and completed by the student, restructuring of text through informal outline procedures, and summaries developed according to specific rules. Many of the strategies might be considered study strategies as well as comprehension strategies. One useful feature of the chapter is the use of activities for teachers to help illustrate the points made.

89. Meyer, Bonnie J. F. "Organizational Aspects of Text: Effects on Reading Comprehension and Applications for the Classroom." PROMOTING READING COMPREHENSION. Edited by James Flood. Newark, Delaware: International Reading Assn., 1984, pp. 113-138.

Meyer reviews current research related to text structure and summarizes the findings in relation to the impact of text structure on comprehension and recall as well as practical implications for the selection of textbooks and for improving comprehension in the classroom. She identifies the interrelationship between organizational patterns and the hierarchy of ideas. Other variables examined are the kinds of signaling provided in the text and the role of the length, complexity and familiarity of the text.

90. Meyer, Bonnie J. F., and G. Elizabeth Rice. "The Structure of Text." HANDBOOK OF READING RESEARCH. Edited by P. David Pearson, Rebecca Barr, Michael L. Kamil and Peter Mosenthal. New York: Longman, 1984, pp. 319-351.

Meyer and Rice examine, in some detail, various systems for analyzing text structure. They begin with an historical perspective pointing out that although educational researchers

have only recently begun investigating the topic of text
structure, educators have been teaching patterns of
organization to students for some time. Although the analyses
and comparisons of various prose analysis systems for both
narrative and exposition are oriented more toward research than
toward instruction, the discussion nevertheless presents a
thorough framework for understanding much of the research and
research related problems in this area.

91. Santeusanio, Richard P. "Distinguishing Main Ideas and
Absorbing Data." A PRACTICAL APPROACH TO CONTENT AREA
READING. Reading, Massachusetts: Addison-Wesley, 1983, pp.
67-135.

The author recognizes the interrelationship of three areas of
reading that are frequently taught separately: levels of
comprehension, patterns of organization, and main ideas and
details. The last is "subsumed" by the patterns of
organization and both of these may be expressed by the writer
and identified by the reader on a literal or an implied level
of comprehension. The emphasis in this chapter is on numerous
strategies to teach main idea/details, data or listing of
information, and comparison/contrast. The examples are very
detailed and drawn from different areas of the secondary school
curriculum.

92. Santeusanio, Richard P. "Recognizing Sequence and
Cause/Effect." A PRACTICAL APPROACH TO CONTENT AREA READING.
Reading, Massachusetts: Addison-Wesley, 1983, pp. 137-196.

The author details possible student problems and difficulties
with comprehending sequence and cause/effect, suggests teaching
strategies, and gives examples from various content areas. The
approach is practical; the suggestions are clear and detailed;
the material is helpful in addressing a particularly
troublesome area for high school students.

93. Tierney, Robert J., and James Mosenthal. "Discourse
Comprehension and Production: Analyzing Text Structure and
Cohesion." READER MEETS AUTHOR/BRIDGING THE GAP. Edited by
Judith A. Langer and M. Trika Smith-Burke. Newark, Delaware:
International Reading Assn., 1982, pp. 55-104.

The authors examine, in some detail, four aspects of text
analysis. Propositional analysis is concerned with the
relationships between idea units. Cohesion examines the
"linguistic mortar which connects the text together" (p. 70).
Story grammars and event chain formulations provide a framework
for examining the structure of narrative texts. The structural
relationships of ideas and concepts, and mapped patterns
reflecting these relationships are viewed as a means of
comprehending expository texts. The chapter, which is
concerned with theory and research, provides a thorough
foundation for understanding the basic concepts. Some
suggestions are made to teachers within this perspective.

94. Vacca, Richard T. "Perceiving Organization in Text Materials."
    CONTENT AREA READING. Boston: Little, Brown, 1981, pp. 139-
    157.

    Vacca presents a brief theoretical foundation for a very
    practical discussion of text organization. He includes
    organizational patterns (listing, time, comparison/contrast and
    cause/effect) and an overriding pattern of hierarchy of ideas
    (main idea/details). He gives guidelines for constructing
    pattern guides and concept guides as well as numerous, detailed
    examples from various content areas.

                              Periodicals

95. Alvermann, Donna E. "Restructuring Text Facilitates Written
    Recall of Main Ideas." JOURNAL OF READING 25 (May 1982):
    754-758.

    The author suggests, on the basis of a limited study, that
    students' comprehension and recall can improve if they develop
    a graphic organizer based on a different organizational pattern
    from that used in the text. For example, in a selection in
    which items are listed, the students develop a graphic
    organizer comparing and contrasting the listed items. This
    strategy seems to highlight the relevant information and serve
    as a "cueing device" for the main idea.

96. Armbruster, Bonnie B., and Thomas H. Anderson. IDEA MAPPING:
    THE TECHNIQUE AND ITS USE IN THE CLASSROOM OR SIMULATING THE
    "UPS" AND "DOWNS" OF READING COMPREHENSION. (Reading
    Education Report No. 36.) Urbana: University of Illinois,
    Center for the Study of Reading, October 1982.

    Idea mapping, a "diagrammatic representation of information
    in text" (p. 10), emphasizes the relationships between ideas.
    By using a set of frames and symbols the reader can comprehend
    text using either a bottom-up or top-down approach.
    Information can be organized into an idea map, or the idea map
    can serve as a framework for predicting what will be included
    in the text. The authors provide examples and ideas for
    including this strategy in classroom instruction.

97. Arnold, Martha Thompson. "Teaching Theme, Thesis, Topic
    Sentences, and Clinchers as Related Concepts." JOURNAL OF
    READING 24 (February 1981): 373-376.

    Mastery of the concept of "main idea" in expository text in
    the reading class can be transferred to literature as well as
    to speaking and listening, and expository and creative writing.
    The author makes several useful suggestions to the teacher for
    doing this.

98. Bartlett, Brenden John. "So This Is The Main Idea: Where Use
    of an Author's Top-Level Structure Helps a Reader." Paper

presented at the Annual Meeting of the World Congress on Reading, Manila, Philippines, August 5-7, 1980. 25pp. (ED 200 954)

Bartlett proposes that training in the use of top-level structure (organization patterns) facilitates the reader's recognition, comprehension and recall of the main idea. Research by the author and others is cited in support of this hypothesis.

99. Bowman, Margie, and Linda Gambrell. "The Effects of Story Structure Questioning Upon Reading Comprehension." Paper presented at the Annual Meeting of the American Educational Research Association, Los Angeles, California, April 13-17, 1981. 54pp. (ED 203 301)

Bowman and Gambrell studied the effectiveness of a story structure questioning technique on the reading comprehension of sixth graders. They concluded that this strategy appears to improve comprehension and recall of narratives. The paper provides examples and guidance in using the strategy.

100. Clewell, Suzanne, and Julie Haidemenos. "Organizational Strategies To Increase Content Area Learning: Webbing, Pyramiding, and Think Sheets." Paper presented at the Annual Meeting of the International Reading Association, Chicago, Illinois, April 26-30, 1982. 14pp. (ED 214 139)

The authors present three reading strategies based on text structure that will aid in comprehension of content materials. Webbing and pyramiding are graphic aids which represent main ideas and details and are done after the material has been read. Think sheets are started before the reading takes place, include making predictions about the text, and are completed in small groups after the material has been read. Detailed instructions are given for teaching students the three strategies.

101. D'Angelo, Karen. "Precis Writing: Promoting Vocabulary Development and Comprehension." JOURNAL OF READING 26 (March 1983): 534-539.

Drawing on research that supports the notion that developing writing skills improves reading skills, D'Angelo suggests that precis writing is particularly beneficial because of its stress on "selecting, rejecting, and paraphrasing ideas" (p. 535). In presenting detailed instructions on how to teach precis writing, she emphasizes the critical importance to precis writing of the relationship between main idea and detail. Examples are given for identifying the relationship in reading and incorporating it in writing. In addition, she cites the potential for vocabulary growth in the act of paraphrasing.

102. Donlan, Dan. "Locating Main Ideas in History Textbooks."

JOURNAL OF READING 24 (November 1980): 135-140.

Because main idea or topic sentences frequently appear in positions other than at the beginning of paragraphs, Donlan advocates teaching students to identify the "logical relationships that exist between component sentences" (p. 137) as a way of identifying the main idea of paragraphs. He starts with the relationships between words, then pairs of sentences, and finally sentences within paragraphs. The strategy requires thinking and active participation on the part of the reader and requires teaching on the part of the teacher. "If students cannot find the main idea, it is pointless to ask them to find it. They must be taught how" (p. 136).

103. Escoe, Adrienne S. "Schooling and Scheming: From Research in Reading Instruction toward Information Processing." Paper presented at the Annual Meeting of the International Reading Association, New Orleans, April 27-May 1, 1981. 69pp. (ED 204 735)

Four areas of comprehension are considered: main idea, sequence, cause and effect, and drawing conclusions. The author provides a sequential model of information processing for each area and proposes that we diagnose a student's ability to perform the required strategies at each step and then instruct in the strategies that are lacking. The paper provides numerous specific examples of possible formats for diagnosis with some general implications for instruction.

104. Geva, Esther. "Facilitating Reading Comprehension Through Flowcharting." READING RESEARCH QUARTERLY XVIII (Summer 1983): 384-405.

Flowcharting requires that the reader analyze text structure and diagram the ideas presented and their relationships. The flowchart provides a framework for representing both content and function. The author suggests this is a useful strategy for less skilled readers, particularly those with a deficit in top-down strategies. The article reports on research conducted by the author and includes specific examples showing student improvement.

105. Kent, Carolyn E. "A Linguist Compares Narrative and Expository Prose." JOURNAL OF READING 28 (December 1984): 232-236.

Kent analyzes the differences between narrative and expository text. They differ in the areas of person, orientation, time and linkage (for example, chronological or logical links between information or events). These points are clearly illustrated. Implications for instruction are provided. The author stresses the importance of the teacher's understanding and using the differences in helping students comprehend.

106. Moore, David W., and John E. Readence. "Processing Main Ideas Through Parallel Lesson Transfer." JOURNAL OF READING 23 (April 1980): 589-593.

   After identifying the difficulties students have with the concept of "main idea," the authors suggest that a sequential teaching strategy be used in four parallel tasks. The strategy requires that the teacher model the process of determining the main idea, the student then chooses a main idea from alternatives and finally, generates one on his own. This strategy is used in parallel lessons of viewing pictures, listening to information and reading, orally and silently. The authors provide a number of suggestions for implementation.

107. Olson, Mary W., and Bonnie Longnion. "Pattern Guides: A Workable Alternative for Content Teachers." JOURNAL OF READING 25 (MAY 1982): 736-741.

   Olson and Longnion propose the use of a pattern guide to highlight the organizational patterns used in high school textbooks. They give examples based on listing, cause/effect, comparison/contrast and time order as well as provide a list of structure words to be used in identifying the patterns. The procedure to follow in developing a pattern guide is very explicit and the examples are easy to replicate.

108. Rhoder, Carol. "The Integration of Reading and Writing Instruction: A Strategy for All Teachers." Paper presented at the Annual Meeting of the International Reading Association, New Orleans, April 27-May 1, 1981. 15pp. (ED 210 642)

   Rhoder proposes using graphic organizers, such as grids, maps or networks as ways of organizing both prior and text-based information in reading and writing. She presents specific examples on both a word and a text level. The use of student generated questions as a means of integrating reading and writing is also advocated and illustrated.

109. Rowe, Elise Murphy. "Determining The Main Idea in Secondary School Reading Through The Modified Language Experience Method. A Psycholinguistic Process." Paper presented at the Annual Day of Reading Meeting of the Secondary Reading League, Chicago, Illinois, October 30, 1982. 14pp. (ED 227 462)

   Rowe compares a subskill approach to comprehending the main idea to a meaning approach, which looks first at the meaning of the total paragraph and then at the main idea. She provides an implementation schedule, suggested activities, and complete descriptions of four of the activities.

110. Sadow, Marilyn W. "The Use of Story Grammar in the Design of Questions." READING TEACHER 35 (February 1982): 518-522.

Sadow suggests that, since recall of a story appears to reflect the various elements of a story and the relationships between them, teachers should design questions that aid in identifying and internalizing the structure of stories. They should ask questions based on Rumelhart's story grammar (setting, initiating event, reaction, action, and consequence). These questions can provide knowledge of facts and patterns of relationships as well as a general understanding of stories. The author provides model questions and illustrates them using examples from CHARLOTTE'S WEB.

111. Stotsky, Sandra.   "A Proposal for Improving High School Students' Ability to Read and Write Expository Prose." JOURNAL OF READING 28 (October 1984): 4-7.

Stotsky identifies expository writing as a critical skill in secondary schools that students generally have not mastered. The solution to this problem is twofold: we need to teach expository reading and writing skills together and the instruction should be provided by the reading teacher. There are important differences between narrative and expository text which students may not understand since they generally get little exposure to these differences in elementary school. English teachers have other important objectives, which may preclude a concentration in this area. Her proposal is for a dual literacy program which calls for a restructuring of the reading and writing curriculum. Stotsky's comments deserve consideration.

112. Valmont, William J.   "Instructional Cloze Procedures: Rationale, Framework, and Examples."   READING HORIZONS 23 (Spring 1983):156-162.

Valmont advocates cloze as an instructional procedure because it requires the student to use various kinds of information available from context clues. Probably even more significant, it requires that the student use a variety of thinking skills.   He gives explicit guidelines, with useful examples for cloze instruction in the areas of vocabulary, relationships (including aspects of text organization and inferencing) and personal involvement (including critical reading).   This is a practical, easily adapted article for teachers.

113. Vaughan, Joseph L. Jr.   "Use the ConStruct Procedure to Foster Active Reading and Learning."   JOURNAL OF READING 25 (February 1982): 412-422.

Vaughan proposes the use of "concept structuring" to enable adolescents to read complex content materials. By reading the material three times, each time for a different purpose, the reader is able to construct a graphic overview by first obtaining an overview of the information by identifying the major topics, then studying the material carefully to fill in details on the overview and finally, reexamining any part that was not understood. This strategy helps the reader create prior knowledge where little or none may exist and insure active interaction with the text. The three readings require different purposes and strategies on the part of the reader.

114. Whaley, Jill Fitzgerald. "Story Grammars and Reading Instruction." THE READING TEACHER 34 (April 1981): 762-771.

Whaley provides clear illustrations in discussing Mandler and Johnson's story grammar. She reviews a body of research that supports three hypotheses: story grammar provides a set of expectations, enables comprehension and improves memory of the story.

Comprehending at Various Levels

Books

115. Pearson, P. David. "Direct Explicit Teaching of Reading Comprehension." COMPREHENSION INSTRUCTION: PERSPECTIVES AND SUGGESTIONS. Edited by Gerald G. Duffy, Laura R. Roehler, and Jana Mason. New York: Longman, 1984, pp. 222-233.

Pearson, in a review of current research, concludes that reading comprehension is a complex, interactive process which can be taught. The discussion of inference is particularly interesting because of the conclusion that it is very possible to teach inferencing skills. The teacher needs to determine the steps in the task, provide sufficient practice and feedback and teach some metacognitive skills. The author does not provide specific guidelines for doing this but gives rather a general perspective. In addition, he gives a list of general strategies for teaching reading comprehension.

116. Pearson, P. David, and Dale D. Johnson. "Making Judgments about the Written Word." TEACHING READING COMPREHENSION. New York: Holt, Rinehart and Winston, 1978, pp. 133-152.

This chapter presents detailed, easily replicated examples of techniques for teaching critical reading. The focus on having the student develop his own set of standards in this area is a particularly useful one for secondary teachers.

117. Ringler, Lenore H., and Carol K. Weber. "Comprehending Narrative Discourse: Implications for Instruction." READER MEETS AUTHOR/BRIDGING THE GAP. Newark, Delaware: International Reading Assn., 1982, pp. 180-195.

The relation between categories of inferences and story characteristics is presented in detail with useful examples. The authors propose a questioning strategy, beginning with free recall, then using probe questions, and finally author-, teacher- or student-generated questions. This is especially useful for reading specialists or English teachers.

118. Santeusanio, Richard P. "Evaluating Persuasive Techniques."
     A PRACTICAL APPROACH TO CONTENT AREA READING. Reading,
     Massachusetts: Addison-Wesley, 1983, pp. 197-233.

     In this chapter, the author provides explicit examples of
     persuasive text with corresponding strategies for leading
     students to engage in critical reading. A set of generic
     questions for critical comprehension and examples of study
     guides are particularly useful for content teachers.

119. Trabasso, Thomas. "On the Making of Inferences During Reading
     and Their Assessment." COMPREHENSION AND TEACHING: RESEARCH
     REVIEWS. Newark, Delaware: International Reading Assn.,
     1981, pp. 56-76.

     Trabasso's discussion of inferences and inferencing is very
     clear and well supported with examples. The focus of the
     chapter is on the relation between inferences, story grammar,
     and the comprehension of narrative text. He provides a
     theoretical framework for understanding the process of
     comprehending literature. The discussion of questions is
     particularly explicit and raises a critical issue for
     teachers: do questions assess or promote inferential
     comprehension? The author concludes that we need more
     research.

120. Vacca, Richard T. "Guiding Levels of Comprehension." CONTENT
     AREA READING. Boston: Little, Brown, 1981, pp. 117-138.

     Vacca presents a wealth of examples illustrating why and how
     to prepare three-level guides in many of the content areas. A
     three-level guide is designed to help students perceive,
     understand and use literal, inferential and applied levels of
     comprehension.

Periodicals

121. Carr, Eileen M., Peter Dewitz, and Judythe P. Patberg. "The
     Effect of Inference Training on Children's Comprehension of
     Expository Text." JOURNAL OF READING BEHAVIOR XV (No. 3,
     1983): 1-18.

     The authors, in an experiment using sixth grade students,
     improved inferential comprehension by using a structured
     overview to activate background knowledge, a cloze technique
     to relate previous knowledge to textual information and a
     self-monitoring checklist to enable transfer to new
     situations. The examples given make the procedure used
     particularly clear. The conclusion is that students,
     especially poor readers, can be taught to increase inferential
     comprehension of expository text.

122. Cunningham, James W. "Reading Comprehension Is Crucial But Not Critical." READING HORIZONS 20 (Spring 1980): 165-168.

The author describes a strategy to insure students' active involvement in the process of developing a notion of what is "good," establishing standards for evaluating text and then applying it to a variety of written materials. The procedure is explicit and can be transferred to a variety of settings.

123. Hillocks, George, Jr. "Toward a Hierarchy of Skills in the Comprehension of Literature." ENGLISH JOURNAL 3 (March 1980): 54-59.

Hillocks believes that secondary school students will have difficulty understanding the abstract structure of literature (story grammar) unless they can "deal with the literal and inferential content of the work" (p. 55). Through carefully planned sequential questions moving from the literal to the inferential, he provides a basis for understanding and appreciating literature.

124. Hillocks, George, Jr., and Larry H. Ludlow. "A Taxonomy of Skills in Reading and Interpreting Fiction." AMERICAN EDUCATIONAL RESEARCH JOURNAL 21 (Spring 1984): 7-24.

The authors present recent research results indicating that lower level comprehension enables upper level comprehension. They provide examples from widely read pieces of literature illustrating the literal level of comprehension (basic stated information, key detail and stated relationship) and the inferential level (simple implied relationship, complex implied relationship, author's generalization and structural generalization). They indicate the need for further research but nevertheless draw some implications for instruction. Questions asked by teachers orally and in study guides need to be carefully selected and ordered to insure comprehension and enjoyment of literature.

125. Holmes, Betty C. "A Confirmation Strategy for Improving Poor Readers' Ability to Answer Inferential Questions." THE READING TEACHER 37 (November 1983): 144-148.

The confirmation strategy developed by Holmes is designed to provide a structured, systematic way for students to generate hypotheses (inferences) about a text and then confirm them. The strength of the strategy may be in the fact that the student is continually referred back to the text for data to support the hypotheses. Although the material was developed for upper elementary students, there is much here that can be applied to students having difficulties in the secondary school.

126. Lindquist, Alexa Ann. "Applying Bloom's Taxonomy in Writing Reading Guides for Literature." JOURNAL OF READING 25 (MAY 1982): 768-774.

Lindquist has designed a process guide for literature which students can use independently. The guide, used before, during and after reading, includes generic questions that represent the levels in Bloom's Taxonomy. In addition, it highlights the structural features of the particular genre. The author has included a guide for novels which illustrates the weaving together of levels of comprehension, story grammar, and the process of reading.

127. Riley, James D. "Statement-Based Reading Guides and Quality of Teacher Response." JOURNAL OF READING 23 (May 1980): 715-720.

Riley proposes the use of statements as an alternative to questions in order to stimulate higher levels of comprehension. The judgmental quality of questions is absent in statements. The students' opinions, if supported, are as valid as the teacher's. The author provides contrasting examples of dialogues between students and teacher based on responding to questions or statements. He suggests using statements in a reading guide and as the basis for small-group discussion.

128. Ross, Elinor Parry. "Checking the Source: An Essential Component of Critical Reading." JOURNAL OF READING 24 (January 1981): 311-315.

Ross presents a number of activities designed to help students evaluate the author's background and bias as well as the type of publication being used. All of these activities require that a wide variety of materials be available to the students. The article seems especially useful for social studies teachers.

129. Shirley, Fehl L. "Critical Reading That Makes A Difference." Paper presented at the Annual Meeting of the Claremont Reading Conference, Claremont, California, January 21-22, 1983. 21pp. (ED 225 139)

Five interdependent phases are identified for critical reading: word meaning, suspension of judgment, interpretation, problem solving and insight. Shirley provides a wealth of examples for each phase.

130. Smith, Harriet K. "Using a Journal Article as a Demonstration Lesson." JOURNAL OF READING 25 (January 1982): 346-348.

Smith presents a rationale for teaching students to recognize the importance of factual information, inferences and background knowledge in reading comprehension. She provides an easily replicated way of doing this, while at the same time having reading teachers work with content teachers.

131. Thompson, Loren C., and Alan M. Frager. "Teaching Critical Thinking: Guidelines for Teacher-Designed Content Area

Lessons." JOURNAL OF READING 28 (November 1984): 122-127.

Thompson and Frager put critical reading squarely into the content classroom and under the umbrella of critical thinking. They suggest five guidelines: stimulate interest, generate active involvement by all students, use students' prior knowledge, facilitate transfer, extend instruction over time. They provide clear examples and specific activities for teaching critical thinking.

132. Wilson, Cathy R., and Carol Hammill. "Inferencing and Comprehension in Ninth Graders Reading Geography Textbooks." JOURNAL OF READING 25 (February 1982): 424-428.

Wilson and Hammill review current literature on inferencing and present findings from a study they conducted. Their research indicates that problems of inferencing may arise from lack of background knowledge and/or from an inability to inference. Poor readers may think the task of reading is to decode words, not get meaning. The authors conclude that we need to address the problem of background information and model the process of inferencing during comprehension.

CHAPTER IV

THINKING

The title of this chapter is misleading. It implies we are finally going to be concerned with thinking. In fact, this has been the focus all along. Lira (160) states that:

> Reading is apparently, to a great extent, a reasoning process, in which the student uses his linguistic, experiential, and conceptual schemes to organize information and predict meaning. He reads to determine whether the information contained in symbols confirms, negates or adds to his existing set of information. (p. 3)

Each aspect of reading discussed so far has been viewed from this perspective. Think of the issues raised in Chapter I. The instructional suggestions made so far have generally involved thinking about text, interacting with it, reworking and reorganizing it. Now we will take an even more direct look at how to foster "thinking" about text.

We begin by raising an area of uncertainty and by asking a question. First, the uncertainty. The question of research verification of reading and thinking strategies on the secondary level is a serious issue. In general, we have good research support for many of our ideas about reading strategies used in elementary schools. This is not as true of secondary school reading. Vaughan (145) issues a general, overall caution that is echoed in almost every serious review of research in this area. "It seems clear that research on instructional reading strategies in secondary schools is sparse at best" (p. 77). MacGinitie's sense of uncertainty is present again!

Second, the question. Since different strategies seem to result in different kinds of learning and the retention of different kinds of information Cook and Mayer (85) believe that "it seems unproductive to ask which reading strategy results in more learning; rather, the appropriate approach is to ask how each reading strategy influences 'what is learned'" (p. 104).

To provide a context for this discussion, we need to review and expand our definition of a skilled reader. In Chapter I we looked at Brown's (3) definition of a skilled learner and a skilled reader as one who learns from text, applies a reasoning, problem-solving approach to comprehension and monitors his own progress. Stewart and Tei (174) provide some additional details. Good readers:

> have a knowledge of the reading process
> extract meaning and summarize
> use text structure to find meaning
> are aware of and use a variety of strategies
> choose the effective one for a particular text
> anticipate postreading questions
> engage in self-questioning
> monitor their success in comprehending
> use self-checking strategies.

In addition, Davey (152) suggests that good readers have a meaning orientation to print and use reading strategies to:

> form good hypotheses about meaning before starting to read
> organize information into mental images
> use prior knowledge
> monitor their comprehension as they go along
> have active ways to fix up comprehension difficulties.

The emphasis in these two lists is on strategies, not primarily on traditional reading skills. The focus of this chapter is on strategy lessons. Atwell and Rhodes (150) make a useful distinction here: "Skills lessons are product oriented and convergent--getting 'the answer' is the goal of each lesson" while strategy lessons "promote reading as a constructive process necessitating reader-author transaction of language and thought...encouraging active student involvement in thinking about the text" (p. 702). We will examine a number of thinking strategies that skilled readers seem to use as well as ways of encouraging their use.

Activating and Using Prior Knowledge

Theory

Each chapter so far has stressed the significance of prior knowledge in comprehension and recall, from a general theoretical perspective in Chapter I to the specifics of word knowledge, text structure, inferencing and applied reading in Chapter II and Chapter III. Vacca (146) stresses that prior knowledge reduces uncertainty about the text. As we have seen, this can take many forms.

Prior knowledge is particularly important for the content teacher because of the nature of the material read. Much of it is unfamiliar, often not part of students' daily lives. As Cook and Mayer (85) point out "when prior content knowledge is absent, the text appears to be nothing more than a series of unrelated facts" (p. 95). However, in many cases it is not a question of either/or, all knowledge or no knowledge. Rather, students may have some knowledge, perhaps isolated bits, some appropriate and some inappropriate (134, 159). The job for us, as teachers, is to activate what's there, particularly when the knowledge structure is fragile or seldom used, to assess when knowledge is lacking or is inappropriate, and to help students acquire relevant knowledge. Ultimately, of course, the student has the same responsibilities. "Readers need to be able to acquire relevant content knowledge and to assess when they lack sufficient content knowledge" (85, p. 98).

This all sounds reasonable. The question we must face on Monday morning is "How?" Although research supports the importance of prior knowledge it has not answered all our practical questions on how to activate, assess and acquire it. One of the issues, for example, that has not been resolved is where to start in activating prior knowledge. Do we start with the students' knowledge and language as Langer (134, 135) advocates or do we assume that since the teacher knows the most about the subject we begin there? This is probably the route taken by most teachers. Do we know enough about the process to be ready to make an either/or decision? Probably not.

One strategy that is often suggested to activate prior knowledge is the use of a structured overview. Vaughan (145) states that "the waters surrounding structured overview as a prereading strategy are murky; however, when factors such as student participation, text structure, and where to focus conceptual discussion are examined more thoroughly, researchers may resolve the confusion" (p. 73). Rickards (169), in looking at Ausubel's advanced organizers, concludes that "while Ausubel's theory has many shortcomings, it is well worth salvaging" (p. 10). Again, we can feel the mantle of MacGinitie's uncertainties floating around our shoulders.

In the same vein, how do students acquire prior knowledge? We can teach them about text structure and provide them with that kind of specific, fairly limited prior knowledge. It is a different matter to try to teach them all the prior knowledge they may need to read a history text successfully. Again, the literature can only make suggestions here, not give final, definitive answers.

Practice

Suggestions relating to prior knowledge seem to fall into four categories: activating starting with the teacher's level of knowledge, activating starting with the students' level of knowledge, assessing the level of knowledge, and adding to the level of knowledge before reading begins. In reviewing these suggestions, consider how many of them are integrated approaches, in which a number of activities have been combined to provide a complete strategy. Notice also that many of them are suitable for the content teacher.

To activate and use prior knowledge starting with the teacher's knowledge:

1. Provide a structured overview or graphic organizer based on content information and/or text structure "to help guide students in organizing prior knowledge into conceptual

frameworks, to fill information gaps in students' backgrounds
and to blend these experiences with new content" (18, pp. 715-
716). (18, 85, 140, 142, 145, also see Chapter III)

To activate and use prior knowledge starting with the student's
knowledge:

1. Use an Anticipation Guide in any subject area where students
    have some background knowledge and/or preconceived ideas. This
    is beginning with the students' store of knowledge. Students
    agree or disagree with prereading statements prepared by the
    teacher which are designed to reflect students' probable
    backgrounds and beliefs. They then read to confirm, reject or
    modify their prior knowledge. This strategy can also encourage
    predictions about the text. Carefully planned questions can
    also help activate prior knowledge. (137, 138, 142, 146, 148)

2. Use the Guided Writing Procedure. This strategy is designed to
    activate and use students' prior knowledge to write, read and
    rewrite. Before reading students generate a list of words or
    phrases associated with the topic (see Chapter II), develop a
    graphic organizer and use it to write a short paragraph. After
    the text is read, further drafts are written and critiqued.
    (138, 142)

To assess prior knowledge:

1. Use all student-generated prior knowledge activities as informal
    assessment devices. (142)

2. Provide students with a means of assessing as well as activating
    prior knowledge. PReP is a three-step instructional/assessment
    paradigm to be used by groups of students before reading. (134,
    143, 145, 158)

3. Teach students to use metacognitive strategies to identify
    missing or weak knowledge areas. (170)

To add to or create prior knowledge:

1. Use reading to create prior knowledge. Have students read
    topically related texts on different reading levels so that the
    knowledge acquired in the easier text aides in comprehending
    more difficult texts. This is a powerful argument for a multi-
    text approach in content area reading. (140, 151)

2. Provide a rationale and purpose for rereading as well as a
    structure such as the ConStruct procedure in order to create
    prior knowledge through reading. (113, 145)

3. Create prior knowledge through a variety of means other than
    reading, such as lectures, films, handouts, charts. (151)

4. Use questions as a possible way of creating knowledge. For
    example, they may be a means of linking prior information about

text structure to the story line in narratives. (172)

5. Encourage the restructuring of prior knowledge to accommodate new knowledge by analyzing preconceptions, questioning, inferring, evaluating, encouraging confrontation, and supporting students in what may sometimes be an uncomfortable process. There are many similarities between this idea and reading on various levels! (136, 179)

In all of these activities classroom atmosphere plays a critical role. Students must feel free to take risks if they are honestly going to expose their level of prior knowledge and evaluate its appropriateness and sufficiency (134).

Predicting

Theory

Related to prior information are predictions. If you have some prior information about dogs, no matter how minimal that information is, you anticipate (predict, formulate a hypothesis) that an article on the feeding of puppies will deal with certain topics: numbers of feedings per day, times of feedings, kinds of food (regular dog food or special puppy food, water and/or milk). Not only will you predict topics, you will also predict some of the content. Because of what you also know about babies, you will hypothesize that puppies will need to be fed a number of times each day (and maybe each night!) and will probably need some special food. You are making what Collins and Smith (30) call predictions or hypotheses about what will happen. You come to the text with expectations and you read the text in that light. The predictions are part of the active process of reading.

According to Kimmel and MacGinitie (157), because you possess relevant schema or background information you can distinguish important from unimportant elements in the text. As you read you formulate new hypotheses that in turn activate other schema. Something in the text may trigger your recall of feeding a baby in the middle of the night. Are you going to have to do that with a puppy? You accept or reject a hypothesis depending on the fit of new information. "The formulation and testing of relevant hypotheses requires a flexible approach to a task. It is necessary that hypotheses be held tentatively, for they may need to be changed or discarded before a correct set of hypotheses is arrived at" (ibid., p. 15). Making predictions can also arouse interest and motivation as well as improve comprehension (161). Before you buy a puppy, you certainly are motivated to read the article carefully to find out about those middle of the night feedings!

Practice

Think of the soccer player reading the soccer article and the chemistry text in Chapter I. He made predictions as soon as he started to read about soccer but didn't have the background knowledge to do this when he was reading about chemistry. We have already looked at the problem of helping him acquire that knowledge. Once it is acquired, he may still be hesitant, not comfortable enough with his own competence in the subject to predict consistently. This is the challenge. Because successful readers appear to use prediction strategies, we need to devise ways of teaching all students to do this.

1. Model the process of formulating and evaluating hypotheses while reading aloud to students, giving the reasons for a hypothesis, evidence against it and any confusions or doubts you have. It is important to have students try this after you have modeled the procedure. (30)

2. Before reading, have students use the title or an overview of the chapter to predict the vocabulary that will be included and/or the meanings of words. (161)

3. Present a title, first sentence, or major heading and have students develop questions they think will be answered. (161)

4. Provide formal guides to be used during independent reading which include questions or statements students use to predict facts, topics or events that will be included in the chapter. After reading students check their predictions and change them if necessary. (30, 161)

5. Use predicting as part of other strategies, such as the Anticipation Guide (see Activating and Using Prior Knowledge) or the Directed Reading-Thinking Activity (see Asking and Answering Questions).

6. Use prediction for both convergent and divergent outcomes. Don't have students just predict for facts; have them predict a sequence of events. Create a situation that arouses curiosity and requires resolution; pose a conflict to be resolved or a problem to be solved. (146, 150, 160)

Asking and Answering Questions

Theory

It is particularly important to examine the role of questions carefully because as Moore, Readence and Rickelman (137) point out "they are a major device, if not the major one, in the instructional repertoire of teachers" (p. 13). Teachers frequently have had little training in asking questions. Unfortunately, to compound the problem, students frequently have no strategy for answering questions. They may try to guess the answer the teacher is expecting without having a real strategy for determining the answer based on the text. The focus of this discussion is on questions for instruction which will encourage thinking about and comprehending the text and that can be asked by the teacher, the text, or the student.

Teacher- (or text-) generated questions can be asked at three points in the reading process: before, during and after reading.

Prereading questions:

1. activate prior knowledge. (137, 148)

2. can focus attention on concepts or details which have been highlighted. (85, 137, 142)

3. can limit comprehension to the information asked. (140, 142)

4. provide motivation for reading. (137, 142, 148)

Interspersed questions:

1. can have "forward" or "backward" effects, serving as pre- or post-questions. (85)

2. promote interaction with text for poor readers or for those who might not reflect as they read. (145, 156)

Postreading questions:

1. motivate the reader to read carefully without limiting attention, since he does not know what question will be asked. (85, 140)

2. enhance overall comprehension and retention of text as well as incidental learning. (85, 142)

3. induce review and consolidation of material read. (141, 154, 169)

4. aid in restructuring and integrating the text. (85)

5. can "inhibit" integration of new information and prior knowledge if questions are explicit. (140)

6. can limit attention if the same type of question is asked after each section of the text. (85)

7. "shape" the way the student studies the text by suggesting areas to examine. (147)

Student-generated questions can:

1. help the reader integrate text and prior knowledge. (141)

2. entail deep processing of the text and thus improve comprehension. (137)

3. promote comprehension monitoring. (141, 170)

So far, we have looked at two aspects of the topic--who is

asking the question and when it is being asked? A third aspect is the level of the question being asked. This has already been examined in Chapter III. Raphael and Gavelek (141) cite numerous studies documenting that most questions asked by teachers at all grade levels are literal, textually explicit questions. Unfortunately, it is difficult to find many who disagree with their conclusion.

Finally, recent literature has focused on the content and purpose of questions and has suggested that questions can:

1. require processing relevant parts of the text. (167)

2. focus on integrating information and concepts. (Ibid.)

3. encourage useful "elaborations." (Ibid.)

4. require restructuring of the text. (85)

5. build internal and external connections. (Ibid.)

Vacca (147) cautions that in developing questioning strategies, we should not focus on "either/or" but should consider a variety of strategies, since, as we have seen, different questions at different places in the reading will perform different functions.

So far, we have examined only part of the problem--asking the question. What about answering the question? Everyone who has taught (or has been a student!) has been witness to Vacca's (ibid.) description of the student who randomly tries to guess the answer the teacher wants or writes everything he can think of in hopes that he will hit on the "right" answer. Students often do not have any other strategy for answering the question.

Raphael and Gavelek (141) believe that we need to teach students about the question-answer relationship. In their studies, using students up to the eighth grade, question answering was a particular problem with middle- and low-ability students. However, teaching students the source of answers, based on the Pearson and Johnson model of textually explicit, textually implicit and experientially based information (see Chapter III) appeared to be useful.

In addition, Page (140) suggests that the response the student is expected to make can influence the quality of the answer. "Questions requiring an overt response produce better performance than questions not requiring an overt response" (p. 62). Remember the arguments advanced in Chapter I about the mutually reinforcing activities of reading and writing?

A great deal of research has been done on many aspects of questioning. As Graves and Clark (156) indicate, the field of asking adjunct questions has been well researched and many conclusions validated. However, there are still areas of uncertainty. Cook and Mayer (85) believe that we have documented that questions "improve learning" but that we need research on "how various adjunct question manipulations influence the encoding process" (pp. 115-116). A number of practical strategies have been developed and researched, with results that still raise questions. ReQuest, for example, has been validated with narratives but not with expository text, according to Vaughan (145). Cook and Mayer (85), on the other hand, contend that there is little empirical support at all for this strategy. Other strategies have been verified with elementary or college students but not with secondary. For example, the research conducted on the Directed Reading-Thinking Activity has been done with elementary not secondary students (85). Rickards (169) has raised questions about the research itself, stating that the "adjunct question paradigm does not match the typical way in which in-text questions are presented" (p. 8).

Raphael and Gavelek (141) have raised a number of yet unanswered questions about the relationship between question asking and question answering. How do all the variables interact? How does the classroom teacher use questions to meet the varied needs of students in large group discussions? How can we develop students' abilities to generate their own questions and transfer them to a variety of reading materials?

Practice

Questions are an important instructional activity. Our task is to insure that they result in a "thinking" approach to reading and reading comprehension. The need to provide a classroom atmosphere conducive to risk-taking has been identified in other areas. It is certainly critical in the area of questioning (147, 160). Consider the following suggestions.

To develop teacher-generated (and text-generated) questions:

1. Identify the purpose of the questions and the information you want the students to attend to in planning the level and position (before, during, after reading) of the questions. Plan to use a variety of levels and of positions to achieve overall comprehension. (85, 137, 142, 147, 148, 167, Chapter III)

2. Use open-ended oral questions in a strategy such as the Directed Reading-Thinking Activity (DR-TA) which goes from the top-down ad is designed to help students understand the process of reading and make predictions while reading. This approach can also help students make the transition to asking their own questions. (85, 137, 147, 176)

3. Use open-ended oral questions in combination with a highly structured format which goes from the bottom-up, such as the Guided Reading Procedure (GRP). (147)

4. Provide written Question Guides or a Guide-O-Rama to accompany the text which will lead the reader through the material. (147, 176)

5. Develop a list of specific questions that can be used for any selection. These can focus on the concepts and their interrelations or on the structure of the text. They can be used for class discussion or for independent reading of the text. (126, 174, Chapter III)

6. Vary the group size during oral questioning. Questioning during one-to-one instruction may relate prior knowledge to new knowledge more effectively than questioning of a whole class. Questioning during small group instruction can provide motivation and interchange of knowledge and ideas. (141)

7. Use questioning strategies that integrate a number of approaches such as Referential questioning which includes questions on morphemes and word meanings, direct and personal analogies and the synthesis of new and prior information. (178)

   To develop student-generated questions:

1. Provide for a transition between teacher-generated and student-generated questions by modeling questions. Formulate questions under different conditions using a "phase-out/phase-in" or a reciprocal questioning strategy, such as ReQuest, with students eventually formulating their own questions before, during and after reading. (85, 137, 141, 142, 145, 147, 160, 171)

2. Encourage the use of text structure as a basis for formulating self-generated questions. (88, 170, 172)

3. Teach students to develop a variety of self-questioning strategies such as anticipating postreading questions, using "wh" questions which can be adapted to any text, or turning titles and headings into questions that might be answered in the text. (108, 161, 162, 171, 174)

4. Encourage self-generated questions at different times during the reading process: before for anticipating and predicting, during for focusing and after for studying and remembering. (135)

   To develop students' question-answering strategies:

1. Teach students to analyze what the question is asking for, what the question words mean and how sources of information can be identified. (155)

2. Identify textually explicit, textually implicit and script implicit questions with your students. Use a technique such as Question-Answer Relationship (QAR) that has been used with students through eighth grade. This can also serve as a metacognitive strategy. (141, 166)

3. Allow students to look back into the text for answers. Your goal here is instruction, not assessment. (140)

4. Encourage specific, overt responses to questions in written as

well as oral form. (140)

Monitoring Comprehension

Theory

Comprehension monitoring is part of a larger category of
metacognitive skills. Few textbooks in reading, until very
recently, have contained references to metacognition or
comprehension monitoring. However, "as research increasingly
reveals, metacognition plays a vital role in reading" (149, p. 2).
This topic is increasingly becoming part of the literature on
reading (133). We have already referred to the concept; now we need
to examine the "rapidly exploding literature on this topic" (177, p.
329) more closely and explore its implications for reading
instruction.

First, let's look at some definitions.

Stewart and Tei (174): "In general terms, cognition refers to
using knowledge possessed; metacognition refers to a person's
awareness and understanding of that knowledge....Cognition
implies having skills; metacognition refers to awareness of and
conscious control over those skills" (p. 36).

Wagoner (177): "Both 'metacognition' and 'cognitive monitoring'
apply to knowledge about cognition in general. 'Comprehension
monitoring,' by contrast is viewed as applying mainly to
reading comprehension" (p. 329).

Pitts (164): "A vital component of reading comprehension is the
ability to monitor or judge the quality of one's understanding.
This awareness is a metacognitive skill called comprehension
monitoring. It 'entails keeping track of one's ongoing
comprehension success, ensuring the process continues
effectively, and taking remedial steps when necessary'" (p.
516).

Armbruster, Echols, and Brown (149): "Metacognition involves
not only knowing what one does and does not know but also
knowing what to do to remedy comprehension failures in order to
increase learning. This knowledge is metacognition about
strategies. Researchers have focused on two different kinds of
strategies: 'fix-up' strategies to resolve comprehension
failures, and studying strategies to enhance storage and
retrieval (where comprehension failure is not necessarily an
issue)" (p. 14).

This discussion will focus on the comprehension monitoring
aspects of reading; the next chapter will look at studying
strategies. Comprehension monitoring for some readers may be a
conscious process, one that involves knowledge and control.
Armbruster, Echols, and Brown (149) suggest that reading to learn
includes four variables: the text, the task, strategies, and learner

characteristics. The reader must know about all these variables before he can control them. Wagoner (177) adds that the reader's knowledge of his particular strengths and weaknesses in relation to these metacognitive variables will influence the strategies he applies.

One of the implications of the notion of knowledge preceding control is that, as Palinscar and Brown (163) point out, comprehension fostering strategies can often also be comprehension monitoring strategies. Many of the strategies already discussed fall into this category. The advantage to both teachers and students is obvious. We can give students one strategy to use for two purposes. For example, we can give students knowledge about text structure to use as a comprehension monitoring strategy as well as a comprehension enhancing strategy.

The text identifies a problem. I read the text and understand the problem. If there is a problem, there is probably a solution, or at least a discussion of possible solutions. Do I understand the solution? If I don't, then I have identified a comprehension failure and must take steps to correct it. I might go back and reread the text to see if I missed the solution. Maybe I misunderstood the problem.

The development of cognitive monitoring seems to be related to age. Wagoner (177) reviewed much of the research in the area of comprehension monitoring and concluded that "people get better at comprehension and monitoring of comprehension as they get older" (p. 344). Pitts (164) agrees but adds a caveat. "The older children get, the better their comprehension monitoring skills....Still, comprehension monitoring is not automatically developed with age" (p. 517).

What are some of the factors that may be involved? Baker and Brown (2, 133) suggest that not only is age involved but also level of reading ability. "The evidence is clear that less experienced and less successful readers tend not to engage in the cognitive monitoring activities characteristic of more proficient readers" (2, p. 44). Tierney (175), after reviewing a number of his own studies, concludes that secondary students have a narrow view of reading, lack the strategies needed to comprehend and "lack both the awareness and abilities by which to self-regulate their own behavior" (p. 5). Santeusanio (185) suggests that there may be several reasons why secondary students don't monitor their own comprehension. They may be discouraged by difficult material or may not be interested in the material. Many students seem to have an unquestioning belief in the printed word, which makes them passive readers. Finally, teachers may have assumed much of the responsibility for monitoring comprehension without expecting students to do it.

Research results have been encouraging about teaching comprehension monitoring strategies which can have a positive effect on comprehension and recall. Tierney (175) also reviewed a variety of research projects in different areas including teaching self-regulating strategies in inferencing, summarizing, questioning, identifying and using text structure. The results documented his hypothesis that we can teach self-regulating skills and they will have an impact on comprehension and recall (pp. 5-7). This conclusion is echoed in other sources (133, 149, 153, 164).

Practice

Wagoner (177) suggests that "research is surely at an early stage of investigating monitoring strategies" (p. 342) but the literature can provide some guidelines for helping students develop effective strategies. Effective strategies require active participation on the part of the reader. This is certainly not the first time that particular phrase has been used to describe the reading process or some aspect of it! We will look at two aspects of the problem: first, strategies students can use in monitoring comprehension and, second, how to teach these strategies to students.

To develop students' comprehension monitoring strategies:

1. Insure that they have a knowledge of the reading process as a prerequisite to control of the process. (30, 149, 153, 162, 174)

2. Use comprehension fostering activities as comprehension monitoring strategies (133, 152, 163). A variety of activities have been suggested as performing both functions, with the caveat that students must know when, where and how to apply them (149). These may include:

   answering or anticipating questions posed by the teacher or the text. (163, 174)

   self-generating questions. By asking questions that he cannot answer, the reader is aware of his own level of comprehension. (141, 163, 164, 170, 174)

   recognizing and using text structure. (14, 170, 174)

   summarizing the text. If you can't produce an adequate summary, you may not be comprehending fully. (163)

   using thinking skills in an ongoing process of comprehending and monitoring that comprehension. These include questioning, clarifying and predicting. (133)

3. Encourage the use of coping skills. This might entail a script in which the reader tells himself to slow down, check his reading, ignore an unknown word, etc. This may be effective, at least in the short run, with students who have reading and comprehension fostering skills but need to learn to control and use them. (163)

4. Provide some list or form students can use for self-regulation

of the comprehension process and of their success in it. This may be a list showing sources of difficulty; it may be a rating scale for comprehension; it may be a list of questions to be used with any selection of a given type; it may be a set of rules governing a procedure or a series of steps to take; it may be a code the reader applies to indicate his state of mind while reading. (121, 141, 152, 153, 163, 164, 173, 174, 175, Chapter III)

5. Develop fix-up strategies to be used when the student has determined a failure in comprehension. This can involve a sequence similar to the coping strategies but is to be used after comprehension has failed rather than while a strategy is being applied. (30, 149, 153, 162, 164, 170)

To instruct in comprehension monitoring:

1. Model effective strategies orally. Talk students through the process of reading. Let them know what you're thinking as you process the information. Talk about the comprehension successes and failures you're having and how you are detecting them and fixing them up. (30, 152, 153, 163, 164, 175)

2. Provide written guides modeling the process, particularly for difficult text. This is called by names such as Guide-O-Rama or glossing. The intent is to provide marginal or intratext notes detailing the process of reading and monitoring comprehension. (139, 142, 147, 168)

3. Fade out the support you provide. It is critical that students begin to monitor comprehension on their own. Remember the characteristics of good readers! (139, 163)

4. Allow for discovery learning. Tierney (175) holds that while we need to model we also need to provide opportunities for students to work with the material and come up with their own strategy. They are "more apt to learn how to access that strategy as well as use the strategy spontaneously" (p. 13). (175)

5. Identify levels of metacognitive ability. The ability to use and verbalize the use of a strategy are evidence of mastery of the strategy. There are, obviously, levels leading to that mastery where a student may be able to use but not verbalize or may understand the strategy but can't use it or verbalize it. (14, 174)

6. Plan for a variety of strategies. One comprehension monitoring strategy will not work in every situation. (14, 164)

7. Insure application by providing for practice and transfer to content texts. (14, 152, 153, 175)

8. Provide motivation to use the strategies once they have been learned by making students aware of their importance and usefulness. The problem of motivation cannot be overemphasized.

(163)

Implicit in this discussion of developing comprehension monitoring strategies in students is the notion that the classroom atmosphere must be such that students feel free to risk admitting that they don't understand.

Suggestions For Implementation

This is another area that lends itself well to cooperative efforts between the reading specialist and the content teachers.

1. Provide an atmosphere conducive to risk-taking.

2. Think of thinking strategies as related and interconnected. Teach them that way.

3. Help students develop a variety of strategies that they can draw on depending on the text and on their need and purpose. "We do not know a better-worse or first-second sequence of strategies" (135, p. 41).

4. Provide instruction and practice in strategies that can be used before, during and after reading. (140, 143, 145, 177)

5. Plan joint inservice workshops with the academic departments and the reading department, using many of the strategies in this chapter as a basis. Use required course texts to develop and apply the strategies.

Summary

Thinking is the bottom line!

BIBLIOGRAPHY

Books

133. Baker, Linda, and Ann L. Brown. "Metacognitive Skills and
      Reading." HANDBOOK OF READING RESEARCH. Edited by P. David
      Pearson, Rebecca Barr, Michael L. Kamil, and Peter
      Mosenthal. New York: Longman, 1984, pp. 353-394.

      Metacognition, according to the authors, includes knowledge
      and regulation of cognition.   Baker and Brown present a
      comprehensive and clear review of metacognitive research in
      both reading for meaning (comprehension) and reading for
      remembering (studying). The developmental perspective taken
      is particularly useful for secondary teachers since they show
      that "younger and poorer readers do not monitor   their
      comprehension as effectively as older and better readers" (p.
      378). Because the emphasis is on research, the implications
      for instruction are somewhat general but very optimistic. We
      can teach metacognitive skills and they can make a difference
      in a student's performance.

134. Langer, Judith A. "Facilitating Text Processing: The
      Elaboration Of Prior Knowledge."   READER   MEETS
      AUTHOR/BRIDGING THE GAP. Edited by Judith A. Langer and M.
      Trika Smith-Burke. Newark, Delaware: International Reading
      Assn., 1982, pp. 149-162.

      Langer reviews research related to the storage and retrieval
      of items in memory and the role of prior knowledge in
      comprehension, recall and text processing. She proposes an
      activity, PReP, to be used before reading in which students
      recall words associated with the concept, evaluate their
      usefulness in the material to be read, and discuss any new or
      elaborated   ideas.   The   activity   is   an
      "instructional/assessment paradigm" allowing the teacher to
      identify students who may have difficulty learning from the
      text and providing students with a means of activating and
      elaborating prior knowledge.   Practical illustrations and
      instructional aids make the activity very clear and easy to
      apply in a secondary content classroom.

135. Langer, Judith A. "The Reading Process." SECONDARY SCHOOL
      READING: WHAT RESEARCH REVEALS FOR CLASSROOM PRACTICE.
      Edited by Allen Berger and J. Alan Robinson.   Urbana,
      Illinois: ERIC Clearinghouse on Reading and Communication
      Skills and the National Conference on Research in English,
      1982, pp. 39-51.

      Reading is viewed by the author as a complex task, requiring
      interaction between the reader and the text and involving the
      construction of meaning. Because of these complexities we
      need to help students develop a variety of strategies for
      reading. Langer examines the roles of prior knowledge and

metacognition in reading comprehension. A particularly useful feature of the chapter is the chart included for strategies for teachers to use before, during and after students read.

136. McNeil, John D.   "Restructuring Schemata."   READING COMPREHENSION: NEW DIRECTIONS FOR CLASSROOM PRACTICE. Glenview, Illinois: Scott, Foresman, 1984, pp. 58-81.

McNeil addresses a critical issue in reading comprehension: how to help students accommodate new information into an existing knowledge structure when the new information may require changes in the existing structure. His emphasis in all strategies is on confronting discrepancies and on examining and evaluating them. He leads us into areas where students may be uncomfortable, where we may sometimes hesitate to go. His strategies are useful, clear, and precise enough to replicate. He includes an activity to use with teachers to demonstrate the problems encountered by students.

137. Moore, David, W., John E. Readence, and Robert J. Rickelman. "Asking and Answering Questions." PREREADING ACTIVITIES FOR CONTENT AREA READING AND LEARNING. Newark, Delaware: International Reading Assn., 1982, pp. 13-25.

The teacher's task is to lead students from answering teacher-generated questions to generating their own questions. The chapter presents a series of techniques designed to accomplish this, including guidelines for teacher questions on various levels as well as reciprocal questions involving both teacher and students. Student questioning is phased in with three strategies.

138. Moore, David, W., John E. Readence, and Robert J. Rickelman. "Forecasting a Passage." PREREADING ACTIVITIES FOR CONTENT AREA READING AND LEARNING. Newark, Delaware: International Reading Assn., 1982, pp. 26-34.

Forecasting a passage activates prior knowledge, involves the student in predicting content, highlights important content and motivates the student to read actively. The three techniques of discovery learning, the anticipation guide and the guided writing procedure are described in detail.

139. Otto, Wayne, and Sandra White. "Editors' Epilog: Look to the Interaction." READING EXPOSITORY MATERIAL. Edited by Wayne Otto and Sandra White. New York: Academic Press, 1982, pp. 279-290.

The interaction between the reader and the text, with all of its ramifications and various directions, is reviewed by the authors. They propose that "glossing," a technique designed to enhance both the process of reading text and the comprehension of the content as a way of not only addressing reader-text interaction but also meeting the needs of teachers. Marginal and intratext notes provide the student

with a guide while reading.   The goal is to "fade" out,
leaving the reader with a metacognitive strategy he can use
while reading.

140. Page, William D. "Readers' Strategies."   SECONDARY SCHOOL
      READING: WHAT RESEARCH REVEALS FOR CLASSROOM PRACTICE.
      Edited by Allen Berger and H. Alan Robinson.   Urbana,
      Illinois: ERIC Clearinghouse on Reading and Communication
      Skills and the National Conference on Research in English,
      1982, pp. 53-66.

      Page   reviews research relating to readers' strategies
      before, during and after reading. He addresses a variety of
      issues including advanced organizers, questions and study
      skills. In each area he points out the uncertainties as well
      as promising directions for instruction.

141. Raphael, Taffy E., and James R. Gavelek. "Question-Related
      Activities and Their Relationship to Reading Comprehension:
      Some   Instructional   Implications."   COMPREHENSION
      INSTRUCTION: PERSPECTIVES AND SUGGESTIONS. Edited by Gerald
      G. Duffy, Laura R. Roehler, and Jana Mason.   New York:
      Longman, 1984, pp. 234-250.

      The   authors present a clear overview of questions and their
      role in reading comprehension and comprehension monitoring.
      The distinctions between other-generated and student-generated
      questions are particularly useful in planning instruction. In
      addition, Raphael and Gavelek report on a body of research
      dealing with question-answer relationships, pointing out that
      questions can be textually explicit (the answer is clearly
      stated in the text), textually implicit (the answer must be
      drawn from various parts of the text) or scriptually implicit
      (the answer is related to the text but depends on the reader's
      prior knowledge). Because of the nature of content reading,
      this discussion is especially relevant for the secondary
      teacher. The focus of the chapter is on current research with
      a view toward possible instructional implications.

142. Readence, John E., Thomas W. Bean, and R. Scott Baldwin.
      "Comprehension Strategies in Content Areas." CONTENT AREA
      READING: AN   INTEGRATED   APPROACH.   Dubuque,   Iowa:
      Kendall/Hunt, 1981, pp. 128-155.

      The   authors cite three psychological principles as a basis
      for their discussion of comprehension strategies.   These
      include the need to apply prior knowledge, to comprehend at
      various levels, and to organize information for long-term
      retention.   They propose a number of practical strategies
      based on these principles, including anticipation guides,
      study guides, graphic organizers, and questions.   A
      particularly useful notion is the stress they place on active
      instruction on the part of the teacher at all stages of the
      reading process--before, during and after reading.

143. Robinson, H. Alan, and Kathleen Schatzberg. "The Development of Effective Teaching." BECOMING READERS IN A COMPLEX SOCIETY. Eighty-third Yearbook of the National Society for the Study of Education, Part 1. Chicago, Illinois: The University of Chicago Press, 1984, pp. 233-270.

This chapter is based on the premise that all teachers need to "view reading instruction as an integral part of their curricula" (p. 233). To this end, Robinson and Schatzberg provide a brief overview of instructional strategies to be used before, during and after instruction. Many are discussed including, to name only a few, developing and activating schema, prediction, metacognition, and questioning. A particularly interesting part of the discussion deals with the need to integrate strategies in planning instruction. Finally, the authors examine the role of preservice and inservice training to enable teachers to provide the kind of instruction secondary students need.

144. Tierney, Robert J., and James W. Cunningham. "Research on Teaching Reading Comprehension." HANDBOOK OF READING RESEARCH. Edited by P. David Pearson, Rebecca Barr, Michael L. Kamil, and Peter Mosenthal. New York: Longman, 1984, pp. 609-655.

A major aim of this chapter is to examine promising areas of future research and possible methodologies that might be used. However, in moving toward this goal, the authors have provided an extensive overview of current research relating to comprehending and learning from text. They examine strategies to be used before, during and after reading, including building, enriching and activating prior knowledge, questioning by teacher and student, using advanced organizers and study guides, summarizing, comprehension monitoring, and using sentence and text structure. In all of these areas the difficulties with the current research are raised.

145. Vaughan, Joseph L., Jr. "Instructional Strategies." SECONDARY SCHOOL READING: WHAT RESEARCH REVEALS FOR CLASSROOM PRACTICE. Edited by Allen Berger and H. Alan Robinson. Urbana, Illinois: ERIC Clearinghouse on Reading and Communication Skills and the National Conference on Research in English, 1982, pp. 67-84.

Vaughan examines a wide variety of instructional strategies in light of current research findings in secondary schools. He concludes that the research is "sparse at best" (p. 77). Many of the strategies used by teachers come under his scrutiny: SQ3R, ReQuest, PReP, structured overviews, adjunct questions, previewing, advanced organizers, graphic postorganizers, and semantic mapping. For these, and others, he suggests the kinds and amounts of current empirical support and some possible constraints or limitations. The reader is left with a sense of uncertainty, which may have been the author's intention.

146. Vacca, Richard T.   "Reducing Uncertainty Through Prediction
      and Curiosity Arousal."   CONTENT AREA READING.   Boston:
      Little, Brown, 1981, pp. 89-113.

      Vacca highlights the teacher's role in reducing a student's
      uncertainty about the text to be read by providing
      instructional situations that will enable the student to
      anticipate the content, activate and relate prior information
      and raise questions to be verified. The techniques discussed
      include, for example, arousing curiosity through the
      presentation of problems to be solved, conflicts to be
      resolved, and values and attitudes to be examined. Techniques
      for predicting include anticipation guides and previewing.

147. Vacca, Richard T. "Questions and Questioning." CONTENT AREA
      READING. Boston: Little, Brown, 1981, pp. 159-191.

      Vacca presents a thorough overview of oral and written
      teacher-generated questions. He presents and illustrates a
      variety of strategies for posing questions as well as examines
      when, how and why we should be questioning. The emphasis, for
      the most part, is on the teacher. Detailed examples are
      useful in understanding the strategies and in transferring
      them to various content areas.

                           Periodicals

148. Annacone, Dominic, and Richard Sinatra. "Raising The Level Of
      Content Study Through Question Planning." Paper presented
      at the Annual Meeting of the International Reading Assn.,
      Atlanta, Georgia, April 23-27, 1979. 11pp. (ED 194 866)

      The authors view question planning from two perspectives.
      Both prereading questions and questions that accompany or
      follow the reading should stimulate thinking, accommodate
      existing knowledge and arouse curiosity.   In addition
      prereading questions can be used to make predictions about
      issues and content. They also propose that questions can be
      used to enhance comprehension on a variety of levels and can
      be used independently to preview new materials. The specific
      examples of questions are very helpful in applying the
      authors' ideas.

149. Armbruster, Bonnie B., Catharine H. Echols, and Ann L. Brown.
      THE ROLE OF METACOGNITION IN READING TO LEARN: A
      DEVELOPMENTAL PERSPECTIVE. Reading Education Report No. 40.
      Champaign, Illinois: University of Illinois at Urbana-
      Champaign, Center for the Study of Reading, April 1983.
      32pp. (ED 228 617)

      According to the authors, metacognition involves both
      knowledge of the process of thinking and learning and the
      control a student has over the process.   In relation to
      reading to learn metacognition includes four variables. The

text is the first variable and includes the features that influence comprehension such as topic, vocabulary, syntax, and, most important, text structure. A second variable is the task. Task requirements include knowing that the purpose of reading is to obtain meaning and knowing how to modify reading behaviors in response to various tasks. The reader must be able to estimate the degree of learning he has with respect to demands of the task and be able to predict his performance on the task. The third variable involves the strategies engaged in by the learner to store and retrieve information from the text. Last is the variable of learner characteristics, such as ability and motivation, that influence learning. The learner must control and coordinate these four variables. Knowledge precedes control which means that the learner must know about all these variables before he can control them. In discussing these variables and possible instructional implications, the authors review a large body of relevant, current research. The report is particularly useful because of its developmental perspective.

150. Atwell, Margaret A., and Lynn K. Rhodes. "Strategy Lessons as Alternatives to Skills Lessons in Reading." JOURNAL OF READING 27 (May 1984): 700-705.

The authors emphasize the importance of reading, talking and thinking as a means of developing strategies for understanding text. Atwell and Rhodes give specific examples, one based on prediction of content and the other on prediction of word meaning and word relationships. The distinctions between skills lessons and strategy lessons are clear and useful.

151. Crafton, Linda K. "Learning from Reading: What Happens When Students Generate Their Own Background Information?" JOURNAL OF READING 26 (April 1983): 586-592.

Reading "multiple topically and conceptually related materials" (p. 592) can be a strategy for developing unfamiliar concepts. Crafton found that 11th-grade students who read two texts on the same unfamiliar topic and were trained in verbalizing the reading, thinking and questioning process as they read the second passage, comprehended at higher levels, were more active in the process of reading and were better able to personalize the topic than a control group who read two texts on different, unfamiliar topics and also verbalized the process. She concluded that the experience of reading allowed the reader to construct background information. A major implication for the classroom is the need to provide a variety of texts on different readability levels for students.

152. Davey, Beth. "Think Aloud--Modeling the Cognitive Processes of Reading Comprehension." JOURNAL OF READING 27 (October 1983): 44-47.

Davey suggests that poor comprehenders lack the thinking

strategies needed to deal with comprehension problems. She
defines and illustrates five needed skills that can be taught.
They include making predictions, developing images from the
text, relating new and prior information, monitoring ongoing
comprehension, and actively applying fix-up strategies. The
author presents ways these can be modeled by the teacher for
the student and ways they can be transferred to classroom
situations.

153. Davey, Beth, and Sarah M. Porter. "Comprehension-Rating: A
      Procedure to Assist Poor Comprehenders." JOURNAL OF READING
      26 (December 1982): 197-202.

      The authors have developed a procedure to improve
      comprehension that focuses on some common problems of poor
      readers. By modeling the process of comprehension, teachers
      stress a meaning orientation to print. By rating
      comprehension (I understand or I don't understand) students
      attend to meaning while reading. By establishing criteria for
      understanding (an elaborated and defined rating system) and
      identifying the source of difficulty (word or idea), students
      begin to acquire control. Finally, by using a checklist of
      fix-up strategies, students can evaluate their own success in
      comprehending and improve.

154. Duchastel, Philippe C. "Testing To Aid Text Processing."
      Paper presented at the Meeting of the International
      Symposium on Text Processing, Fribourg, Switzerland,
      September, 1981. 10pp. (ED 215 326)

      Duchastel proposes that testing, in the form of
      postquestions, consolidates the learning experience that has
      taken place. Testing has more than an assessment function; it
      has an instructional function, "similar to practice or
      rehearsal" (p. 3). The author suggests that every class
      should end with a test, possibly an ungraded self-test. He
      indicates the need for further research in the testing effect.

155. Gordon, Belita. "Teach Them to Read the Questions." JOURNAL
      OF READING 26 (November 1982): 126-133.

      Gordon proposes that in order to perform well on reading
      tests students must be taught to read the passage and to read
      the questions. In this article, she concentrates on teaching
      them to read the questions. Her approach includes identifying
      questions that can be answered by scanning for information or
      meaning and those questions that cannot be answered this way.
      She advocates predicting possible sources of answers as well
      as predicting alternative vocabulary. In addition, she
      presents a script for students to use in monitoring their
      comprehension of the questions. The article provides
      suggestions for answering questions, taking tests, and self-
      monitoring of success in these two areas. Explicit examples
      are given.

156. Graves, Michael F., and Donna L. Clark. "The Effect of Adjunct
     Questions on High School Low Achievers' Reading
     Comprehension." READING IMPROVEMENT 18 (Spring 1981): 8-13.

     The authors review research relating to the effect on
     comprehension of adjunct questions and conclude that this is
     an area where strategies have been empirically validated.
     They present their research, using 185 high school low
     achievers, in which comprehension was significantly greater
     for students in the interspersed postquestion condition than
     for final questions or no questions. However, the final-
     question condition produced significantly more comprehension
     than the no-question condition.

157. Kimmel, Susan, and Walter H. MacGinitie. HYPOTHESIS TESTING
     IN READING COMPREHENSION. Technical Report #14. New York:
     Columbia University, Teachers College, 1981. 34pp. (ED 219
     744)

     Readers construct hypotheses about text that has been read
     and will be read which are based on the text and on prior
     information. Kimmel and MacGinitie review a wide body of
     research which suggests that this is an active process
     requiring flexibility on the part of the reader. The
     discussion is detailed, relating the research findings on
     schema activation and hypothesis formulation and evaluation to
     research on the cognitive style of learners and on reading
     theories. The report presents a thorough review of the
     literature.

158. Langer, Judith A. "Examining Background Knowledge and Text
     Comprehension." READING RESEARCH QUARTERLY XIX (Summer
     1984): 468-481.

     Langer reports on research conducted with sixth-grade
     students comparing the effect of PReP activities with general
     motivational discussion of the topic to be read and no
     activity in assessing and activating prior knowledge. She
     found that although PReP had been designed to increase
     students' awareness of their level of prior knowledge, it
     might "even generate some limited new concept awareness
     through focused group discussion" (p. 479). The PReP
     activities appeared to raise comprehension of average and high
     achievers but not of the low achievers. The author raises a
     number of questions that need to be examined through research.

159. Lipson, Marjorie Youmans. "Learning New Information From
     Text: The Role of Prior Knowledge and Reading Ability."
     JOURNAL OF READING BEHAVIOR XIV (1982): 243-261.

     Lipson investigated the impact of prior knowledge on
     children's ability to learn new information. The subjects,
     equally intelligent average and poor readers, demonstrated the
     critical importance of prior knowledge in reading
     comprehension. In fact, they used it as a basis of

comprehension even when it was contradicted by the text. The author discusses the implications of the findings, particularly the problem of readers making inappropriate inferences and recalling incorrect information because of the reliance on incomplete or inaccurate prior information.

160. Lira, Juan R. ACTIVE COMPREHENSION IN PROGRESS.   October 1980. 30pp. (ED 195 927)

Lira reviews current literature on comprehension and proposes that we teach students a strategy of predicting, locating, organizing, remembering, and evaluating in order to insure active comprehension. The examples given to illustrate the various aspects of the strategy and the discussions of student and teacher behavior make this monograph particularly interesting to teachers.

161. Nichols, James N. "Using Prediction to Increase Content Area Interest and Understanding." JOURNAL OF READING 27 (December 1983): 225-228.

The author presents a series of practical suggestions for formal and informal prediction guides designed to arouse student interest and encourage active reading in order to verify the predictions. The material is easily replicated by secondary teachers.

162. Nist, Sherrie, L., Kate Kirby, and Annice Ritter.   "Teaching Comprehension Processes Using Magazines, Paperbacks, Novels and Content Area Texts." JOURNAL OF READING 27 (December 1983): 252-261.

The authors present a detailed, useful analysis of how to use a variety of reading materials to help students understand and control the process of reading, monitor and fix up comprehension failures, develop a positive attitude toward reading, generate interest in topics and materials, develop self-questioning strategies and organize information through mapping.

163. Palincsar, Annemarie Sullivan, and Ann L. Brown.   RECIPROCAL TEACHING OF COMPREHENSION-MONITORING ACTIVITIES (Technical Report No. 269).   Champaign, Illinois: University of Illinois at Urbana-Champaign, Center for the Study of Reading, January, 1983.

The authors advocate a comprehensive approach to comprehension monitoring. It includes skills training in specific task appropriate strategies (summarizing, questioning, clarifying and predicting). In addition, students are given self-regulation training (to monitor the application and success of these skills) and awareness training (to be cognizant of the importance and usefulness of the skills and the monitoring activities). Palincsar and Brown report on the positive results obtained with students in three different experiments using a modeling approach to training students in these three levels of instruction.

164. Pitts, Murray M. "Comprehension Monitoring: Definition and Practice." JOURNAL OF READING 26 (March 1983): 516-523.

Comprehension monitoring is critical to success in reading; older, better readers monitor more successfully than younger, poorer readers. Based on these conclusions from theory and research, Pitts suggests that readers be made aware of obstacles to comprehension and be taught self-questioning and fix-up strategies to improve their comprehension monitoring skills. This can be done effectively by the teacher modeling the various strategies.

165. Raphael, Taffy E. "Teaching Learners About Sources of Information for Answering Comprehension Questions." JOURNAL OF READING 27 (January 1984): 303-311.

Raphael reports on her research with elementary and middle school students which was concerned with teaching them to know, identify and use the source of answers to questions in order to improve comprehension. The results indicate that students can improve the quality of their answers. The strategy seems particularly useful for average and low readers.

166. Raphael, Taffy E. IMPROVING QUESTION-ANSWERING PERFORMANCE THROUGH INSTRUCTION. Champaign, Illinois: University of Illinois at Urbana-Champaign, Center for the Study of Reading, March 1982. 64pp. (ED 215 303)

Raphael presents a four-session program to teach students to identify and use the question-answer relationship in text. She bases the program on the Pearson and Johnson taxonomy of textually explicit and implicit questions and scriptually implicit questions. Detailed instructions and materials are included for use by teachers and students. Most of the material is on a fairly low reading level and can serve as a training program for poor secondary readers or as an introductory exercise for better readers. In either case, as the author points, the transfer to the student's own text is critical.

167. Reder, Lynne M. "The Role of Elaboration in the Comprehension and Retention of Prose: A Critical Review." REVIEW OF EDUCATIONAL RESEARCH 50 (Spring 1980): 5-53.

This review of comprehension and retention draws together research findings from the fields of educational psychology, psychology, and artificial intelligence. The author discusses areas of critical importance to secondary school teachers concerned with reading: advanced organizers, questions, prior knowledge, text structure, theories of discourse, and inferences. A useful list of references provides the serious students with a starting point for investigating these topics.

168. Richgels, Donald J., and Ruth Hansen. "Gloss: Helping
      Students Apply Both Skills and Strategies in Reading Content
      Texts." JOURNAL OF READING 27 (January 1984): 312-317.

      Richgels and Hansen define gloss notations as marginal notes
      that direct the reader's attention to particular features of
      the text. They provide clear guidelines and examples for
      preparing gloss notations. The authors point out that "while
      gloss has not been thoroughly researched, there have been some
      promising applications of the technique" (pp. 312-313).
      References are included for these applications.

169. Rickards, John P. "Notetaking, Underlining, Inserted
      Questions, and Organizers in Text: Research Conclusions and
      Educational Implications." EDUCATIONAL TECHNOLOGY 20 (June
      1980): 5-11.

      Rickards provides us with a thorough review of the
      literature in the target areas. In addition to identifying
      and clarifying relevant issues, the article is a useful source
      of references for those wanting further study in these areas.

170. Sanacore, Joseph. "Metacognition and the Improvement of
      Reading: Some Important Links." JOURNAL OF READING 27 (May
      1984): 706-712.

      Sanacore presents a clear, although brief, explanation of
      many of the critical areas of theory and research relating
      metacognition and reading. He suggests a number of classroom
      applications including some specific suggestions and
      guidelines in the areas of student-generated questions, text
      structure, study strategies, and obstacles to comprehension.

171. Shapiro, Edythe, R. "Training Remedial Reading Students to Use
      Questioning Techniques." TECHNIQUES 1 (July 1984): 67-72.

      The author examines the varieties of questions and their
      role in comprehension and comprehension monitoring. The focus
      is on teaching students to ask their own questions by
      beginning with the teacher identifying the kind of question
      that could be asked of a selection, telling why it is being
      asked and relating it to the active processing of the text.
      Next, the teacher models the process of generating questions.
      Then, the group of students generates questions. Finally,
      each student generates his own questions. The procedure
      advocated is clearly explained.

172. Singer, Harry, and Dan Donlan. "Active Comprehension:
      Problem-Solving Schema with Question Generation for
      Comprehension of Complex Short Stories." READING RESEARCH
      QUARTERLY XVII (No. 2, 1982): 166-185.

      Singer and Donlan report the results of an experiment

conducted with fifteen 11th-grade students in which the
students were trained to use schema-general questions based on
story grammar to generate story-specific questions.
Comprehension was significantly higher for the experimental
group. Although there were certain shortcomings to the study,
discussed by the authors, the results are intriguing to
secondary teachers. The questions used in the study represent
the concerns of English teachers in teaching comprehension of
literature. The notion of students' developing their own
questions, reading actively and monitoring their own
comprehension is appealing.

173. Smith, Richard J., and Velma Dauer. "A Comprehension-
Monitoring Strategy for Reading Content Area Materials."
JOURNAL OF READING 28 (November 1984): 144-147.

Smith and Dauer propose that students use a code to record
their cognitive and affective reactions while reading content
material. The code might differ according to the subject but
would include reactions such as: "A" = Agree, "B" = Bored, "C"
= Confused (or Clear), "D" = Disagree (or Difficult) etc. The
responses are recorded and then discussed in a group.

174. Stewart, Oran, and Ebo Tei. "Some Implications of
Metacognition for Reading Instruction." JOURNAL OF READING
27 (October 1983): 36-42.

The authors review current research on metacognition and
reading, examine the implications of this line of research and
make suggestions to teachers for instructional strategies.
They recommend providing students with knowledge about the
reading process, knowledge of the sources of meaning in text
and how to use them, and strategies for comprehending
including predicting, searching, questioning, and summarizing.

175. Tierney, Robert J. LEARNING FROM TEXT. Reading Education
Report No. 37. Champaign, Illinois: University of Illinois
at Urbana-Champaign, Center for the Study of Reading,
January 1983.

Tierney examines appropriate reading behaviors leading to
comprehension, reviews his own and others' research on the
behaviors secondary students actually exhibit and concludes
that the discrepancies here may be helped by developing self-
regulating strategies in secondary readers. The guidelines he
proposes for developing these strategies and instructing
students are especially useful for anyone teaching in a
secondary school. They include relevance, explicitness,
student as informant, self-regulation and application. Clear
examples are provided for applying these to teaching text
patterns.

176. Van Jura, William J. "The Role of Questioning in Developing
Reading Comprehension in the Social Studies." JOURNAL OF
READING 26 (December 1982): 214-216.

The author examines both oral and written questioning strategies including the Directed Reading-Thinking Activity (DR-TA) and the Guide-O-Rama. His focus is on actively involving the student in the process of reading and "learning to learn" through questions. The aim is to develop students' abilities to ask their own questions.

177. Wagoner, Shirley A. "Comprehension Monitoring: What It Is and What We Know About It." READING RESEARCH QUARTERLY XVIII (Spring 1983): 328-346.

Wagoner limits her review of metacognition to comprehension monitoring of connected discourse. The focus is on reading but studies related to listening are also considered. She makes a useful distinction between "knowing about comprehending" and "knowing how to comprehend" or between recognizing that there is a problem and using fix-up strategies to take care of the problem. The review of the literature is comprehensive and highlights the various paradigms and research techniques that have been used. Areas of needed additional research are identified and general conclusions are presented based on the studies. The article is important reading for anyone interested in an overview of the research base of comprehension monitoring.

178. Wood, Karen D., John E. Readence, and John A. Mateja. "Referential Questioning: A Strategy for Enhancing the Reader-Text Interaction." READING HORIZONS 22 (Summer 1982): 263-267.

The authors identify the importance of the "connection between the concepts to be taught, the vocabulary necessary to teach them, and the experiences of the readers who are to learn them." They propose a questioning strategy to be used before, during and after reading which relies on metaphor and analogy relating prior experience and the target concept or referent. The instructions are clear, with explicit examples. A particularly useful feature of this strategy for content teachers is the stress on building vocabulary as part of the questioning process.

179. Yesw, Rose N. "QUIRES: An Approach to Improving Thinking Skills in Grades 9-16." NEW ENGLAND READING ASSOCIATION JOURNAL 18 (WINTER 1983): 29-34.

Yesw reports on a strategy designed to improve thinking skills in all areas of verbal comprehension including reading. It is related to Piaget's cycle of learning and change: equilibrium, disequilibrium, accommodation, assimilation. When new information is encountered, students begin by generating questions, preferably before beginning. They infer from the information, relate new information to old information, evaluate the new through standards they establish and synthesize their information. Examples of probing questions are included for every stage of the strategy.

CHAPTER V

STUDYING

In this chapter we will look at two major kinds of study strategies. The major focus is on study strategies that help students organize, remember and retrieve the information they have comprehended. First, though, we will take a brief look at two of the study skills students identify as needed, indeed as critical, for their success in school: reading rapidly and taking tests.

To begin, we need a framework for understanding studying. Vacca (188) sums it up for us very succinctly. Studying requires that you <u>do</u> something with information. "Studying is an intentional act....Studying is an unhurried and reflective process" (p. 195). Mayer (196) is quite specific in examining how to help the reader "creatively apply the new information, as well as to retain the presented information" (p. 30). The act of doing involves selecting, organizing and integrating. However, Alvermann and Ratekin (189) add another dimension here. "Merely 'having' knowledge of strategy routines is not in itself adequate for effective study behavior" (p. 240). Students also need metacognitive knowledge of themselves as knowing effective strategies and knowing when and how to use them.

A common assumption is made that all students receive instruction of some kind in study skills in secondary school. Unfortunately, Simpson (203), in a review of current studies, found that this is not always the case. When instruction is provided it is not always systematic and does not always require that the student master and use a variety of study strategies independently in a variety of situations. In addition she found that when students did have knowledge of study strategies, they were not able to monitor their progress and effectiveness in using them. Finally, she found that students tended to use a generic strategy without consideration of its effectiveness for a particular content area or without the ability to adapt it to meet particular content needs. Her conclusion gives us food for thought.

There has been a proliferation of reports about U.S. school graduates lacking basic skills, yet one critical area-- graduates' independent learning strategies--has been virtually ignored by the media. Reading educators, focusing on students' skills and difficulties in learning from texts, have found that students do not have the mature and efficient strategies necessary for learning on their own. (p. 136)

In general, effective studying seems to occur when students:

1. understand the purpose and outcome of the studying process. (180, 188, 189, 202)

2. focus attention and select what is to be studied. Some aspects of the text are more important than others and have more relevance for the purpose the student or teacher has identified. (85, 183)

3. process the information during studying at different levels or depths. (85, 180)

4. build connections both between prior and new information and between the various new bits of information. (85, 196)

6. organize the information in a meaningful way. (183, 187, 196)

7. encode the information in a useful way, one related to the purpose and outcome of the studying process. The notion of encoding specificity involves the idea that the way in which the information is encoded determines how it is stored, which in turn determines which retrieval cues will access it. (180)

8. take into account course and task characteristics as well as student characteristics in determining specific study activities. (202)

9. spend time on the task of studying and space the studying time. (183, 188, 189)

Now, consider what students often seem to do when left on their own. They read everything at the same speed trying to "get through" the chapter before dinner, t.v., the game, etc. The rate may be fast or slow depending on their skills as readers, their perception of the reading process, and their motivation and purpose in reading. They underline the text while reading it, probably using a yellow highlighter; then they review the text the night before the test, probably rereading the underlining. What research is suggesting is certainly much more demanding in terms of effort and time. "Not surprisingly, these techniques that are likely to yield the highest learning benefits also have the greatest costs in student time and energy " (180, p. 236). Our responsibility, as reading teachers and as content teachers, is to make the pay-off clear to students when we are instructing them in study skills.

Think back over prior chapters. Suggestions for teaching students vocabulary and comprehension strategies have been made that can also be study strategies. For example, the technique of identifying and using organizational patterns has been introduced as a comprehension strategy but as was pointed out, it also aids in the recall of information. The use of active comprehension techniques such as networking or mapping the organizational patterns meets Vacca's criteria of studying. This overlap between a strategy you use to teach comprehension and a strategy the student uses to study

has, of course, many advantages. The student practices the strategy
during reading or content instruction. He is required to transfer
it to new material. When he is proficient in using it he can
recognize its usefulness and apply it as a study strategy.

It will certainly be no surprise, at this point, to learn that
there are yet again unanswered research questions, this time
relating to study strategies. The questions raised frequently
involve verification of the effectiveness of the strategy in general
and verification of the effectiveness of the strategy for this
particular age group. For example, Anderson and Armbruster (180)
found only a few studies of networking and mapping, with just two
showing "promising results" (p. 235) for networking with college
students, both deaf and hearing, and one showing "facilitative
effects" (ibid.) for mapping using middle school students.
According to Vaughan (145) mapping has been verified as a useful
strategy for college students but not adolescents.

Changing and Adapting Reading Rate

Theory

Think about reading rate and flexibility in the context of
theories of the reading process and of the role of metacognition in
reading. If a student understands the process of reading and is
able to monitor his own process and progress, he should be able to
change his speed, reading rapidly or slowly depending on his prior
knowledge and abilities, his purpose, the text characteristics and
the outcome desired. Think of our reader reading the account of the
soccer game and the chemistry text. He is reading the chemistry
text in order to take a 200-item multiple choice test. He is
reading the article on the soccer game to see if his name is
mentioned. His strategy and speed should be different in the two
situations. Because the interaction of these variables is critical
in defining and achieving speed and flexibility appropriate to the
situation, readers need to develop different rates (182, 184, 186,
201).

Problems in the area of reading rate and flexibility may be
indicative of problems in other areas. Perhaps the student doesn't
understand the process of reading. Perhaps he is not able to
monitor his own process and progress as he reads. Perhaps he hasn't
been trained or encouraged to change and adapt his rate. If there
has been (or still is) a great deal of emphasis on oral reading, the
student has been taught to attend to every single word. Skimming
requires that he not attend to every word. If most of the questions
asked have been (or still are) literal-level questions, the student
may be afraid that if he doesn't read every word he will miss that
one detail that's on the test.

Memory and Moore (199) report on a recent study which cited
skimming and scanning activities as "among the least important of
the reading activities that might be taught" (p. 469) according to
middle and secondary school teachers. Yet think of yourself using

this book as a source for information on various topics.   You are
not going to read every single word of every sentence on
metacognition if you are looking for a metacognitive strategy
related to text structure.   You are going to be selective.   Your
rate is going to be flexible, identifying sections dealing with
metacognition or comprehension monitoring (you need a list of
possible identifiers), and reading rapidly while looking for key
words relating to the specific area of text structure.   Then, you
slow down and read more carefully once you hit the key words.   Since
your purpose is to learn about specific strategies, you will have to
read very carefully once you find them in order to copy the
appropriate citations.   In this process you are an active, critical
reader, making decisions as you read.

        Students, pressured by the many demands on their time and
required to read an increasing volume of material, almost
universally want to read faster.   They generally don't think about
reading flexibly.   To verify this, take an informal survey of your
students!   The trick is to maintain or even improve comprehension
while at the same time varying the rate to meet the demands of the
situation.   How can we do this?   Gibson and Levin (182) in summing
up much of the literature in the area of rapid reading concluded
that "there is no magic route to reading speedily with good
comprehension" (p. 548) but the "best way" is to work on the causes
of slow reading.   They cite many of the areas we have been concerned
with, particularly in the areas of vocabulary and comprehension.
Early and Sawyer (181) agree.   "But more is needed....Rapid reading,
so long as the materials being read are within the realm of the
half-known and partly familiar, can be trained by specific
techniques and sustained practice" (p. 429).

        Research has not generally been supportive of rate improvement
programs that have relied on mechanical rate controllers which
seldom take the realities of the reading process into account.
Early and Sawyer (ibid.) suggest "if machines are already part of
your equipment, use them sparingly, chiefly for motivational
purposes.   Your whole purpose is to move students away from the
support of external pressures toward the establishment of an inner
drive for fluency" (p. 430).   Tonjes and Zintz (186) concur.
"Expensive mechanical devices serve best only as initial motivating
devices" (p. 123).

Practice

1. Use lists of reading situations or a variety of reading
    materials to introduce the notion of variability in reading
    rate. (184, 185, 186)

2. Provide practice in timed reading, using classroom materials and
    incorporating comprehension checks. (184)

3. Present guidelines for skimming including developing key words
    as well as pacing activities. Either you pace the students in
    their skimming or give them material that demonstrates how to
    skim. Use cloze activities to provide practice in comprehending

without attending to every word. (181, 185)

4. Relate skimming and scanning to comprehension strategies such as
    text structure and critical reading. (193, 199)

5. Use content materials and the content classroom to assess
    flexibility in reading and to provide instruction. (201)

Taking Tests

Theory

Taking tests is an anxiety-producing activity for most
students. If you had read in the beginning of this chapter that
there would be a test at the end, wouldn't you get a twinge of
anxiety wondering why, what and how? There are two aspects to test
taking: first, we must reduce anxiety about taking the test; second,
we must improve performance on the test. The two, in practice, are
closely related.

Tryon (204), in reviewing a wide variety of approaches to
reducing test anxiety, concluded that "almost all treatments seem to
be effective in reducing self-reported test anxiety; even a credible
placebo pseudotherapy reduces test anxiety" (p. 364). This is
certainly reassuring. There are psychological and physiological
options that might reduce test anxiety, however, that are not
practical options for us as teachers. One option that does seem
practical is to improve student confidence and test-taking skills by
teaching "test-wiseness." Lange (194) defines this as "a set of
skills that enables a test taker to use the form and characteristics
of tests and test situations 'to receive a score commensurate with
the abilities being measured'" (p. 740). In addition, an important
aspect of taking tests, of course, is knowing the subject matter and
knowing that you know it. Most of Chapters III and IV, as well as
the reminder of Chapter V, are concerned with this second variable.

Practice

1. Provide suggestions on how to study for tests, anticipating the
    kinds of questions that might be asked on essay or objective
    tests. (184)

2. Develop test taking strategies that can apply to any test, such
    as the using time, avoiding errors, guessing and reasoning
    deductively. (195, 198)

3. Teach students how to analyze questions in order to identify
    what they are asking for and what are possible sources of
    information. (155, 184, 185, 200)

4. Encourage use of a strategy to eliminate multiple choice
    responses. (200)

5. Teach a metacognitive script students can use as they take

tests. This is an "internal dialogue" (155, p. 129) the student
has with himself that reminds him of the purpose and function of
each part of the test--the directions, the questions, the words
used, the kind of response expected--and leads him through the
test. (155)

6. Give practice tests and model the procedure for taking the test.
(194, 195, 200)

Underlining, Notetaking and Summarizing

Theory

Santeusanio (185) quotes Pauk as saying that:

Real learning takes place only through self-teaching. The
instructor may pour forth the choicest words of wisdom, and the
student may hear them, and even write them in his notebook but
unless he takes these words, and rethinks them in his own
words, visualizes them, crystallizes and assimilates them,
internalizes them, the words from lectures or books will make
no positive difference in his life, academic or otherwise.
(pp. 236-237)

Compare this statement to what students usually do and to what
the literature suggests they should do.

Underlining, according to Mayer (196), aids in selecting
information. It directs attention to the text and to particular
items in the text but does little to organize that information or
build connections between bits of information or information and
concepts. Notetaking and summarizing perform similar functions of
selecting, understanding, organizing and remembering information. A
common distinction between notetaking and summarizing is that the
former is done while listening or reading and the latter is done
after listening or reading. According to Cook and Mayer (85, pp.
104-106) there are a number of possible ways that notetaking,
summarizing and underlining can influence learning. These include:

directing attention toward certain information and away from
other information.

limiting attention because of the difficulty of attending to
two tasks at once.

encouraging verbatim encoding and, thus, verbatim recognition
or recall.

allowing for student organization of information.

providing opportunity for building connections with other
information and for reacting to and evaluating information.

Two issues related to notetaking are raised by McAndrew (197).

First, does the value lie in the act of taking notes ("encoding" hypothesis)? He points out that the research here is uncertain at best but, that in order for notetaking to have value students must do something besides make a verbatim transcription. Second, does the value lie in having a way to store the material for further study ("external storage" hypothesis)? McAndrew states that taking notes is not enough, students must study them afterwards. There is much support for this second view (85, 168).

Notetaking, according to Anderson and Armbruster (180) has the potential for being an effective strategy because it allows students the opportunity to rework the lecture or the text, perhaps at a deeper level. They cite the limited research on effective notetaking and suggest it is most effective if students know what is expected as a result of the notetaking. Thus, they will focus their efforts and perhaps process at deeper levels in order to meet the expected outcome. Many of the same comments apply to summarizing. It is difficult, according to them, to find research supporting summarizing as a useful activity. It is probably useful "if the student is actually reordering and reworking the text in order to construct an abstract and if the criterion task requires the retrieval of deeply processed main ideas" (p. 233). Formal outlining, according to these authors, may be an effective studying technique but it is very time consuming to learn because students need extensive training in order for it to be productive. A danger is that they may use the format but process text superficially.

The implications of research for practice are clear. The conditions for effective studying must be incorporated into the skills of underlining, notetaking and summarizing.

Practice

In considering any of the possible alternatives for these particular study skills, you and your students need to evaluate the amount of time needed to learn the strategy and the time needed to apply it to a particular text. Look at the importance of the text, the amount of information to be learned and the ease of applying the strategy. Before teaching any strategy consider whether students can use it in more than one classroom or content area.

1. Give instruction in "constrained" underlining which avoids irrelevant and unimportant material. Relate this to instruction in main idea and detail. Suggest restricting underlining to one or possibly two sentences per paragraph to encourage deep processing of the material. Use underlining only for material that does not need close study. Stress the need to study and use the underlined material. (85, 169, 197)

2. Give instruction in how to listen and take notes by presenting a lecture with a listening guide or with opportunities to take and compare notes with each other and with you. (184, 187, 188)

3. Work with content teachers in how to give lectures so students can take notes. (85, 197)

4. Begin instruction in taking notes on reading by providing a study guide which is designed to "mirror the thinking process by which a reader extracts information from the text" (184, p. 143). The important elements of the text will be highlighted and identified by the questions and the comments in the guide. (184)

5. Relate notetaking and outlining to comprehension strategies. The use of text structure as the basis for notes is a particularly useful one. Use either the structure used in the text or restructure the text to make it more meaningful. (88, 181, 196)

6. Demonstrate the use of free-form outlines, such as the "array," pyramid or radial outline or idea line before moving toward the more formal, conventional outline. This is particularly useful for less mature readers. The emphasis is on the content not the form of the outline. (88, 181, 184, 188)

7. If you use formal, conventional outlines for notetaking give detailed instruction, practice and transfer, using a variety of content materials. ' (180, 181, 184, 185, 187)

8. Present a strategy for reworking verbatim notes such as the Verbatim Split Page Procedure (VSPP), the Cornell system with a Recall Column, the "T-Note" System or the Notetaking System for Learning (NSL). The verbatim notes on one side of the page are reorganized and expanded to include omitted items, to categorize information and to include previously presented information or prior knowledge. (183, 185, 187, 188, 191)

9. Model the process of summarizing and provide instruction and practice in using rules for summarizing. Brown, Campione and Day (13) suggest: deletion of unnecessary and/or redundant material, substitution of a superordinate term or event for a list of items or actions, and selection or invention of a topic sentence. Relate instruction in summarizing to instruction in the main idea. (13, 88, 135, 184, 187, 192)

10. Relate notetaking to summarizing. Write the information in the author's words while taking the notes; then rewrite in a summary using your own words or summarize each section before proceeding to the next section. (85, 183)

11. Have a variety of strategies available for notetaking and summarizing such as mapping, filling in or constructing a structured overview, completing an anticipation guide. (180, 181, 185, 187, 190)

12. Encourage the use of these study strategies as metacognitive strategies. The key here appears to be to insure that students receive practice in understanding the process they are using, overseeing that process and applying the skills to a broad variety of materials. (13, 133)

SQ3R

Theory

Study methods, such as SQ3R, have been used for a number of years. The strategy involves: Survey, Question, Read, Recite, Review. Variations on the strategy have been developed which adapt it to the various content areas.

The research support for this strategy is slim at best. Santeusanio (185) cites the fact that it has not been fully researched and the research that has been done has not completely supported the results. Anderson and Armbruster (180) state that there is "little research to review" (p. 236) and the studies that have been done are inconsistent and difficult to interpret. Vaughan (145) questions its value and cites the lack of research. Cook and Mayer (85) say there is "not a great deal of empirical support for it" (p. 117).

There are problems using the strategy. The student may not look at the chapter as a whole (185). The headings in the text may be inappropriate and the student may have trouble turning them into questions that relate to the main idea (180). Reading the chapter or unit in this fashion may not relate to the task the student is expected to do after reading (180). The student may be reluctant to give up old strategies and use one that requires a great deal of effort (145, 181).

Why do we include this strategy in textbooks on reading in the content areas? Probably, partly because teachers think it will work. As Vaughan (145) suggests, it requires that the student be an active participant. In addition, reading a chapter is a big job for some students and, according to Santeusanio (185), it is a way to begin. Perhaps the problem with SQ3R is that teachers have not provided students with sufficient instruction and practice in a complex strategy (145). If the strategy seems to have some value we might consider how to solve some of the problems associated with it. However, we cannot forget the problem of the lack of research support.

Practice

1. Provide direct instruction and model the process. (145, 181, 183, 184, 185, 187)

2. Provide ample practice and insure transfer to content materials. (170, 185)

Writing

Theory

The connections between reading, writing and thinking have been discussed in a number of different contexts. These connections can be used to advantage in studying material (181). It has also been proposed that "one of most effective ways to commit information to long-term memory is to write it in your own words" (142, p. 151). In addition, remember the principle of encoding specificity--we remember items the way we have encoded them. Anderson and Armbruster (180) believe that encoding is critical to the studying process. "Almost any (study) technique can be effective if its use is accompanied by focused attention and encoding in a form and manner appropriate to the criterion task" (p. 236).

Practice

Many of the writing activities already discussed are relevant here. Consider also two designed specifically as study strategies.

1. Teach students to use the Guided Writing Procedure (GWP). This strategy integrates prior knowledge and prediction with summarizing by having students begin writing before reading and then revise the content of their writing after reading. (138, 142)

2. Use REAP, a strategy designed to "sharpen" reading, thinking and writing skills. The strategy requires that students: Read, Encode (written retelling in the reader's own words), Annotate (a written annotation which may take a variety of forms in order to synthesize understanding which goes beyond a verbatim reproduction of the text), and Ponder. (85, 145, 184)

Suggestions for Implementation

This is obviously another area where reading specialist and content teacher can work together.

1. Introduce and model the strategies, either to individuals or to content classes. Practice and transfer can be provided by both the reading and content teachers.

2. Encourage student questions. Interactive instruction is critical but particularly in this area. Students will not use study strategies unless they understand completely how to apply and transfer them.

3. Be sure that students perceive the usefulness of the strategy taught and the kinds of materials it can be used with. This is essential if the strategy is to be used independently.

4. Insure that students have a variety of strategies they can use with different materials and at different points in their studying--before, during and after reading.

5. For all of the above to take place and for students to become proficient in the use of study skills, it is imperative that time be allotted in the secondary school schedule for direct

instruction in study skills for many of the students.

6. Instruction and practice should be provided in the various content areas, using a variety of text, with the expectation and requirement that the strategies will be used independently.

7. Study strategies should be developed with a metacognitive component. Include a list of steps and/or rules, a script or a set of questions in the instructional process for students to use to determine when they should apply the strategy and to monitor their success in using it.

Simpson (203) offers a suggestion that is already in place in many school districts but certainly not everywhere. She suggests the formation of a school-wide reading committee composed of elementary and secondary content teachers. Their charge would be to examine whether study skills are being taught now and how we know they are, what specific strategies are being taught, and whether these strategies are relevant. Existing reading committees might be refocused to examine these questions.

Summary

In developing study skills, we must shift the locus of control from the teacher to the student. At some point he must accept the responsibility for studying, for reworking the information, and for putting it in a form that is meaningful to him, connects to his prior knowledge and reflects the author's underlying structure and meaning. This is asking a lot of students, much more than we are often asking now and much more than many students are giving now. In fact, for many students the real problem may be not the acquisition of strategies for studying but the motivation for transferring them to content areas and using them independently.

BIBLIOGRAPHY

Books

180. Anderson, Thomas H., and Bonnie B. Armbruster.   "Reader and
      Text--Studying Strategies."   READING EXPOSITORY MATERIAL.
      Edited by Wayne Otto and Sandra White. New York: Academic
      Press, 1982, pp. 219-242.

      The authors define studying as "reading with the requirement
      that students will also perform identifiable cognitive and/or
      procedural tasks" (p. 219).   In examining common studying
      techniques   such   as   notetaking,   outlining,   summarizing,
      student-generated questions and SQ3R, Anderson and Armbruster
      point   out   the   paucity of relevant, current research. They
      believe that for these techniques to be effective, they must
      be related to the task the student will eventually perform.
      This is often not the case. They highlight the difficulties,
      particularly for SQ3R where the task to be done after reading
      is not part of the process. They raise an important question
      for teachers to consider in teaching any study strategy.   Is
      the study strategy appropriate to the final task   and   is   the
      result worth the time and effort the student must expend in
      order to learn and apply the strategy?

181. Early, Margaret, and Diane J. Sawyer. "Studying = Reading +
      Writing."   READING   TO LEARN IN GRADES 5 TO 12. New York:
      Harcourt Brace Jovanovich, 1984, pp. 403-435.

      The authors make a impassioned plea for more writing in
      secondary   schools   as   a   way of   learning and as a way of
      studying.   They   present   clear,   detailed   examples   of
      notetaking, outlining, mapping, SQ3R, writing a research
      paper, and taking tests.   An interesting and potentially
      important admonition is the caution that we should consider
      teaching study skills to "at least the lower half of those
      bound for college" (p. 434).

182. Gibson, Eleanor J., and Harry Levin. "Rapid Reading: Whether,
      When, and How?"   THE PSYCHOLOGY OF READING. Cambridge,
      Massachusetts: The MIT Press, 1975, pp. 539-549.

      The message is clear. Rapid reading does not come from
      moving the eyes faster but from knowing how to read well. We
      need to focus on flexibility as well as speed always within a
      framework of comprehension.   The authors review research in
      this area and relate their discussion to a larger context of
      how we acquire and practice reading.

183. Readence, John E., Thomas W. Bean, and R. Scott Baldwin.
      "Reading/Study Strategies in Content Areas."   CONTENT AREA
      READING: AN   INTEGRATED   APPROACH.   Dubuque,   Iowa:
      Kendall/Hunt, 1981, pp. 156-171.

Underlying the strategies discussed in this chapter are the learning principles of limited capacity to attend and the importance of rehearsal in acquiring, retaining and recalling information. Practical suggestions are given for listening and notetaking, locating information, and reading and responding in daily assignments.

184. Roe, Betty D., Barbara D. Stoodt, and Paul C. Burns. "Reading-Study Skills." SECONDARY SCHOOL READING INSTRUCTION: THE CONTENT AREAS. Boston: Houghton Mifflin, 1983, pp. 105-156.

The discussion includes a wide variety of study skills with explicit illustrations and directions for teaching them to students. The authors have included study methods such as SQ3R, outlining and notetaking, locating information, following directions, using graphic aids, varying reading rate and remembering information.

185. Santeusanio, Richard P. "Developing Self-Directed Study Techniques." A PRACTICAL APPROACH TO CONTENT AREA READING. Reading, Massachusetts: Addison-Wesley, 1983, pp. 235-270.

The focus of this chapter is on developing readers who can "independently learn information from textbooks and other chapters" (p. 236). All of the techniques are geared toward this end. They include SQ3R, notetaking, outlining, mapping, test-taking, comprehension monitoring, and reading at varying rates. The discussion is particularly useful because the author not only defines and illustrates each technique but also presents a brief review of current research.

186. Tonjes, Marian J., and Miles V. Zintz. "Adapting Rate for Efficient Comprehension." TEACHING READING/THINKING/STUDY SKILLS IN CONTENT CLASSROOMS. Dubuque, Iowa: Wm. C. Brown, 1981, pp. 97-131.

The authors relate rate and flexibility in reading to characteristics of the reader and the text. The emphasis is on maintaining or improving comprehension. A very useful feature of this chapter is the inclusion of activities to be used by teachers or students to demonstrate the basic concepts. In addition, suggestions are made for teaching students strategies to adapt their reading rate.

187. Tonjes, Marian J., and Miles V. Zintz. "Improving Study Skills." TEACHING READING/THINKING/STUDY SKILLS IN CONTENT CLASSROOMS. Dubuque, Iowa: Wm. C. Brown, 1981, pp. 203-252.

In order to become independent learners, students must locate, organize, interpret and use and/or apply information. Tonjes and Zintz examine and give explicit directions for teaching a wide variety of study skills under these categories. Many of these are the traditional kinds of study skills we have often advocated but not always had success

with, such as notetaking and SQ3R. The authors suggest that
the reason for this limited success is that teachers are not
comfortable with study skills.   They provide a wealth of
activities and examples to overcome this problem.   In
addition, they provide guidelines and activities for locating
information,   developing   listening   skills,   outlining,
establishing study habits, and taking tests.

188. Vacca, Richard T. "Study Strategies." CONTENT AREA READING.
      Boston: Little, Brown, 1981, pp. 193-221.

      Vacca's aim in developing study strategies is to involve the
      student and enable him to do something with the information he
      has read.   The emphasis is on instructing the student in
      gradual steps to use and apply the strategies discussed.   The
      author views outlining and notetaking as methods not only of
      recording information but also of clarifying relationships.
      The use of visual arrays, pyramids and radials is suggested as
      a way of introducing outlining and notetaking. Visual aids
      from a variety of content areas are presented along with
      suggestions for teaching students to use them in comprehending
      text.

Periodicals

189. Alvermann, Donna E., and Ned H. Ratekin. "Metacognitive
      Knowledge About Reading Proficiency: Its Relation To Study
      Strategies and Task Demands." JOURNAL OF READING BEHAVIOR
      XIV (1982): 231-241.

      Alvermann and Ratekin, using average 7th- and 8th-grade
      readers,   examined the hypothesis that a reader's self-
      knowledge "about his or her own proficiency in meeting
      specific   task demands" (p. 238) affects his choice of
      strategies in studying for a test. They found that average
      readers who perceived of themselves as having low proficiency
      in studying for tests used inactive strategies and, in fact,
      did not score as well in essay tests as did average readers
      who perceived of themselves as being able to perform the
      required task. They drew some tentative conclusions from the
      data: metacognitive knowledge about reading proficiency seems
      to affect the choice of study strategies;   7th- and 8th-
      graders seem to have limited knowledge about the wide range of
      strategies available; knowing about a strategy does not insure
      that it will be used.

190. Davidson, Jane L.   "The Group Mapping Activity for Instruction
      in Reading and Thinking." JOURNAL OF READING 26 (October
      1982): 52-57.

      Davidson recommends that each student make a map of the text
      after reading. Then the group compares the maps made by each
      student.   The discussion helps students gain insight into the
      reasoning processes of others as well as their own.   The

mapping aids in retention and recall. Various examples are given based on one text.

191. Davis, Archie, and Elvin Clark. "High Yield Study Skills Instruction." Paper presented at the Annual Meeting of the Plains Regional Conference of the International Reading Association, Des Moines, Iowa, October 22-24, 1981. 12pp. (ED 208 372)

The authors present detailed information on teaching students chapter mapping, previewing and "T-note" making. Ten keys are provided for effective previewing. The examples and information on "T-note" making are particularly useful. By dividing the notebook paper into three parts with each part used for a different kind of information, students are required to organize, manipulate and think about their notes.

192. Hare, Victoria Chou, and Kathleen M. Borchardt. "Direct Instruction of Summarization Skills." READING RESEARCH QUARTERLY XX (Fall 1984): 62-78.

Hare and Borchardt adapted Brown and Day's list of rules for summarizing in a study conducted with high school students in which they determined that "carefully delineated instruction in summarization skills positively influenced students' use of summarization rules and the quality of their summarization products" (p. 75). The difficulties caused by failure to identify implicit main idea are discussed. The discussions of summarization skills and of the components of direct instruction are particularly useful.

193. Jacobowitz, Tina. TEACHING PREVIEWING TECHNIQUES TO HIGH SCHOOL STUDENTS. 1980. 13pp. (ED 212 982)

The author relates previewing to identifying and using the text structure independently in order to comprehend and recall information. She suggests active surveying and skimming, techniques ordinarily reserved for increasing speed and flexibility, as ways of also allowing students to "grasp" the macrostructure of the text. This in turn allows them to predict content and read actively and selectively. Active surveying is similar to surveying with the additional tasks of readers generating questions and predicting answers. Active skimming also involves questioning and predicting. A useful, detailed outline is provided for each strategy.

194. Lange, Bob. "Promoting Test-Wiseness." JOURNAL OF READING 24 (May 1981): 740-743.

Lange reviews a number of monographs dealing with the topic of test-wiseness and concludes that students can improve in their abilities to take tests. The review suggests a number of strategies, such as teaching students how to eliminate unlikely answers, use cues in questions and use time appropriately during the test. Lange does not include any details but provides references to use in researching the question of test-wiseness further.

195. Markel, Geraldine. "Improving Test-Taking Skills of LD Adolescents." ACADEMIC THERAPY 16 (January 1981): 333-342.

   The focus of the article is on the problems learning disabled students have taking tests. As the author reminds us, many of these problems also apply to the regular high school population. She suggests there are five possible areas of concern: anxiety management, problem-solving skills, assertiveness, study and test-taking skills and self-management skills. The suggestions made are fairly general but provide a starting point for dealing with these problems.

196. Mayer, Richard E. "Aids to Text Comprehension." EDUCATIONAL PSYCHOLOGIST 19 (Winter 1984): 30-42.

   The study strategies of underlining, notetaking, and outlining are put into the broad context of the tasks of selecting important information, organizing information within a text and integrating old and new information. The focus is particularly useful for encouraging students to move beyond underlining (selecting) to notetaking and outlining (organizing). A review of much of the research in this field is presented as are implications for instruction.

197. McAndrew, Donald A. "Underlining and Notetaking: Some Suggestions from Research." JOURNAL OF READING 27 (November 1983): 103-108.

   McAndrew reviews research conducted over the past decade and draws some educational implications for the teaching of underlining and notetaking. In both cases he stresses the need to teach students how to perform the skill and to encourage study of the material afterwards. Of particular interest is the discussion of how instructors should structure the lecture and prepare handouts.

198. McPhail, Irving P. "Why Teach Test Wiseness?" JOURNAL OF READING 25 (October 1981): 32-38.

   We need to teach test wiseness (the ability to use test characteristics in order to score well) to help students whose future often rests on their scores and to help educators by improving the validity of tests. McPhail gives specific lists of skills and examples of lessons designed to meet this objective.

199. Memory, David M., and David W. Moore. "Selecting Sources in Library Research: An Activity in Skimming and Critical Reading." JOURNAL OF READING 24 (March 1981): 469-474.

   The authors combine teaching the skills of skimming and of critical reading together in an activity specifically aimed at library research. The strategy is well explained and has much appeal to high school teachers and students. It represents reading skills as clearly relevant to the content classroom and, thus, should have appeal to students.

200. Parrish, Berta W. "A Test to Test Test-Wiseness." JOURNAL OF READING 25 (April 1982): 672-675.

Parrish provides a test to be used as an introduction to teaching test-taking skills to secondary school students. She includes multiple choice, true/false, fill in the blanks, matching, and following directions.

201. Patberg, Judythe P., and Janell B. Lang. "Teaching Reading Flexibility in the Content Areas." READING HORIZONS 21 (Summer 1981): 211-219.

Readers need to be flexible, adapting their rate and strategy to the material and to their purpose. Patberg and Lang believe assessment and instruction in this can and should be done in the content classroom. They provide three strategies for assessment including examples and discuss in general the question of how to instruct.

202. Rohwer, William D. "An Invitation to an Educational Psychology of Studying." EDUCATIONAL PSYCHOLOGIST 19 (Winter 1984): 1-14.

Rohwer presents a comprehensive review of research on studying and proposes a "preliminary conception" of the variables and their relationships. Course and text characteristics vary and are "determinants of both study activities and of the influence of student characteristics on these activities" (p. 9). Student characteristics also vary. The article deals with the various possible interactions among these variables. The need for directed and extensive research is emphasized.

203. Simpson, Michele L. "The Status of Study Strategy Instruction: Implications for Classroom Teachers." JOURNAL OF READING 28 (November 1984): 138-142.

Simpson, after reviewing recent research, concludes that students are leaving high school without the study skills they need to be independent, mature, efficient learners. This can be traced to three reasons. First, students have not always been taught study strategies; when they have been taught the instruction has been incomplete and there has been no requirement that the strategy be used with new material independently. Second, students cannot monitor their progress or effectiveness in using a strategy. Third, they have learned generic strategies and have not been taught to identify the demands of particular content areas in choosing or adapting strategies. Simpson provides guidelines for overcoming these problems: set up a district-wide reading committee to evaluate study skills taught; provide direct instruction in study skills by teaching rules, modeling strategies, and giving guided practice; teach and reinforce appropriate study strategies in content areas; and develop an expectation that students will learn independently.

204. Tryon, Georgiana Shick. "The Measurement and Treatment of Test Anxiety." REVIEW OF EDUCATIONAL RESEARCH 50 (Summer 1980): 343-372.

The author has reviewed literature in this field looking at both the results of the studies and the research designs used. A wide range of treatment conditions is examined and a general conclusion drawn that most treatments can to some extent reduce test anxiety. They do not necessarily change test performance.

CHAPTER VI

MOTIVATING

Anyone who has ever been in a classroom has been witness to the problems associated with motivation. Early and Sawyer's (207, pp. 241-243) description of the unmotivated student is disturbingly close to reality. There are the reluctant readers and learners who haven't the "time or taste" for reading; they get Cs, maybe Bs, by listening to the teacher, "borrowing" others' notes, maybe skimming the text or using knowledge gained from television or their parents. But, they don't read. We also have the bored, disinterested students who do not read. School is boring. The subject matter is boring. The textbook is boring. They are "tuned out." They need to be "turned on." Finally, there are the students who are poor or mediocre readers. Reading is a lot of work; it takes a lot of time and effort. It just may not be worth it!

This is a very serious aspect of secondary school instruction in all areas, but particularly in the area of reading. Motivation is at the heart of becoming an effective reader and of reading to learn. In both the short and long run, the student must have some reason for pursuing and completing the task. "Walberg and Uguroglu (1980) conclude that student motivation is a necessary condition for learning and that increasing the other factors such as quality and amount of instruction at great cost will be relatively fruitless if student motivation remains at low levels" (241, p. 102).

In addition, motivation to read and to learn has another implication, which we will not pursue but will mention. Visit a secondary school. Observe student behavior in the classrooms. Compare classrooms. Wlodkowski (241) cites the "increasing evidence...that classroom teachers themselves identify the teachers' failure to motivate as their number one problem in discipline and control today" (p. 102). Could this be a factor in the behaviors you observe in some classrooms?

Motivation is mentioned in almost every text on educational psychology and in most texts on elementary reading. Unfortunately, you cannot assume it will be included in a text on secondary reading even though the NAEP (34) found that although students recognized it was important to read, the percentage who read daily declined with age. It is possible that students are not motivated enough to read in the face of competing demands on their time. A problem in motivation exists on the secondary level but we do not always address it.

The problem is compounded because of the existence of different theories of motivation, with different implications for the classroom. MacGinitie (p.xi) warned us that "we desperately need a way of seeing in the dark. We naturally feel the need to be certain that what we do is right" (p. 679). Be forewarned. There is, at the present time, no absolute certainty as to how best to motivate students to read and learn from their reading but your classroom experiences have undoubtedly convinced you that we must deal with the problem.

Using Techniques that Motivate

Theory

Before we look at what theorists say about motivation, make a list of some of the conditions you think of as necessary for motivation. Your list probably includes some variation on the following items:

Interest: Students need to be interested in text and/or the topic. The interest may come from their prior knowledge, the relevance of the text or topic to their lives or their aspirations or the teacher's efforts at arousing interest.

Self-evaluation and success: Students need to feel that they can succeed. They may believe this because we tell them they can do it or they may have had successful experiences in the past.

Value: Students need to think that the job is worth doing. Elementary students will often do something because we tell them to; secondary students need to feel it's worth doing.

If these are the conditions, how do we motivate? We provide interesting materials, tell students they can do it, provide appropriate tasks at which they will succeed, and show them why they need to master the skill or learn the information.

We have made some predictions. We have identified what may be some of the affective aspects of motivation and some of the things that we as teachers can do to improve motivation. Now we need to confirm, reject or alter these predictions by looking at some current theories. This review of theory is only a cursory overview and you may want to draw on the references provided or texts in educational psychology or learning theory for more depth and details.

The Expectancy X Value theory reflects many of our predictions. "The degree of effort that individuals will put forth in attempting to reach a particular goal will be a function of the value they place on reaching the goal and their expectancy of being able to reach it if they do make the effort" (213, p. 200). If I like the text and think it's important to read it, and am sure I have the ability to succeed in reading it, I will be motivated to make a substantial effort to complete the reading. According to Wigfield and Asher (211) most theorists in this tradition have looked at affective not cognitive motives for valuing the goal and making the effort to reach it.

The self-efficacy theory is an example of a theory that has included both affective and cognitive variables in motivation. "Effort derives primarily from expectations for success, or self-efficacy....The strength of belief in one's ability to perform is a more critical influence on behavior in challenging situations than either task incentives or actual personal skill" (217, p. 91). The student uses information from his social environment to construct this expectation. He bases it on his past performance, the influences of others, his psychological state. We have already identified most of these as variables. These are the ones we expect to be involved in motivation. In addition though, some "internal reasoning processes as precursors to motivation processes" (ibid., p. 89) are included. Bandura suggests task analysis processes such as "selective attention, personal standard setting, and self-observation during the task" (ibid.).

Brophy (213) has made two contributions to our thinking here. First, he is concerned that frequently the emphasis is put on the effort part of the process and not on the value. He asserts that "valuing the actual processes of learning (as distinct from their outcomes) should be included as basic to motivation to learn" (p. 201). In addition, he recognizes that learning in a classroom is a cognitive act and that there is an important cognitive aspect to motivation, citing particularly the metacognitive aspects of learning.

The attribution theory (211, 217, 237) is also an example of the stress on cognitive aspects of motivation. This theory also is concerned with expectancy and value but emphasizes that reasoning processes rather than affective processes are the basis for determining the expectancies and values. The causal factors generally associated with motivation in this approach are ability, effort, task difficulty and luck. These can operate on two dimensions: stability (is the causal factor changeable or not?) and locus of control (is the causal factor personal or environmental?). The learner attributes potential success or failure to the various causes and performs according to his perception of the dimensions. "This kind of self-control over learning gives students a sense of responsibility for their achievement and produces 'a continued disposition to achieve'....This persistence, an aspect of motivation, is neglected when motivation is thought of as a gimmick used only to arouse student curiosity through interesting materials or games" (237, pp. 687-688).

We are beginning to see the learner as more purposefully in control, as organizing the task and what he does to accomplish it. Corno and Mandinach (217) propose the notion of self-regulated learning consisting of "specific cognitive activities, such as deliberate planning and monitoring, which learners carry out as they encounter academic tasks" (p. 89). Corno and Mandinach tie this notion in to both expectancy and attribution. "Together these form a set of student interpretive processes useful for accomplishing a variety of academic tasks" (ibid.). The student, not the teacher, is in control of his own motivation.

Finally, consider the Time Continuum Model. Rather than propose another theory, Wlodkowski (241) uses a cognitive approach to integrate various theories of motivation chronologically at the beginning, middle, and end of learning activities. His model aids the teacher in "systematically selecting and using motivational constructs (strategies) of any origin based on the six major factors of the model: attitude, need, stimulation, affect, competence and reinforcement" (p. 104). The focus is on using different aspects of different theories in different learning situations.

As is the case with so much of the literature in the field of education and educational psychology, concerns have been raised about the research. Brophy (213) notes that much of the research in the field of motivation has been conducted in play situations, not work situations similar to school setting and that the focus has been, until recently, on the affective not the cognitive aspects of motivation. Corno and Mandinach (217) echo this by citing the need for studies that integrate learning, motivation and instruction in the classroom. Wigfield and Asher (211) hit even closer to home. Their concern about motivation research is that it is sparse in the field of reading.

We have already expressed an uncertainty about the fact that there are a number of ways of looking at motivation. We have no set formula to propose for achieving motivation in students. In fact, students have probably have individual differences in their "sensitivity" to the variables discussed (217). In addition, it may be that some alternative approaches to motivation are more effective in some situations than in others. Teachers "need to view motivation as a multidimensional construct....stemming from a combination of student, task, and instructional characteristics" (ibid., p. 105). Students need "to become adroit at strategy shifts across tasks, and even within certain complex tasks" (ibid., p. 106). It may be as Wlodkowski (241) proposes. We may need a "continuous and interactive motivational dynamic" (p. 105).

However, in spite of the uncertainties, look how far we've come from where we started. We have a number of new notions about motivation. We still have the affective variables but we have added cognitive variables. We no longer think in terms of the teacher being in charge of motivating the student but now consider the student as an active agent in the process. Motivation is not static but may change within a task. Motivation is not concerned solely with accomplishing the task today but with accomplishing many learning tasks in the future and with valuing learning--both its processes and products. Now we need to look at some of the techniques suggested in the literature to see how to help the students described in the introduction reach this point.

Practice

What are you going to do tomorrow morning when the third period
class arrives (you know what THAT group is like!) or sixth period
when THAT student comes in (you know who I mean!)? Unfortunately,
most of the suggestions in the literature cannot be implemented that
quickly. Rather, motivation is a long-term process. However, let's
look at some of the suggestions.

A number of the strategies suggested involve setting up the
task so the student can succeed, develop appropriate expectations,
and assume control while performing the task with a reasonable
amount of effort.

1. Identify student interests in topics and materials. Begin to
   engage students in learning through their interests. (11, 209)

2. Identify student attitudes toward reading. Do students have
   negative or positive attitudes toward reading as a means of
   personal development, as a way of progressing in job or school
   hierarchies, and as an avenue for enjoyment? (227)

3. Provide a variety of materials, based on different interests,
   abilities, and attitudes. This relates to a number of the
   variables discussed: the affective role of interest and the
   cognitive appraisal of a student's ability to perform the task.
   (11, 209, 214)

4. Clarify the objectives of the lesson and assignments as well as
   procedures to be followed. Keep assignments short enough so
   they can be handled successfully. Students can begin to assume
   control when they know what to do and what the expectations are.
   (11, 207, 229, 237)

5. Give students choices in both the task and in materials to be
   used. The choices may need to be constrained at first and
   gradually broadened. (207, 209, 225, 237)

6. Provide opportunities for students to set their own goals. They
   may be more likely to see the value in the task if they have had
   a part in identifying and formulating it. Many students will
   need help with this in the beginning, with you providing
   guidance and choices. Goal setting gets at the problems of
   locus of control, the self-regulation of motivation, and
   realistic expectations. (237)

Other suggestions relate cognitive learning skills and
strategies to motivation.

1. Identify and teach needed basic skills. No amount of student
   effort or value will suffice if the student lacks the basic
   skill needed for the task. (211)

2. Teach students to learn how to learn so that they can develop a
   sense of cognitive competence and do the job independently as

well as value the process and products of learning. This
includes the thinking and studying strategies already discussed,
such as generating questions, summarizing and monitoring
comprehension. (213, 217, 237)

3. Show students how to generate and control their own interest in
    material not immediately appealing. This can include
    understanding and monitoring their processes of interest
    activation, comprehending text and self-questioning. The
    student is in control and is self-regulating the process. (161,
    232, 238)

Another group of techniques relates to the affective state that
teachers can help create to increase motivation.

1. Assume that students will succeed in the task. At the same
    time, maintain high expectations and standards. Students often
    perceive themselves as we perceive them. (229)

2. Reduce anxiety so the students are relaxed and receptive to
    learning. In test situations, however, students should probably
    be less relaxed and oriented toward producing an acceptable
    performance. (213)

3. Use rewards and punishments carefully. This is a very complex
    topic and deserves more study than we can give it here. This is
    another place where your courses in educational psychology are
    useful. For example, a reward may focus the student's
    motivation on getting the task done, not on learning the skill
    related to the task. "Read and complete these two pages on
    identifying the main idea. Then we will see the movie." It's
    inspiring to see how quickly everyone finishes the two pages but
    have they learned the skill? (213)

4. Use encouragement which evaluates the activity or the task, not
    the person. (237)

5. Give feedback related to specific goals, not general grades.
    (213, 225)

6. Stress the positive aspects of the task for the future.
    Brophy's example is useful. Don't stress that you'll never
    graduate from high school if you don't learn to read. Instead
    stress that you need to read to get a good job when you graduate
    from high school. (213)

A final group of techniques is concerned with how the teacher
structures the classroom.

1. Model appropriate behaviors. This enables the student to be
    confident of how to proceed and gives him a means of monitoring
    his use of the process and his progress in completing the task.
    This is not the first time that modeling behavior has been
    discussed! (211, 213, 217, 238)

2. Provide an atmosphere conducive to risk-taking. Encourage student participation. Again, a repeat topic! (220, 229, 230, 238)

3. Provide time during school for independent reading activities. (207, 209, 215, 238)

Using Materials that Motivate

Theory

The literature dealing with the use of materials to motivate has two main focuses. The first focus, the role of interest in motivation, we have already examined. Interest in the topic and/or the material is a way of engaging the student in the task but is only part of motivation. It is not all of it. Providing interesting materials will not carry most students through a difficult task. However, it may well get the student started and keep him going while acquiring some of the skills, strategies and confidence he needs to tackle topics and materials which may not be top on his list. The second focus, how to use these interests in developing motivation, remains to be examined in the context of choosing and using materials.

Students' interests in topics and materials seem to be age-related. Tonjes and Zintz (11) found that "after age ten and up to adulthood there appear to be three overriding themes; the search for self-identity, how they relate to others and the process of becoming an adult" (p. 35). These three large areas of interest, in fact, can provide us with a wide variety of materials. We need to remember, though, that what is interesting to one student, may not be interesting to all students. This suggests the need to identify individual student interests and to provide a variety of materials for members of a class to read (211). It also suggests the need to have a variety of different kinds of materials on the same topic. Tonjes and Zintz (11), for example, recommend science fiction for the science student and light historical novels for the reluctant historian. Finally, interests for any individual student can change over time. It is important to re-evaluate them periodically (211).

Practice

Remember that choosing materials is only part of the task of motivating students. However, it is a part that we can identify fairly easily and can use to begin the process and sustain motivation while other strategies are developing.

1. Provide materials that deal with the interests, concerns and problems of adolescents. This might include books on social situations and peer relationships of concern to teenagers, value systems relating adolescent culture to the larger society or particular individual problems such as divorce. This means suggesting science fiction, biographies, teenage romances, contemporary fiction, sports books, lyrics from popular songs.

It also means not necessarily requiring a reaction paper or a book report. (11, 206, 210, 212, 219, 224, 225, 226, 230, 233, 236, 240)

2. Introduce materials written by other students. The content will probably be interesting and the material can serve as a model and a motivator for your students to write materials for others to read. Remember the connection between reading and writing? (223, 230)

3. Use controversy and conflict in topics and materials as a means of generating interest, motivating students to read, and insuring involvement in the completion of the task. We also suggested this as a way of involving students in activating prior knowledge and predicting. (228)

4. Don't forget humor as a motivator. Use puns, jokes, funny stories to teach the subtleties of language as well as main idea and important detail. (216, 231)

6. Use interests generated by the content and the media of television as a basis for introducing school topics and materials. Use the books on which shows are based. Provide scripts for shows which can be obtained from the networks or from adolescent magazines. Use television topics as background information for other reading. (207, 215, 234)

5. Make reading practical. Use real materials. These can be on a fairly low level, such as job applications or they can be more complex, including college and/or loan applications. (221)

7. Relate school materials to local issues, by identifying an issue of significance to students and by requiring research and reading of local sources to resolve the issue. The number of parking spaces adjacent to the local high school is of concern in many suburban schools. The topic might be a more significant one, such as following the path of a fellow student who has been charged with drug peddling as he goes through the judicial system. (207)

8. Provide a wide variety of paperbacks, magazines and other reading materials related to a particular content area. This might include biographies, historical novels, science fiction. This does not mean abandoning the textbook; it does mean providing additional options. (161, 205, 207, 208, 209, 218, 222, 235, 239)

Suggestions for Implementation

The need for reading teachers and content teachers to work together has been pointed out in a number of situations. It is particularly critical in the area of motivation, especially with the current emphasis on the cognitive aspects of motivation. No matter how interesting the content teachers make the course or what

fascinating reading materials are chosen, the student still needs to
perceive himself as able to accomplish the task of reading and
learning from the reading and must have the cognitive skills to do
this.   Many of these skills are the thinking and studying skills we
have discussed.

We can add the need to include another person here--the
librarian.   The librarian should prove an invaluable resource in
researching and choosing materials.

Summary

A great danger in secondary school, to which we are all prey,
is that of becoming so involved with imparting the knowledge of our
subject and/or with teaching the skills of reading that we forget we
are dealing with young people who may not have the same dreams and
desires that we do.   They have an agenda which may or may not
coincide with ours. Fortunately, they often remind us of this with
a vengeance.   They don't allow us to take motivation to read for
granted.

We cannot, and should not, hope to achieve unanimity in our
goals and objectives with all students but we do need to agree that
reading is a way of learning content and is an enjoyable activity.
We can reach this goal by using both affective and cognitive
motivational strategies in working with reluctant, unmotivated
readers.   Many of these strategies are the same ones students can
use to comprehend, study, and monitor their own progress.   They
become successful and are motivated to attempt and try new tasks.
At the risk of sounding glib, success breeds success.

Lamberg and Lamb (209) assert that "fortunately, ways to
improve motivation are very simple, very inexpensive, and very
powerful" (p. 332). For teachers, faced with the realities of the
secondary classroom, the ways don't always seem that simple although
they may be inexpensive. But, they are possible. How powerful they
are depends on the teacher, the student, the task, and the
instructional situation. However, in spite of these complexities
and uncertainties, we can improve students' motivation to read and
to learn from reading.

BIBLIOGRAPHY

Books

205. Bishop, David. "Motivating Adolescent Readers via Starter
     Shelves in Content Area Classes." MOTIVATING RELUCTANT
     READERS. Edited by Alfred J. Ciani. Newark, Delaware:
     International Reading Assn., 1981, pp. 44-70.

     Bishop advocates including a shelf of paperback books
     related to the subject of the content classroom. The fact
     that the books are readily available will increase the
     likelihood that they will be read. A wide range of available
     books increases skills and motivates students to read
     independently. This unusually practical and helpful chapter
     contains guidelines for each step of the process, from
     identifying sources for choosing the books to incorporating
     paperbacks into the classroom. A large annotated bibliography
     of sources is included. Some of the items are not current but
     the secondary teacher can still identify useful books and the
     addresses of potential sources from the list.

206. Ciani, Alfred J. "Recent Adolescent Literature: An
     Alternative to the Serials." MOTIVATING RELUCTANT READERS.
     Edited by Alfred J. Ciani. Newark, Delaware: International
     Reading Assn., 1981, pp. 35-43.

     Ciani analyzes serial novels and concludes that because of
     the repetitiveness of plot and the often biased nature of
     these books, as well as their cost and the time needed to
     choose them, teachers should avoid them. Instead he suggests
     contemporary adolescent fiction, science fiction, sports books
     and other nonfiction. In each case he provides a useful
     annotated bibliography.

207. Early, Margaret, and Diane J. Sawyer. "What To Do About Kids
     Who Won't Read." READING TO LEARN IN GRADES 5 TO 12. New
     York: Harcourt Brace Jovanovich, 1984, pp. 241-270.

     The authors provide guidance in using a number of strategies
     to increase student motivation and interest, including
     Sustained Silent Reading, oral reading, television in the
     reading program, and motivation within the content classroom.
     The critical role of the teacher in providing enthusiasm and a
     model is highlighted.

208. Haag, Enid E. "Enriching Content Classrooms through
     Collateral Reading." TEACHING READING/THINKING/STUDY SKILLS
     IN CONTENT CLASSROOMS. By Marian J. Tonjes and Miles V.
     Zintz. Dubuque, Iowa: Wm. C. Brown, 1981, pp. 305-333.

     Haag believes that textbooks must be "supplemented by a

large and varied collection of pertinent collateral material"
(p. 305). The author provides many suggestions for assembling
this collection. The list of sources is particularly useful,
covering general sources as well as ones specific to each
content area. Procedures for teaching students to locate
information are also given in general and for each content
area.

209. Lamberg, Walter J., and Charles E. Lamb. "Developing Positive
Attitudes Toward Reading." READING INSTRUCTION IN THE
CONTENT AREAS. Chicago: Rand McNally, 1980, pp. 329-346.

The authors suggest that in order to develop motivation to
read the teacher allow for self-selection of reading
materials, provide time in the day for regular independent
reading, insure that students read a variety of kinds of
materials, administer interest inventories and monitor student
reading. Specific suggestions are included, particularly for
the interest inventories.

210. Smith, Cyrus F., Jr. "Motivating the Reluctant Reader through
the Top Twenty." MOTIVATING RELUCTANT READERS. Edited by
Alfred J. Ciani. Newark, Delaware: International Reading
Assn., 1981, pp. 26-34.

Occasionally the lyrics of a popular song are suitable for
teaching poetry and can provide a unique opportunity for
motivating the reluctant reader. Smith gives complete
examples with a number of interesting suggestions for
initiating and following up this kind of lesson. The emphasis
is on teaching reading and reading related skills based on the
student's interest in popular music and musicians.

211. Wigfield, Allan, and Steven R. Asher. "Social and
Motivational Influences on Reading." HANDBOOK OF READING
RESEARCH. Edited by P. David Pearson, Rebecca Barr, Michael
L. Kamil, and Peter Mosenthal. New York: Longman, 1984, pp.
423-452.

The authors review some of the general research in
motivational theory, including a particularly clear discussion
of attribution theory with its emphasis on cognitive
determinants of motivation. The discussion of home and school
influences on reading, even though focused mainly on
elementary children, is interesting and useful to the
secondary teacher as a background in understanding students.
Teachers' perceptions of students and ways of interacting
with them can have varying effects on motivation and
achievement. Although the emphasis in this chapter is on
research that has been and should be conducted, there is much
food for thought here for teachers. In addition, the authors
draw some tentative conclusions about race and socio-economic
status as factors in motivation and achievement.

Periodicals

212. Auten, Anne. "All About Adolescent Literature: Pro and Con."
     JOURNAL OF READING 28 (October 1984): 76-78.

     Auten defines young adult literature as that written
     primarily for adolescents and primarily read by them. She
     reviews problems with using this type of literature which have
     been cited in recent ERIC articles. Problems include the
     limited forms YA literature takes, difficulties for the reader
     of moving from it into adult literature, and problems for the
     teacher in using it effectively. She also reviews the
     positive features of YA literature and suggests ways it can be
     used effectively. The bibliography is short but useful.

213. Brophy, Jere.   "Conceptualizing Student Motivation."
     EDUCATIONAL PSYCHOLOGIST 18 (Fall 1983): 200-215.

     Brophy presents a comprehensive review of theories of
     motivation after examining the particular requirements for
     motivation in school work settings as contrasted to play
     settings. He proposes that we must motivate students not just
     to learn but to value learning. To that end, he suggests
     activities that involve students in learning to learn, self-
     monitoring, and problem solving. They focus on task processes,
     not just task outcomes, on the cognitive, not just the
     affective. Teacher modeling is seen as one effective way of
     stimulating students to value learning and to learn how to
     learn.

214. Carbo, Marie.   "Reading Styles Change Between Second and
     Eighth Grade." EDUCATIONAL LEADERSHIP 40 (February 1983):
     56-59.

     Carbo studied the reading styles of 293 students from grades
     two, four, six, and eight. She investigated the role of
     environmental, emotional, sociological and physical stimuli in
     planning reading programs. The comparison of second and
     eighth graders in particular highlights the need to provide a
     diversity of materials for older students, to allow them to
     make choices, and to provide time for independent, individual
     reading.

215. Coley, Joan D. "Non-Stop Reading for Teenagers: What We Have
     Learned and Where We Go From Here." Paper presented at the
     Annual Meeting of the College Reading Assn., Louisville,
     Kentucky, October 29-31, 1981. 9pp. (ED 211 951)

     Coley reviews current research generated by the Reading
     Enrichment/Achievement Demonstration Project (READ). The
     program consists of sustained silent reading using paperbacks.
     The research studied results from 1,100 students in
     alternative schools, community-based programs and junior high
     schools. Areas of student interest in terms of topics and
     kinds of reading materials were identified. The project

demonstrated that students "grow toward maturity" (p. 8) and enjoy reading when they can practice their skills with interesting materials.

216. Colwell, Clyde G. "Humor as a Motivational and Remedial Technique." JOURNAL OF READING 24 (March 1981): 484-486.

For some students, with problems in reading and writing, school is a "hostile environment." Humor is seen by Colwell as one way of alleviating this and motivating students. He provides a number of specific suggestions, most more suitable to the reading specialist than the content teacher.

217. Corno, Lyn, and Ellen B. Mandinach. "The Role of Cognitive Engagement in Classroom Learning and Motivation." EDUCATIONAL PSYCHOLOGIST 18 (Summer 1983): 88-108.

The authors propose that self-regulation processes are of critical importance in the classroom learning-motivation cycle. Self-regulation is one form of cognitive engagement in which the student is alert to incoming information, is selective, connects new knowledge to old, plans a performance routine, and monitors and checks his performance. The emphasis in the proposed model is on a cognitive approach to motivation.

218. Dole, Janice A., and Virginia R. Johnson. "Beyond the Textbook: Science Literature for Young People." JOURNAL OF READING 24 (April 1981): 579-582.

Popular science books can motivate the student who is reluctant to read the textbook and can provide a resource for the student unable to read the text. These fiction and nonfiction books also provide needed background information and relate science concepts to real life. Suggestions are made for the science teacher, reading teacher and librarian to work together. A list of science books in different areas is also included.

219. Gallo, Donald R., Ed. "Living with Adolescent Literature." CONNECTICUT ENGLISH JOURNAL 12 (Fall 1980): 1-190.

This special journal issue contains a wealth of useful, classroom-oriented articles which all focus on the theme of adolescent literature. Suggestions are made on what to use, how to use it, and how to involve students in the act of reading. Many of the major themes of adolescents are discussed, such as role models, parent relationships, drugs, and power. Special interest groups are included: blacks, urban students, Mexican-Americans, females.

220. Gold, Patricia Cohen, and David Yellin. "Be the Focus: A Psychoeducational Technique for Use with Unmotivated Learners." JOURNAL OF READING 25 (MARCH 1982): 550-552.

Gold and Yellin base their motivational technique on current reading theory.   Content lessons are structured with a prereading discussion in which each student must agree or disagree with a fact, idea, concept or issue from the text. Then each student reads silently to confirm or reject his position.   Last, postreading discussion reviews information, summarizes, identifies missing areas and suggests areas for further research and reading. The distinctive feature of this technique is that each student is required to speak for two minutes without interruption. He is the focus person.   The authors suggest that this procedure attacks the problems of "passivity,...low level of risk taking and low degree of self-confidence" (p. 550). Through this technique the student is motivated.

221. Gottsdanker-Willekens,   Anne   E.   "FUNctional   Folders: Independent Applied Reading Materials." JOURNAL OF READING 25 (May 1982): 764-767.

The author uses real materials to motivate and folders to encourage independence in this strategy.   The examples of possible real world materials for the various content areas are especially useful. She also provides guidance in setting up the folders.

222. Guerra, Cathy L., and DeLores B. Payne. "Using Popular Books and Magazines to Interest Students in General Science." JOURNAL OF READING 24 (April 1981): 583-586.

Guerra and Payne suggest that popular science literature can help in overcoming the problem of motivating general science students.   They recommend biographies, science fiction, informational books, and a variety of magazines. They provide suggestions for activities and sources for additional information on choosing science books.

223. Hatcher, Barbara.   "Cultural Journalism Publications for Reluctant Readers." JOURNAL OF READING 23 (February 1980): 424-429.

Cultural journalism magazines focus on local people, local activities and local ways of dealing with human needs and problems. The articles are written and edited by students for students. Because of these characteristics Hatcher believes that they are uniquely suited for the reluctant secondary school student. Not only are the articles relevant to the concerns and problems of the reader but they also can extend the reader's background and perspective. The article contains a useful list of publications and addresses which identifies those that have an ethnic emphasis.

224. Holbrook, Hilary Taylor.   "Adolescent Literature: More Than Meets the Eye." JOURNAL OF READING 25 (January 1982): 378-381.

Holbrook reviews a number of recent monographs and speeches published by ERIC on the topic of adolescent literature. She concludes that adolescent literature in the secondary classroom can motivate the most reluctant reader and even "spark a lifetime interest in reading" (p. 378). She identifies reading preferences and provides an excellent list of sources for the secondary teacher to use in selecting a wide variety of books designed to appeal to adolescents.

225. Indiana State Department of Public Instruction. METHODS FOR MOTIVATION, GRADES 7-9. Indianapolis, Indiana: Division of Reading Effectiveness, August 1981. 14pp. (ED 210 647)

This monograph relates motivation in reading to the realities and complexities of adolescent life. Interests are identified and ways of providing for those interests suggested as well as ways of providing support and feedback that will encourage students to take charge of their own reading.

226. International Reading Association Literature for Adolescents Committee. "Sources of Information on Young Adult Literature." JOURNAL OF READING 28 (October 1984): 56-62.

This article is a valuable resource for secondary teachers, providing them with a annotated bibliography of periodicals, textbooks and tradebooks that have a major or partial focus on the topic of young adult literature.

227. Lewis, Ramon, and William H. Teale. "Another Look at Secondary School Students' Attitudes Toward Reading." JOURNAL OF READING BEHAVIOR XII (No. 3 1980): 187-201.

Lewis and Teale identify three dimensions of students' attitude toward reading. They have positive or negative feelings about reading as a way of achieving individual development, of attaining success in school, work or life, and of obtaining pleasure. The authors discuss elements of a scale designed to measure these dimensions and relate their model to instructional needs.

228. Lunstrum, John P. "Building Motivation Through the Use of Controversy." JOURNAL OF READING 24 (May 1981): 687-691.

After examining educational, psychological and psycholinguistic theories, the author concludes that controversy is a useful means of motivating the student to engage in the reading process. He provides an example from a history course, incorporating current reading strategies, which illustrates how to accomplish this through all the stages of the reading process.

229. McDaniel, Thomas R. "A Primer on Motivation: Principles Old and New." PHI DELTA KAPPAN 66 (September 1984): 46-49.

McDaniel proposes five principles as the foundation for

motivating students: invite success, use cooperative learning, maintain high expectations, focus attention on the task, and provide for interaction in the classroom. The article provides many examples of classroom behavior and a rating scale for teachers to evaluate themselves as motivators.

230. McWilliams, Lana, and Dennie L. Smith. "Decision Stories: Language Experience for Adolescents." JOURNAL OF READING 25 (November 1981): 142-145.

The authors provide clear examples and directions on developing decision stories written by students based on real-life problems and situations. Students critique and respond to each other's stories. The emphasis is on building motivation, personal growth, and thinking and communication skills.

231. Nilsen, Don L. F., and Alleen Pace Nilsen. "An Exploration and Defense of the Humor in Young Adult Literature." JOURNAL OF READING 26 (October 1982): 58-65.

Nilsen and Nilsen compare and contrast teenage and adult views of humor. Teenage students are leaving childhood and entering adulthood. Their experience with life has been limited but they urgently want more. These factors influence the language, allusions and topics that teens find humorous. The article analyzes some current literature and provides guidance for previewing other works. Humor is motivating to students; it is also a way of enabling them to become manipulators of language.

232. Ortiz, Rose Katz. "Generating Interest in Reading." JOURNAL OF READING 27 (November 1983): 113-119.

Oritz takes the point of view that the reader has an important responsibility in generating interest in a text. The interest does not reside solely in the text. It is a state of mind in which we approach and interact with the text. The article is concerned with ways students can generate interest in materials that are not immediately appealing. These include activities such as highlighting the elements of interest, monitoring the process of arousing interest and interacting with the text through questioning and predicting. The author also includes suggestions for workshop activities for students and teachers.

233. Parrish, Berta W. "Put a Little Romantic Fiction into Your Reading Program." JOURNAL OF READING 26 (April 1983): 610-615.

Parrish confronts the issue of including teen romances in a secondary reading program and concludes, why not? She examines the characteristics of the romances, their probable sources of appeal, and their positive and negative aspects. She holds that they should be part of a wide range of books available to teens. Since they are so popular, we should accept them and use them as a way of encouraging reading and of reading other types of books. A list of publishers is included.

234. Potter, Rosemary Lee. "The Link Between Reading Instruction and Commercial Television: Is This a Bandwagon?" JOURNAL OF READING 24 (February 1981): 377-381.

This article contains some interesting, practical suggestions for using the appeal of television as a motivating force in reading including reading books or articles that "tie-in" to television programs in some way as well as the production scripts and condensed scripts. Reading and thinking skills might be taught using the programs themselves. Potter raises a series of important questions regarding research needs in this area and the proper balance between television and books in the classroom.

235. Povsic, Frances F. "Russia in History--Historical Fiction and Biography for Junior High School Students." JOURNAL OF READING 25 (January 1982): 350-359.

This annotated bibliography of historical fiction and biography provides a source for content teachers who want an alternative or supplement to the history textbook.

236. Ross, Beth, and Nancy Simone. "Reading Interests of Tenth, Eleventh and Twelfth Grade Students." M.A., Ed. Thesis, Kean College of New Jersey, April 1982. 65pp. (ED 215 329)

The authors surveyed 300 students in the target grades and found evidence of a decrease in the amount of time spent reading outside school compared with previous research. A range of reading interests were identified, including science fiction for males and romance novels for females.

237. Stone, Nancy R. "Accentuate the Positive: Motivation and Reading for Secondary Students." JOURNAL OF READING 27 (May 1984): 684-690.

Stone reviews three theories of motivation: achievement motivation, locus of control and attribution theory. All three, she feels, stress the adult as a self-governing learner, who needs to organize information as a way of controlling his environment. She make specific suggestions for the teacher to increase student motivation.

238. Van Jura, Sarah A. "Secondary Students at Risk: Two Giant Steps toward Independence in Reading." JOURNAL OF READING 27 (March 1984): 540-543.

The goal for high school students is to become independent readers. Van Jura suggests that students often have the ability but are unwilling to take chances in reading. To overcome this, two approaches are discussed. In one approach the student is motivated to read by capitalizing on his interests, providing a classroom atmosphere conducive to reading and allowing for and encouraging opportunities for reading. This may not be sufficient. The second approach stresses students' need for a variety of reading behaviors, including questioning, predicting, previewing and predicting in order to increase comprehension and independence. These give them confidence that they can read and the motivation to do it.

239.. Wilton, Shirley M. "Juvenile Science Fiction Involves Reluctant Readers." JOURNAL OF READING 24 (April 1981): 608-611.

Wilton capitalizes on adolescents' interest in STAR WARS and STAR TREK by using juvenile science fiction as a way to help them "discover the excitement of a printed page" (p. 608). She identifies three categories of science fiction: technological, sociological, and psychological. A bibliography and examples of each type are provided for students through grade nine.

240. Winfield, Evelyn T. "Relevant Reading for Adolescents: Literature on Divorce." JOURNAL OF READING 26 (February 1983): 408-411.

Winfield recognizes that students' personal problems can have a negative effect on motivation and encourage withdrawal from the learning process. By providing students with reading material appropriate to the problem, we allow them to put the problem into the perspective of "modern society." The use of adolescent fiction dealing with divorce can "afford the teachable moment for some of your tuned-out students" (p. 411). The article contains an annotated bibliography of novels and other resources for use in the secondary classroom.

241. Wlodkowski, Raymond J. "Making Sense Out of Motivation: A Systematic Model to Consolidate Motivational Constructs Across Theories." EDUCATIONAL PSYCHOLOGIST 16 (Summer 1981): 101-110.

Wlodkowski proposes a Time Continuum Model of Motivation which carries the teacher and student through three phases of any learning activity. In the beginning phases, the focus is on student attitude and needs. During the learning activity, the emphasis is on the stimulation of the student by the activity and on the affective or emotional experience of the student while learning. In the ending stage, the model stresses the feeling of competence the student has acquired and the reinforcement received. Various theories of motivation are incorporated into this one theory. A clear example is provided.

CHAPTER VII

ASSESSING SECONDARY READING AND STUDYING

Assessment. This is a word that can strike terror into the hearts of the uninitiated secondary teacher. "I haven't had any courses in it." "I don't have have time to test. I have to teach science (or math, or English, or social studies)." Yet, as we have seen, reading levels attained vary; skills mastered vary; strategies used vary. It's very discouraging to find out after the midterm that a few (some, all) students have had difficulties with the text. Lamberg and Lamb (255) believe that "information about students' reading ability can and should be an integral part of the instructional planning by the content-area teacher" (p. 159). This "not only provides helpful information, but saves time by eliminating trial and error methods in teaching" (242, p. 112).

The intention of this chapter is not to take the place of an intensive course in reading diagnosis, rather its purpose is to introduce the topic of assessment, suggest some areas to test, give an overview of standardized testing as well as some strategies for informal testing and propose some ways that content teachers and reading specialists can work together.

Understanding Assessment

Assessment and Decision Making

Lamberg and Lamb (255) define assessment as the "systematic collection of information about a student's reading" (p. 154). The literature suggests that assessment is done for a variety of reasons:

1. To make decisions about programs. We need to describe and evaluate programs to acquire funding for specific programs, state aid and/or accreditation or to verify our programs to school boards and parents. This kind of testing is generally static; it looks at what has been achieved as of the moment of testing. Johnston (249) calls this "administrative" testing; we can all picture "downtown" being interested in the results of the standardized tests used for these purposes. Teachers are also interested because of the impact on their particular programs. Program evaluation focusing on product will use standardized tests; program evaluation focusing on process will use techniques such as observations to identify what is happening. (243, 244, 249, 258, 260)

2. To monitor student progress by comparing students to each other and to a norm. We use this information to categorize students, to place them in appropriate groups. Again, administrators will be involved in testing for these purposes but so will classroom teachers and reading specialists. This may be how your groups and classes are determined. This kind of standardized group testing has questionable utility for making instructional decisions but may send up a warning signal about some members of the group. (249, 258, 260)

3. To gather data that are useful in making instructional decisions about individual students. This kind of testing is dynamic and can be adjusted for the individual. Here is the testing that is at the heart of what goes on in the classroom and the reading center. This can be formal, standardized testing using diagnostic tests or informal testing in the classroom or the reading center. (249, 258, 260)

There are, obviously, substantial reasons why we should test students' reading abilities. The danger is that we test because it's that time of year, the principal expects us to test, the student's file has blanks that need to be filled in regarding testing. Those reasons are not good enough. The key word here is "decision." Johnston and Pearson (254) warn that "no one should ever give a test (standardized or teacher-made) unless he or she intends to use the data to make a decision about an individual or a group" (p. 127). In fact, this emphasis on assessment for the purposes of decision-making appears repeatedly in the literature (258, 260, 290).

Who needs the information that will be obtained? Who will make the decisions? Early and Sawyer (243) suggest that there are three groups of people who are concerned with the results of any testing program in addition to the program administrator: the reading teacher, the content teacher and the student. The first two groups you probably expected. Why students? One reason might be motivation. They may be motivated to improve their scores. The answer, undoubtedly, goes deeper than that. Remember in Chapter I, Brown, Campione and Day (13) identified the need for the learner to understand all of the variables involved in learning. Assessment is one way for the student to find out how he stands in regard to those variables. These three constituencies all have a stake in the outcome of the testing program; all need to understand it and be involved in it.

Zigmond and Silverman (290) have taken our original definition of assessment one step further. "Assessment is the process of gathering data for the purpose of making decisions about or for individuals" (p. 163). They have made an important addition.

Theoretical Approaches to Assessment

There are a variety of theoretical approaches that are suggested in the literature.

Product vs. Process.   The first approach focuses on the measurable, observable products of reading. Can the reader answer an inference question?   Skill checklists, informal inventories, vocabulary tests, comprehension questions are all ways of testing for the product. The process approach looks at how the student is able to infer. Can he identify the source of the inference? Is it two textually explicit statements? Is it a combination of text and background knowledge?   Interviewing during or after reading is one way of assessing this.   Hansell (274) in looking at student assessment discusses a "models perspective" which suggests that we should not think of either/or; rather "the comprehension process is related to its products" (p. 699). We should look at both process and product, using a variety of strategies (such as the cloze procedure), encouraging students to preview the text and establish hypotheses about the content, and preparing teacher questions to assess prior knowledge (247, 274).   Farr and Wolf (244) concur although they are looking at program evaluation.

In the product vs. process debate, Cioffi and Carney (265) are squarely on the side of process. They advocate that

> examiners focus on process rather than product, assess the influence of prior experience, examine the circumstances under which behaviors do or do not occur, and perceive the testing situation as an interaction between teacher and student that involves observation and communication. (p. 765)

Bottom-up vs. Top-down.   Do we start with a student's skill levels and his ability to use them to begin the process of comprehending or do we assess his reading abilities from the perspective of his ability to reason about the text and use prior knowledge to organize information and make connections? Otto and Smith (47) have summarized some of the thinking here.

> The skills-centered model falls short in terms of (a) the validity of diagnosing reading problems by testing isolated parts of the total process and (b) its lack of direction for reassembling specific skills once they have been learned. The meaning-centered model falls short in that it does not provide for the explicit diagnosis and instruction that may be required to help students correct specific problems or eliminate specific deficits.

> In other words, neither model is adequate by itself. (p. 26)

Johnston (250) concurs. "While reading may be reasoning, that does not preclude it from having subskills" (p. 10). This is reminiscent of Crismore's (14) continuum of focusing on the message to predicting the message. Vacca (263) looks at the problem squarely from the point of view of the content teacher and holds that "reading is a meaning-based process and that content reading makes sense when teachers guide it without fragmenting the process into a wide array of subskills. The same applies to the evaluation process" (p. 281). Henk, Readence and Mason (275) are adamant. "It is hard to imagine how these subskills, so irrevocably bound to one another in actual reading, can be assessed and/or taught in a discrete fashion" (p. 73). The problem is that for all of us it is much easier and often neater to assess bottom-up skills than it is to assess top-down reasoning.

Cognitive. This approach examines how the text and the reader interact to enable comprehension to occur. Samuels (282, 283) proposes that reading is a constructive process with the reader constructing meaning based on the interaction of the reader and the text. He identifies external and internal factors that impact on this which need to be included in an assessment of reading. External factors include quality of instruction, text characteristics and the time allowed for the task. Internal factors include intelligence, language and decoding abilities, background knowledge for topic and text structure, metacognitive strategies and motivation.

Johnston (250) using a cognitive approach identifies two categories of cognitive strategies: one set includes all the reasoning strategies used to construct meaning from the text and from the reader's head and the other set includes comprehension monitoring strategies. In order to assess reading comprehension he (251) goes on to state that the examiner must look at the text and its characteristics, the fit between the text and the reader's prior knowledge, the source of answers to questions, and the task demands of the assessment procedure.

There are some commonalities among these approaches. In fact, to us as teachers some of the lines between them appear fuzzy. It seems, however, that we are no longer solely stressing skills; we are also stressing reasoning processes and cognitive strategies. We are no longer looking just at the reader. We are considering the text and its characteristics in assessing a student's potential for success or failure. We are examining the instructional setting as well as what we are asking the student to do. These developments in our thinking about the assessment process have clearly come from our current thinking about reading (268). These views of assessment also reflect the kinds of information needed by the reading specialist and the content teacher to plan programs for groups of students and to adapt programs for a particular student.

Perhaps, at this point, we need to add to our definition of assessment. Johnston (251) holds that:

Assessment of reading comprehension requires interpretation of an individual's performance of some task which is based on information from a given text within a given context. Thus, performance on the test will depend on characteristics of the text, the nature of the task, and the context, as well as the person's reading abilities and prior knowledge. (p. 20)

This definition comes closer to expressing some of the theoretical concerns associated with the process of assessment. It also begins to suggest what should be included in an assessment

procedure. Brown, Campione and Day's (13) model for considering
problems for learning from texts includes task characteristics,
learner strategies and processes, text characteristics and learner
characteristics. Current proposals for assessment procedures
suggest items from these four categories (252, 266, 286). This is a
far cry from reading a passage, identifying the main idea, answering
comprehension questions and defining a word from its context.
Unfortunately, this latter model is the one that prevails in the
assessment of comprehension (266). If an assessment procedure is to
result in meaningful and useful decisions, it must be related to the
instructional/learning process. We must begin to consider
additional and different ways of assessing reading achievement.

Kinds of Tests Used in Assessment

In order to understand assessment in the secondary school, we
need to identify some broad categories of tests, making a
distinction between standardized/nonstandardized and formal/informal
tests. The terminology here can be confusing to say the least.
Lamberg and Lamb (255) identify standardized tests as those which
are developed using large groups of students to establish the
representativeness of the responses. These authors include norm-
referenced (the student's score is compared to a distribution of
scores) and criterion-referenced (the student's score is compared to
a previously determined performance level) tests. These can both be
considered as formal tests because of the way they have been
developed. Readence, Bean and Baldwin (260) illustrate another way
of defining the terms. "Formal tests are often called standardized,
norm-referenced tests" (p. 77). They equate standardized and norm-
referenced. They emphasize the use of established norms or the fact
that "the quality of a given score is interpretable only by
comparison with scores acquired by others" (ibid.). By this
definition, they consider criterion-referenced tests as informal
tests because norms are not used as standards for comparison. In
both cases all other tests are informal tests.

The problem area here is the slot for criterion-referenced
tests. We will go with Lamberg and Lamb and consider most
criterion-referenced tests as formal, standardized tests. Many have
been developed commercially and, as Pearson and Johnson found (258),
"in the past decade mathematically based techniques for determining
item numbers, score cutoffs, and other criteria have been developed;
these have legitimized criterion-referenced test construction in the
eyes of testing theorists" (p. 203). However, those criterion-
referenced tests developed by teachers based on observation,
experience or a few students will be considered informal tests.

Thus, for the sake of simplicity we will equate formal and
standardized and informal and nonstandardized. Standardized will
include all tests developed using "mathematically based techniques"
(ibid.). Informal tests include "teacher-made tests, observation
protocols, or interviews. They are curriculum specific rather than
general measures of knowledge of skill" (290, p. 164).

Assessment: Concerns and Constraints

In examining commercial tests and planning informal testing procedures, there are a number of factors you need to consider.

1. The time needed to test. This is a very practical concern for the secondary teacher. The focus is on teaching content, not on testing. In addition, the content teacher deals with many students each day, far too many to test each one individually. However, testing may prove to be a time-saver in the long run if learning can be made more efficient and effective. (154, 242, 249, 290)

2. The relationship of prior information to the comprehension questions asked. The designers of tests generally try to find or write passages and questions in which all of the information needed to answer the questions comes from the passage. The questions are passage dependent. We can measure passage comprehension because the student cannot rely on prior information to answer the questions. However, identifying and using prior information is an important reading strategy. Without passage independent questions, we don't know how or if the reader is identifying and using prior knowledge. This presents a significant dilemma for us as teachers. (249, 254)

3. The kinds of questions asked, the sources of answers, and the cognitive demands they place on the reader. It has become clear that questions pose many problems for the teacher as well as for the student and that there is a need for further research here. (249, 253)

4. The task used to measure comprehension and recall. Common techniques include free recall, summary, open-ended questions, probe questions, true-false and multiple-choice. The literature on these is certainly of interest to the content teacher because of the cognitive demand placed on the student, the impact on the information comprehended and recalled, and the ease of administration, scoring and interpretation. (51, 249, 273)

5. The availability of the text during questioning. Johnston (249) suggests that when the student is not allowed to look at the text he must rely more on long term memory and the cues he picked up while reading which help him retrieve and organize. When he can look back at the text "more weight is placed on recall of approximate location of the information in the text, knowledge that one should look for it, search strategies, and logical reasoning skills" (p. 61). It may be useful to use both procedures.

6. Reliability and validity. In reviewing standardized tests, the teacher must be concerned with the questions of whether the test is measuring what it says its measuring and whether it can do it repeatedly (249, 261, 262). In the case of nonstandardized, informal tests, teachers must deal with the difficulties of

establishing validity and reliability or of the consequences of not achieving these goals (246, 258, 290).

Choosing and Using Standardized Tests

Kinds of Standardized tests

There are a number of different kinds of tests that are used in secondary schools for the three purposes we have already identified. Let's take a brief look at each kind, focusing on group tests since they are widely used and form the basis for most educational decisions.

Reading achievement and survey tests. These are norm-referenced and measure achievement in reading. They generally use multiple choice to measure vocabulary and comprehension, although some of the more recent ones use a modified cloze technique (258). In addition to being used for program evaluation and comparison of students, sometimes they are used to establish minimal competency for graduation purposes (261). (242, 258, 261, 266)

Criterion-referenced tests. These are commercially prepared tests which use statistical procedures to provide a basis for establishing the criteria for skill mastery. They identify separate skills that contribute to reading comprehension, present situations in which they are tested, and establish criterion for demonstrating mastery. Because they isolate skills, they are said to be diagnostic and useful for instructional planning as well as evaluation of progress and programs. However, this representation of reading as a set of subskills has been questioned, particularly on the secondary level. In addition, questions have been raised about the means for establishing the criterion level and the degree of reliability and validity of these tests. (253, 258, 261, 280)

Minimum competency tests. Many of these use a criterion-referenced format. The problem of what to include and how to establish a cutoff for passing also exists here. Norm-referenced tests are also used. The tests may be developed either by the particular state or by a commercial publisher. The aim of these tests is to have the student demonstrate that he has attained a minimal competency in the skill or subject, in this case reading. The purpose of many of these tests is to provide a way of determining who will graduate from high school and who will not. At the least, they will determine which students need more instruction in reading. A decision is certainly made on the basis of these tests. The stakes, in fact, can be very high. (243, 253, 261, 266)

Diagnostic reading tests. Because this is not a book on testing, we will not discuss an important use of formal tests, that of diagnosis of individual students. The topic is complex, with a variety of tests available, and is more appropriate for another source. The use of these tests is generally limited to reading specialists. The time needed to administer and interpret them is prohibitive for the content teacher. The discussion of diagnosis of individual students will be limited to informal assessment procedures which can be done by both the reading teacher and the content teacher. However, there is one widely used, group administered, reading diagnostic test, the Stanford Diagnostic Reading Test. (243, 261)

Concerns about Tests

Consider some of the criticisms made about our current procedures and the tests used in assessing reading comprehension.

1. Tests assume that comprehension is only concerned with product, not with process. They do not "measure the processes involved in the construction of meaning from a text nor do they evaluate an individual's ability to manage those processes" (278, p. 33). They do not provide information on how the student arrived at his answers or failed to arrive at them. They frequently reflect a "bottom-up" approach to reading. (254, 258, 266, 268, 275, 278, 289, 290)

2. Vocabulary tests which give a single score based on a restricted sample may rely "too heavily on the assumptions of a static population of isolated words and on an overly restricted view of how we generate and use words in context" (51, p. 110).

3. Tests do not test for different question-answer relationships and different thinking skills. (267)

4. The passages in most tests do not reflect the material students actually read in classrooms, either in length or in structure. (243, 254)

5. "Test taking, in general, is a learned skill" (254, p. 133). Is the student performing well because he knows ways of eliminating inappropriate choices (remember in Chapter V we taught him to do this) or is he performing well because he is comprehending?

Johnston (250) sums it up, stating that "recently there have been some basic changes in our conception of reading comprehension. However, these have not yet been reflected in our assessment procedures" (p. 6). Cole (266) goes further. After reviewing standardized tests in reading, he states:

> Somewhere along the way, we have lost control of one of our most valuable tools in the process of education. As a result of this, educational testing has not grown with the theory and knowledge base of our field. It has continued to assess factors and domains whose utility and even existence have been questioned by modern research and theory--and whose validity has been contradicted in many ways by modern innovations in instructional practice. (p. 2)

Why do we continue to use these tests?

1. They require little time and effort on the part of the teacher. (290)

2. They can provide a starting point for teaching and can indicate students who may need a more thorough evaluation. (255, 260)

3. They provide a consistent way of evaluating programs that can be understood by other professionals and parents without elaborate explanation. (255, 260, 266)

Practice

   Standardized, formal tests are part of the educational scene. They can provide us with important information. We need to recognize their limitations and make the best possible use of the time devoted to testing and of the results obtained. But, how?

1. Become familiar with the variety of standardized tests available as a basis of comparison to the test your district is presently using. In addition to understanding that test better you will begin to formulate your own ideas on testing and tests. At some point you will be involved in choosing tests. (243, 261, 269, 272, 277, 284, 285, 288, 289)

2. Examine the test used in your district very carefully. Consider it in light of what theorists are saying about reading tests. What are the passages like? How is comprehension measured? What kinds and levels of questions are asked? How can they be answered? Are they text explicit or implicit? Are they passage dependent or independent? What kinds of cognitive demands do the questions place on the reader? In order to understand the results of a test, content teachers and reading specialists must understand the test. (249, 255, 267, 268, 276, 280)

3. Understand how norm-referenced scores are reported and what they mean. Grade equivalent indicates "the grade level at which the average student in a norm group had a given number correct" (262, p. 77). This score is open to many misinterpretations. It does not mean that a seventh grader with a score of 12.3 can be put in twelfth grade materials. It means that, compared to other seventh graders, he is doing very well. Percentile rank indicates that a certain percentage of students did less well than your particular student. His score of 64% means he did better than 64% of the students in the norm group. It is possible to construct local norms which help you compare this student to other students in your school district. Stanines are standard scores, on a nine-point scale, with 5 considered the mean. (261, 262)

4. In making decisions based on standardized tests, consider using more than one test (255). The International Reading Association has taken a strong stand on this issue with regard to minimum competency testing. It is "firmly opposed to the efforts of any school, state, provincial or national agency which attempts to determine a student's graduation or promotion on the basis of

any single assessment" (243, p. 140; 261, pp. 311-312).

5. In specific cases use standardized achievement, survey and criterion-referenced tests diagnostically. Once the student has completed the test, go back and probe for more answers to questions, interview to try to find out the "why" and "how" of the student's performance. (256, 276)

These are things we can do now to make the best use of current tests. For the future Cole (266) urges us to become involved in the development of a testing framework that will reflect current knowledge about reading, testing, and students, by making this change part of our "professional agendas" (p. 31), demanding that test publishers and state legislators require "state of the art" (ibid.) tests.

Assembling a File of Informal Tests

Rationale for Informal Testing

One of the messages that comes across loud and clear when you review the literature on assessment is that formal tests are not sufficient for making instructional decisions. Lamberg and Lamb (255) believe that standardized "tests may be useful to administrators concerned with overall evaluation but they may be of little use to the classroom teacher" (p. 158). Readence, Bean and Baldwin (260) are even stronger; standardized reading tests are "virtually useless for instructional decision-making by teachers with regard to the individual needs of students" (p. 76). Vacca (263) is adamant. They "may not provide the specific information content teachers and reading specialists need....It's safe to say that teachers who consult standardized reading tests should do so judiciously" (p. 299). The consensus seems to be that standardized tests can provide indications of the need for further testing (242, 243) but we need to see how the student performs with classroom materials. One of Houck's (32) "barriers" to success for adolescents in reading, identified in Chapter I, was the "failure to collect instructionally meaningful baseline data needed to guide intervention efforts" (p. 30). Standardized tests of the kind described do not seem to yield this kind of information.

In order to begin to get some of the information not generally available from current formal tests, Johnston and Pearson (254) suggest that we must begin to assess "at least informally" (p. 139) important aspects of reading comprehension that "have been neglected in our assessments" (ibid.). Zigmond and Silverman (290) cite the "increasing popularity" (p. 164) of informal assessment procedures and Otto and Smith (47) go so far as to assert that "formal diagnostic reading tests will probably continue to decline in popularity as they are replaced by more informal assessment techniques" (pp. 25-26).

For our purposes, we will consider three main reasons for informal testing in the secondary school. The focus will not be on program evaluation, although Farr and Wolf (244) advocate the use of "responsive evaluation," based on informal procedures, to insure meaningful program evaluations.

1. In content areas it is "necessary to determine those students who can handle the reading assignments; those who need either direct assistance or alternative materials; and those who would most benefit from being exposed to more challenging intellectual discourse. Such instructional decisions can best be made following an informal diagnosis of students in each content classroom" (262, p. 75).

2. We need to know what skills, strategies and background knowledge secondary school students bring to the content classroom in order to determine how to instruct and whether to provide alternative materials.

3. We may need to provide an in-depth diagnosis on a particular student in order to determine the causes and extent of a reading disability as well as provide remedial suggestions. We have used the term "diagnosis" because it is so commonly used. However, Vacca's (263) concern that diagnosis implies finding what's wrong and fragmenting the reading process into little parts to do this, is well taken. He prefers "evaluation" as an ongoing, positive, holistic process.

Practice

There are a number of ways to conduct informal assessment either in the classroom or in the reading center with a view to making instructional decisions. We will examine three aspects of informal assessments: setting up the procedures, looking at the products of reading, and looking at the process of reading. The key to success here is to keep the student's instructional situation in the forefront of your planning.

First, you need a framework for your planning.

1. Decide on your purpose. Do you want to determine the student's reading level, his competence with particular skills? Do you want to assess the student's ability to read a particular text successfully? Do you want to diagnosis how he is going about the task of reading? What are his problems? What is easy for him? Under what conditions and with what kinds of texts is he able to read successfully? Are there instructional variables that make a difference? (252, 265)

2. If your purpose is diagnostic, decide what reading and study skills and strategies you want to assess. Base your list on the characteristics of good readers already discussed and on those items proposed by experts in the field of reading and testing. Include skills and strategies discussed in this book. Consider the particular demands of your curriculum and the various texts used in compiling your list. (252, 266, 282, 286, 290)

3. Vary the task, use a variety of measures, and test frequently.
    Move from a static testing procedure to a dynamic one, "using
    the interaction between tester and examinee to find the
    conditions under which certain tasks can be performed, and how
    much of specified types of assistance is required for the child
    to succeed" (249, p. 53). This may mean using different texts,
    different tasks, pushing the reader as far as you can. It may
    mean providing assistance and gauging its effect. It may mean
    providing trial teaching situations. (242, 247, 249, 252, 263,
    265, 270, 286, 290)

4. Use content materials. (248, 260)

5. Try to insure building a degree of validity and reliability into
    your assessment by including such items as: the careful
    definition of what you are assessing, the use of a sufficient
    number of questions and passages, and the establishment of
    specific criteria for success. (246, 290)

6. Consider carefully how the student will respond. Will the text
    be available to him when he answers the questions? Will he
    summarize, answer open-ended, yes/no, or multiple choice
    questions, match items or use a rating scale? (51, 246, 249,
    273)

7. Examine commercially prepared informal tests to see if they are
    appropriate for your purposes as well as to see how someone else
    has structured the test. (242, 243, 264)

8. Decide on how the test will be administered—to a group or to an
    individual? You also need to consider the amount of time
    available vs. the kinds and depths of information you need.
    (242)

    Second, look at the products or skills of reading, those items
that are generally tested in reading assessments. Does the student
understand words and comprehend? At what reading level? In the
particular text chosen for his content class? Does he have specific
skills needed for reading in the content class? Consider the
following possibilities.

1. Observation. One of the advantages of using observation as an
    assessment technique is that it can be done on a daily basis,
    can be nonthreatening and can provide information based on a
    variety of situations. Start with a checklist of specific
    observable skills. It may help if you can have someone else
    work with the students while you observe. (201, 242, 243, 260,
    281)

2. Graded word list. This gives information about the student's
    ability to recognize words out of content and may be used as a
    starting point to match student to text. (242, 260, 262)

3. Multi-syllable word list. Present a list of long, unfamiliar or
    technical words to begin to identify the student's competency

with common syllabication generalizations. (271)

4. Cloze passage. The use of a cloze passage can give you an indication of whether the student has comprehended the text and whether the text is appropriate for a particular group of students. This technique has a number of advantages. It is easy to construct, can, and in fact should, use the classroom text, can be administered to groups or individuals, can be used repeatedly with no effort on the teacher's part, and can be modified by giving choices for the answers. Some students may find the cloze passage threatening and may need an introduction to the technique. (242, 243, 249, 259, 260, 261, 262)

5. Content Reading Inventory or Group Reading Inventory. Using the classroom text as the basis this can be given at the beginning of the year or the beginning of a unit to determine the student's ability to locate information, comprehend the text, and understand and use vocabulary. and read flexibly and at various speeds. (201, 242, 260, 261, 262, 263)

6. Study Skills Inventory. This addresses the problem of whether the student has the appropriate skills to read flexibly and at various speed. Can he use the parts of textbooks, understand maps and graphs, use reference materials, and recognize special symbols. Can he outline and take notes from the text? (201, 260, 281)

7. Informal Reading Inventory. This can be commercially prepared or teacher constructed. A range of texts of different reading levels and a variety of questions are used to gauge the student's reading level. Sometimes an IRI is developed using materials from different content areas. (242, 261, 264)

8. Criterion-referenced test. This might be teacher-made, using the required text as the source of skills tested. The problems of construction already mentioned in regard to commercially prepared tests, of course, are present with teacher-made criterion tests. The test can be used to indicate mastery of material read or the student's skills in areas such as locating information or identifying parts of the text. (242, 261)

9. Student self-assessment of skills and attitudes. This can be done through rating checklists, group discussions or teacher interviews. The aim is twofold: to have the student become involved in the reading process by identifying specific skill areas where he has difficulties or by identifying positive and negative attitudes and interests; and to help the teacher in planning interesting, motivating instruction. (11, 201, 209, 261, 262, 287)

Third, look at the process of reading. How is the student approaching the task? Is he identifying and using text characteristics? What thinking strategies is he using? Is he identifying and using prior information? Is he hypothesizing and predicting? Is he able to monitor his comprehension? We are certainly dealing with an area of uncertainty here (remember MacGinitie?). We have fewer guidelines here to help us identify and measure ability and growth. However, there is an increasing emphasis on the need for a dynamic model of assessment that will examine the interaction of the reader and the text and the processes being used. Let's consider some of the suggestions that are currently being offered.

1. Observation. Expand your checklist and include items such as the student's ability to make predictions, take risks, check himself. (263, 265, 286)

2. Cloze passage. In addition to showing reading level and comprehension of a specific text, this can also give an indication of how the student is interacting with the text. Instead of deleting every nth word, delete all the words of a particular category, i.e., noun referents, adjectives. Now you are controlling the task and can get an indication of how the reader is processing elements of the text. (249, 259)

3. Content Reading Inventory. This can have a second purpose. Again, use the classroom text as the basis but this time assess the student's prior knowledge through questions before he starts to read and through the vocabulary maps he is able to construct. (263)

4. Text structure inventory. Using passages from texts which illustrate organizational and hierarchical patterns, ask questions designed to highlight the student's abilities to process different kinds of information. (103, 257)

5. "Concurrent" interviewing. While the student is reading, he talks about the things that are going through his mind, identifies problems he's having. You might probe or ask for more information. Your goal is to find out what he knows about the reading process, what strategies he's using, whether he's able to monitor his own comprehension. This is similar to modeling, except the student is doing it and you assessing his performance. (249, 274, 279, 286)

6. Diagnostic teaching. Hansell (247) affirms that "diagnosis is not a one-time test but may be carried out by careful evaluation of ongoing classroom activities" (p. 79). In fact, this approach lends itself well to the content classroom, once the teacher is over the hurdle of assessment panic. Here is an invaluable way of gathering information informally. Use many of the instructional strategies already discussed to get indications about how the student is processing the text. Diagnostic teaching can either be done as a group activity to determine general group abilities and problems or may be done individually as a form of "trial teaching." This is a place for the knowledgeable content or reading teacher to examine the four variables Brown et al. (13) identified (task characteristics, learner strategies and processes, text characteristics and learner characteristics) to determine the best possible learning

situation.   Here are some suggestions.   You will think of many
more as you put these ideas into practice.   (13, 247, 290)

Identifying and using prior knowledge. Ask questions about
prior knowledge before instruction. Give a mastery test on
content at the end of the unit.   If a student does well   on
the pretest and poorly on the mastery test, he probably
didn't comprehend. If he does poorly on the pretest and
poorly on the mastery tests, he may not have the background
knowledge to understand the concept.   Use   PReP,   an
instructional procedure with an assessment component or
develop an anticipation guide.   (18, 134, 142, 247, 254)

Hypothesizing.   Before reading, have students   predict
topics,   subtitles and vocabulary words that might be
included in the text.   (247)

Summarizing. Used diagnostically you can learn a great deal
about how the student perceives hierarchies of information
in the text. By examining each step of the process you can
begin to identify such things as whether he can delete
unimportant information.   (249, 286)

Question-answering.   Can the student determine the source
for the answer to a question. Is it in the text or in his
head?   Before teaching how to answer questions, use the QAR
procedure diagnostically.   Is the student flexible in
responding to various types of questions with a variety of
text? Can he provide documentation for answers?   Are you
asking questions that probe, that require inferencing, that
demand interaction of the text and the reader?   (119, 166,
245, 254)

6.   Student self-assessment.   An interesting suggestion is that
students participate in a course or a unit on "Learning about
Ourselves as Learners."   The purpose of the course is to help
students understand the process of reading and writing and all
of the variables associated with these tasks. The goal is to
enable students to evaluate themselves.   (243)

7.   Text analysis. Look at the demands of particular materials. It
may be that the problem is not with the student or groups of
students. The problem may lie in the text: the convolutions and
complexities of the language and sentences used, the lack of
clarity in developing concepts. More about this when we discuss
readability of text.   (118, 248, 274, 282)

This discussion of assessment has focused entirely on the
information that can obtained by the teacher and by the student to
assist in instructional planning and in learning.   Duchastel (154)
suggests that testing can have another purpose.   "Testing is not
solely a means of assessment but also a means of assisting learning"
(p. 4). Testing, particularly with questions at the end of a
passage,   provides   for   practice   and   rehearsal,   for   the
"consolidation" (ibid.) of learning. In fact, Duchastel suggests

that every period of instruction end with a short test, perhaps an ungraded self-test.

Suggestions for Implementation

Assessment of students must involve both the content teacher and the reading specialist. This is clearly a two-way street.

1. Cooperation can begin with cooperative planning of informal instruments and procedures after discussion of formal testing results. One or more department meetings or inservice workshops might be devoted to this.

2. The content teacher may find from the group assessment that there is a common problem. The reading specialist comes in either to make instructional suggestions or to do further testing with one or more students. The content teacher, after some diagnostic teaching sessions, determines a need for further testing of individual students. They are referred to the reading specialist.

3. The reading specialist, after reviewing records and possibly doing some individual assessment, alerts the content teacher to individual problems.

4. As a result of the reading specialist coming in to the content classroom and presenting some lessons, the content teacher has a chance to observe the class and begin to spot potential problems. Roles may be reversed to provide another perspective.

5. Nowhere is the need for establishing an atmosphere conducive to risk-taking more compelling. We have all seen the student who doesn't answer the questions, assuring us that if he doesn't answer it's because he just doesn't want to, certainly not because he can't. Teachers also must feel free to take risks. Content teachers must grow and learn in this area if their teaching is to be effective and their reading assignments productive.

6. Finally, we must insure cooperation and interaction between all parties to the assessment process if assessment is to reflect reading theory and is to provide us with useful instructional information.

Summary

Reading assessment has an important role in secondary schools. We concur completely with Pearson and Johnson's (258) conclusion that "tests should serve instruction, assisting us in making more rational decisions" (p. 221). There are many ways this can happen. The reality of this happening depends on our gaining expertise and confidence in this area.

BIBLIOGRAPHY

Books

242. Cheek, Earl H., and Martha Collins Cheek. "Content
     Instruction and Reading Diagnosis." READING INSTRUCTION
     THROUGH CONTENT TEACHING. Columbus, Ohio: Charles E.
     Merrill, 1983, pp. 112-141.

     Cheek and Cheek provide an overview of testing alternatives
     traditionally available to the content teacher. They examine
     and review specific tests in the areas of formal diagnostic
     tests (achievement, intelligence, reading) and informal
     procedures (observation, simplified reading inventory, group
     inventory, cloze procedure and informal inventory). In
     reviewing the formal tests, they point out that many of these
     are not diagnostic but can serve as the beginning of a
     diagnostic process. The focus in the examples provided is
     generally on the product of reading.

243. Early, Margaret, and Diane J. Sawyer. "Assessment and
     Evaluation in the Whole-School Program." "Learning about
     Ourselves as Learners." "Diagnosis of Reading
     Disabilities." READING TO LEARN IN GRADES 5 TO 12. New
     York: Harcourt Brace Jovanovich, 1984, pp. 137-211.

     The authors present a comprehensive overview of the role of
     testing in a total school program. They look at the role of
     standardized survey and achievement tests in program
     evaluation and include a summary of a number of widely used
     group reading tests. Informal tests are suggested as a means
     of allowing the content teacher to gain insights into student
     competencies in handling classroom materials. A particularly
     interesting and unique feature is the detailed presentation of
     a unit to be used by students to learn about their own
     strengths and weaknesses in both the process and product of
     reading. Finally, the general range of possibilities are
     explored for diagnosing reading problems in depth.

244. Farr, Roger, and Robert L. Wolf. "Evaluation and Secondary
     Reading Programs." BECOMING READERS IN A COMPLEX SOCIETY.
     Eighty-third Yearbook of the National Society for the Study
     of Education, Part 1. Chicago, Illinois: The University of
     Chicago Press, 1984, pp. 271-292.

     Farr and Wolf assert that in order to make decisions about
     secondary reading programs we must take an "approach that is
     more holistic than 'testing only'" (p. 273). Program
     evaluation must include a critical examination of the program
     in context, what is working and what is not. It involves
     clarification of all elements of a program and should ease the
     process of change as a result. To accomplish this, the
     authors propose "responsive evaluation" in which the people
     involved in the program participate in describing and

evaluating it through techniques such as observations, interviews and surveys. They describe a six-step process to accomplish this.

245. Galda, S. Lee. "Assessment: Responses to Literature." SECONDARY SCHOOL READING: WHAT RESEARCH REVEALS FOR CLASSROOM PRACTICE. Edited by Allen Berger and H. Alan Robinson. Urbana Illinois: ERIC Clearinghouse on Reading and Communication Skills and the National Conference on Research in English, 1982, pp. 111-125.

Galda bases assessment on an interactionist view of reading. There is not one answer, no one correct response to literature. "By assessment we mean consideration and analysis of individual responses rather than comparison with an arbitrary standard" (p. 112). Using this premise, Galda examines how students respond orally and in writing and how we can analyze these responses. The stress here is on the process the student is using: flexibility in utilizing text information and his prior knowledge, documentation provided for answers. The teacher is also expected to be flexible in varying assessment strategies and looking for general patterns of response. The relationship between how students respond to assessment and how we teach is examined.

246. Guerin, Gilbert R., and Arlee S. Maier. "Assessment Approaches." INFORMAL ASSESSMENT IN EDUCATION. Palo Alto, California: Mayfield, 1983, pp. 25-49.

Guerin and Maier give a broad overview of five approaches: norm-referenced tests, criterion-referenced tests, task analysis, survey analysis and diagnostic analysis. In addition, they provide guidelines for the construction of reliable and valid informal instruments. They discuss, illustrate and provide guidelines for multiple-choice questions, short answer essay, long answer essay, true-false questions, matching items, completion items, ratings and checklists. This section can be especially useful for the secondary teacher.

247. Hansell, T. Stevenson. "Informal Diagnosis of Content Area Reading Skills." APPROACHES TO THE INFORMAL EVALUATION OF READING. Edited by John J. Pikulski and Timothy Shanahan. Newark, Delaware: International Reading Assn., 1982, pp. 63-79.

Hansell examines and copiously illustrates three approaches to the informal diagnosis of reading comprehension which focus on the student. The skills approach, the most common, looks at how well the student has mastered reading skills through observation and informal inventories. The introspective approach looks at the process of understanding, mainly through interviews. The models approach attempts to integrate process and product by "viewing student behavior in a variety of reading-thinking situations" (p. 72). The examples given make the three approaches particularly clear. The author concludes that probably no one approach alone is best; rather the teacher must decide on the basis of which approach or combination of approaches will provide the most useful information.

248. Hittleman, Daniel R. "Adaptive Assessment for Nonacademic Secondary Reading." DISABLED READERS: INSIGHT, ASSESSMENT, INSTRUCTION. Edited by Diane J. Sawyer. Newark, Delaware: International Reading Assn., 1980, pp. 74-81.

Hittleman advocates using the particular materials the student is expected to read in order to judge his competence to read them. The problem may lie not in the student's abilities but in the particular characteristics of the material to be read. Examples from vocational, on-the-job materials are included.

249. Johnston, Peter H. "Assessment Methodology." READING COMPREHENSION ASSESSMENT: A COGNITIVE BASIS. Newark, Delaware: International Reading Assn., 1983, pp. 40-69.

According to Johnston, assessment can provide global information about large numbers of students, specific diagnostic information about one student or general comparative information about groups of students. He discusses the constraints on assessment, ranging from practical administrative concerns to issues of test construction. Of particular interest to the secondary teacher is the analysis of the techniques we use to measure reading comprehension. He goes beyond product measurement with its use of free recall and various kinds of questions and includes process measurement using miscues and cloze tasks as well as metacognitive measurement, identifying, for example, self-corrections, protocol analysis and summarizing. We are given a broad range of purposes and alternatives to use in measuring comprehension.

250. Johnston, Peter H. "Defining Reading Comprehension." READING COMPREHENSION ASSESSMENT: A COGNITIVE BASIS. Newark, Delaware: International Reading Assn., 1983, pp. 1-19.

Johnston addresses many of the critical issues of reading comprehension, relating them to the questions of how we assess comprehension. The complexity of the process of comprehension, involving as it does reasoning processes, metacognitive processes and a series of subskills, demands an assessment process that deals with these processes as well as the readily observable products of comprehension.

251. Johnston, Peter H. "Factors Which Influence Reading Comprehension and Its Assessment." READING COMPREHENSION ASSESSMENT: A COGNITIVE BASIS. Newark, Delaware: International Reading Assn., 1983, pp. 20-39.

The author identifies four factors which impact on comprehension and its assessment. These include the characteristics of the text, the appropriateness of text structure and content to the reader's prior knowledge, the sources of answers to questions and the task demands of the assessment process. In examining each of these areas, Johnston begins the process of bridging the gap between reading theory and assessment. The chapter provides a good starting point for identifying areas to be examined in determining "real or apparent comprehension failures."

252. Johnston, Peter H. "New Directions in Reading Comprehension Assessment." READING COMPREHENSION ASSESSMENT: A COGNITIVE BASIS. Newark, Delaware: International Reading Assn., 1983, pp. 70–86.

Johnston identifies areas that should be considered in assessing comprehension including cue systems, background knowledge, dialect, retrieval strategies, production skills, information processing, schema, monitoring skills, comprehension maintenance strategies, summarization rules, reading demands and reading process. He also identifies strategies related to these areas. Although they are not always explained enough to be easily translated into the classroom situation, they do indicate the range of alternatives. In addition, the author examines question construction and test characteristics. Underlying the discussion is the admonition that the examiner must fully understand the process of reading comprehension and the assessment process.

253. Johnston, Peter H. "Assessment in Reading." HANDBOOK OF READING RESEARCH. Edited by P. David Pearson, Rebecca Barr, Michael L. Kamil and Peter Mosenthal. New York: Longman, 1984, pp. 147–182.

The history of reading assessment, according to Johnston, illustrates the problems of developing assessment procedures as a result of accident rather than design and maintaining them "more through societal press than scientific process" (p. 153). The discussion of questions is particularly interesting and useful to the teacher. The author points out that test questions do not assess the process of reading. In fact, it is not always easy to determine exactly how they are assessing comprehension. Availability of the text changes the task of answering the question. He compares and contrasts norm-referenced and criterion-referenced tests and suggests that criterion-referenced tests with their stress on skill mastery do not lend themselves to a view of reading as an interactive process. He raises important questions about tests and test construction that, while addressed to the researcher, certainly have implication for the teacher. He would, in fact, change the focus from the test to the teacher, with the teacher participating in an interactive testing situation and assuming the responsibility for making decisions.

254. Johnston, Peter H., and P. David Pearson. "Assessment:
     Responses to Exposition." SECONDARY SCHOOL READING: WHAT
     RESEARCH REVEALS FOR CLASSROOM PRACTICE. Edited by Allen
     Berger and H. Alan Robinson. Urbana, Illinois: ERIC
     Clearinghouse on Reading and Communication Skills and the
     National Conference on Research in English, 1982, pp. 127-
     141.

     The authors examine three factors that influence reading
     comprehension (prior knowledge, textual cue systems, and
     reasoning strategies) and three aspects of the context in
     which the reading takes place (situational context, reader's
     purpose, and test-taking skills). They identify the
     shortcomings of standardized tests and provide suggestions for
     assessing these areas informally.

255. Lamberg, Walter J., and Charles E. Lamb. "Standardized
     Tests." READING INSTRUCTION IN THE CONTENT AREAS. Chicago:
     Rand McNally, 1980, pp. 153-159.

     Lamberg and Lamb offer a concise, clear but general
     discussion of standardized tests. It is useful for the
     student unfamiliar with the topic and can serve as the
     framework for readings more specific to the area of content
     reading. After discussing the kinds and uses of standardized
     tests for program evaluation and student diagnosis, the
     authors point out clearly that they are probably more useful
     for program evaluation. For the purpose of student diagnosis,
     teachers need to use more than one instrument and should
     include informal testing in the classroom.

256. Liu, Stella S. F. "Reading Diagnosis in the Classroom."
     DISABLED READERS: INSIGHT, ASSESSMENT, INSTRUCTION. Edited
     by Diane J. Sawyer. Newark, Delaware: International Reading
     Assn., 1980, pp. 57-66.

     Liu discusses a number of alternatives for classroom
     diagnosis, including informal reading inventories and word
     analysis skills. An interesting feature is the discussion and
     illustration of how to use a diagnostic probe in testing for
     both comprehension and word knowledge on standardized tests.
     The teacher provides that student with single bits of
     information in an effort to tease out the reason for an
     initial error.

257. Marshall, Nancy. "Discourse Analysis as a Guide for Informal
     Assessment of Comprehension."   PROMOTING   READING
     COMPREHENSION.   Edited by James Flood. Newark, Delaware:
     International Reading Assn., 1984, pp. 79-96.

     Marshall advocates using informal assessment to investigate
     a wide range of student behavior. In this article, she
     proposes using discourse analysis as the basis for formulating
     questions and evaluating comprehension and recall for both
     narrative and expository text in a variety of ways. The

article draws on current research and presents clear examples.

258. Pearson, P. David, and Dale D. Johnson.   "The Assessment of
     Reading Comprehension."   TEACHING READING COMPREHENSION.
     New York: Holt, Rinehart and Winston, 1978, pp. 200-223.

     The authors present a very clear overview of assessment,
     including the purposes of assessment (comparative assessment,
     program evaluation and pupil diagnosis), the differences
     between norm-referenced and criterion-referenced tests, a
     description and critique of each type, and the use of informal
     tests. The discussion will serve as an excellent introduction
     to or review of the general topic of assessment.

259. Pikulski, John J., and Aileen Webb Tobin.   "The Cloze
     Procedure as an Informal Assessment Technique." APPROACHES
     TO THE INFORMAL EVALUATION OF READING. Edited by John J.
     Pikulski and Timothy Shanahan.   Newark, Delaware:
     International Reading Assn., 1982, pp. 42-62.

     Pikulski and Tobin examine the history of the cloze
     procedure, relevant research, construction of a cloze test and
     its uses, as well as variations on the cloze and how to
     construct them. The authors point out the usefulness of the
     cloze in determining the readability of a content text and its
     appropriateness for a student or a group of students. This
     chapter should prove useful to all secondary teachers.

260. Readence, John E., Thomas W. Bean, and R.Scott Baldwin.
     "Assessing Reading Needs in the Content Classroom." CONTENT
     AREA READING: AN INTEGRATED APPROACH.   Dubuque, Iowa:
     Kendall/Hunt, 1981, pp. 74-101.

     The authors present an overview of formal and informal
     testing. They also provide explicit guidance in constructing
     and using the cloze procedure and the content reading
     inventory. Suggestions are also made on using the textbook
     diagnostically and on identifying student attitudes and
     interests.

261. Roe, Betty D., Barbara D. Stoodt, and Paul C. Burns.
     "Assessment Procedures."   SECONDARY SCHOOL READING
     INSTRUCTION: THE CONTENT AREAS. Boston: Houghton Mifflin,
     1983, pp. 271-318.

     The authors provide a comprehensive overview of the various
     ways of assessing secondary school students' reading
     abilities. The focus is on assessment to determine whether
     students possess the reading skills necessary to succeed in
     content area course materials. The authors review and give
     examples of norm-referenced tests, criterion-referenced tests,
     informal tests and minimal competency tests.

262. Tonjes, Marian J., and Miles V. Zintz. "Matching Print with
     Reader, Part II: Diagnosing Students' Levels, Needs, and

Interests."   TEACHING READING/THINKING/STUDY SKILLS   IN
CONTENT CLASSROOMS. Dubuque, Iowa: Wm. C. Brown, 1981, pp.
74-93.

The authors view survey or achievement tests as useful
mainly for program evaluation or ranking groups of students.
They discuss, briefly, the general characteristics of these
tests and the way scores are reported. The focus of the
chapter is on developing informal strategies such as the
Content or Group Informal Reading Inventory, the Cloze
procedure, the Individual Informal Reading Inventory and an
interest inventory.   Examples are included for each.   The
purpose of diagnosis is to match students with appropriate
materials.

263. Vacca, Richard T. "Evaluating for Instruction." CONTENT AREA
      READING. Boston: Little, Brown, 1981, pp. 279-301.

Vacca stresses the need for a continuous process of
evaluation using observation techniques and content area
reading inventories.   He provides specific examples of both
approaches. The focus is on reading as a meaning-based
process, not as separate subskills. Diagnosis, as contrasted
to evaluation, is seen as a static process that is concerned
more with deficiencies than with what students can do.

                          Periodicals

264. Cagney, Margaret.   "Test Review: Johnston Informal Reading
      Inventory." JOURNAL OF READING 26 (March 1983): 530-533.

Cagney describes this as a group test in which the graded
reading   passages   are   high-interest   adolescent   theme
literature. This, as she points, presents a problem in using
the test to place students in expository material. The
inventory also contains a word opposites and a synonyms test.
In spite of the narrow focus of the test and the lack of
evidence of reliability and validity and field testing, the
author   concludes   that   the   examiner   can obtain some
"interesting information about students' reading competencies"
(p. 533).

265. Cioffi, Grant, and John J. Carney.   "Dynamic Assessment of
      Reading Disabilities."   READING TEACHER 36 (April 1983):
      764-768.

Cioffi and Carney advocate an interactive approach to
reading diagnosis to gain insight into not only the reading
skills that the student possesses but also his potential for
progress and the conditions that will foster that growth. The
interaction is between the examiner, the student and the test
with the examiner supplying information, probing, or teaching.
The focus is on elementary students but the basic premise is
one that is also applicable to secondary students.

266. Cole, Jack N.   "Limitations of The Tests in The Light of
      Recent Research in Reading and Learning: Problems,
      Possibilities, and a Program for Change." Paper presented
      at the Annual Meeting of the International Reading Assn,
      Chicago, Illinois, April 1982. 42pp. (ED 214 156)

      Cole throws down the gauntlet, challenging everyone
      concerned with reading assessment and instruction to recognize
      that current reading tests have not kept up with reading
      theory and research.   They are not testing the learner
      characteristics and strategies which are important for program
      planning and instruction. He provides an analysis of eight
      major tests and makes suggestions for content that should be
      included as well as for actions to be taken by all
      constituents in the schooling process.

267. Crowell, Doris C., Kathryn Hu-pei Au, and Karen M. Blake.
      "Comprehension Questions: Differences Among Standardized
      Tests." JOURNAL OF READING 26 (January 1983): 314-319.

      Based on the premises that comprehension abilities develop
      over time and that students in higher grades should be
      "improving in their use of more difficult comprehension
      skills" (p. 315), the authors analyzed six major standardized
      comprehension tests by categorizing the questions asked on two
      dimensions: Pearson and Johnson's taxonomy of text-explicit,
      text-implicit and script-implicit questions; and Crowell and
      Au's classification according to the complexity of the
      thinking process needed to answer the questions.   They found
      that there was considerable variation from test to test in the
      percentage of questions devoted to text-implicit question-
      answer relationship and higher level thinking skills as well
      as variation in the developmental progression of these
      variables across grade levels for any one test series.   The
      authors suggest but do not develop the notion that there seems
      to be a serious discrepancy between what educators consider
      important to evaluate in reading comprehension and what tests
      are actually evaluating.

268. Curtis, Mary E., and Robert Glaser. "Reading Theory and the
      Assessment of Reading Achievement." JOURNAL OF EDUCATIONAL
      MEASUREMENT 20 (Summer 1983): 133-147.

      Curtis and Glaser examine theory and research related to
      reading from a cognitive perspective.   They look at word
      decoding, accessing word meaning, sentence processing, and
      discourse analysis. In each case the authors provide some
      examples, numerous references, and a discussion relating
      reading theory to practices and possibilities in assessing
      reading achievement.

269. Cummins, R. Porter.   "Test Review: The Nelson-Denny Reading
      Test (Forms E and F)."   JOURNAL OF READING 25 (October
      1981): 54-59.

This standardized reading achievement test ranks students according to reading comprehension, reading vocabulary and reading rate. According to the test manual the whole test can be used as a pre- and posttest for program evaluation. The vocabulary subtest can be used diagnostically since it contains both prefixed and nonprefixed words with an appropriate item analysis. Cummins presents a detailed analysis of the test and concludes that it is useful as a screening test and a predictive instrument but cautions against using it for diagnosis or evaluation. His discussion of the difficulties of using the test as a pre- and posttest for program evaluation is particularly thought-provoking.

270. Duffelmeyer, Frederick A. "A Non-Traditional Technique for Testing Vocabulary." READING HORIZONS 21 (Spring 1981): 179-182.

Duffelmeyer is concerned because vocabulary tests generally do not require that students apply their word knowledge by associating the word with an experience. He has developed a technique in which the student reads a paragraph and chooses a word which does not appear in the paragraph but which expresses an idea to which the paragraph alludes. Examples are included.

271. Floriani, Bernard P., and John T. Wolinski. "Divide and Conquer: Syllabication Assessment and Older Students." READING HORIZONS 22 (Fall 1981): 49-53.

The authors developed an informal instrument, using words from the ninth to the thirteenth grade level, to assess secondary students' ability to demonstrate their knowledge of five "high utility" syllabication generalizations. The authors include the survey with permission to reproduce it.

272. Gordon, Belita. "A Guide to Postsecondary Reading Tests." READING WORLD 23 (October 1983): 45-53.

Although Gordon is addressing the question of reading tests on the college level, all of the tests reviewed are also used in high schools. She presents a clear, easy to follow analysis of five tests: Reading Test, McGraw-Hill Basic Skills System; The Nelson-Denny Reading Test, Forms A,B,C,D,E,F; Sequential Tests of Educational Progress, Series II; Stanford Diagnostic Reading Test, Blue Level; and the Stanford Test of Academic Skills, Level II. Gordon includes information on the test, the publisher, the purpose; the test parts and administration time; score reporting; passage content, number and length; comprehension skills; review of validity, manual and norming sample.

273. Guthrie, John T. "Testing Higher Level Skills." JOURNAL OF READING 28 (November 1984): 188-190.

Because testing has such far-reaching implications for

instruction, not only for individuals but also for programs, Guthrie believes that it is critical that reading tests test for significant skills. He reviews the work of Hillocks and Ludlow (124) in which a hierarchy of comprehension skills is described. Guthrie concludes that it is difficult to test for these using multiple-choice questions. We need to employ free-response, essay questions.

274. Hansell, T. Stevenson. "Four Methods of Diagnosis for Content Area Reading." JOURNAL OF READING 24 (May 1981): 696-700.

Hansell addresses the problem of relating the evaluation of reading competency to what we know about the reading process, focusing on the area of content reading. The content teacher needs to find out whether the student can succeed in the particular content materials by diagnosing student weaknesses. Identifying the reading level of the material is a limited approach, because it examines only the material, not the student. The skills approach focuses on the product of reading, while the introspection approach focuses on the process. Both may be concerned with similar topics. Can the student identify the main idea? How does he know it's the main idea? Finally, Hansell examines an approach based on the models of comprehension. This approach sees "skills as interrelated and attempts to explain how the comprehension process is related to its product" (p. 699). In each instance, specific examples are provided.

275. Henk, William A., John E. Readence, and George E. Mason. "A Reaction to Reading Assessment and Intervention: A Broadening of Perspective." SCHOOL PSYCHOLOGY REVIEW 12 (Winter 1983): 71-74.

Henk, Readence and Mason critique an issue of SCHOOL PSYCHOLOGY REVIEW (vol. 11, Summer 1982) which focused on questions relating to reading assessment and intervention. They express concern that school psychologists would gain a narrow view of reading, since the majority of the articles were based on a "bottom-up" approach to reading, with little recognition of other theoretical models. In addition, they review particular articles pointing out the effect that a narrow approach to reading theory has on the problems of assessment. See Ysseldyke and Marston (289), one of the articles critiqued by Henk, Readence and Mason.

276. Hutson, Barbara A., and Jerome A. Niles. "Reconciling Differences in Test Results: Comprehension." READING HORIZONS 23 (Summer 1983): 235-242.

Hutson and Niles present an analysis of reasons for differences in test results. After discussing the problems of inaccurate, misleading or irrelevant test results, they focus on differences in modes of presentation and response, in the levels and kinds of thinking processes required or permitted, and in scoring procedures and criteria for success. Although most of the examples are on the elementary level, the discussion highlights the problems that plague teachers in understanding and using test results.

277. Kibby, Michael W. "Test Review: The Degrees of Reading Power." JOURNAL OF READING 24 (February 1981): 416-427.

This unusually detailed review of a test describes the DRP as a test of reading effectiveness which gives "the readability level of the most difficult prose a student can comprehend" (p. 418). It is not norm-referenced. Rather it is a series of increasingly difficult passages which measure reading ability on an "absolute scale, not a comparative scale" (ibid.). The measure is readability level. The format is a modified cloze test in which the student selects the missing word from five alternatives. The items deleted have been carefully chosen to measure comprehension; they are not the "nth" word in the passage. The discussion of reliability and validity are useful not only for understanding potential problems with this test but also for providing a model for the reader of what to look for when critiquing this area.

278. Langer, Judith A. THE CONSTRUCTION OF MEANING AND THE ASSESSMENT OF COMPREHENSION: AN ANALYSIS OF READER PERFORMANCE ON STANDARDIZED TEST ITEMS. 1982. 38pp. (ED 216 313)

Langer reports on research designed to examine the process readers use to construct meaning from text, using standardized reading comprehension tests. Subjects represented a variety of ages, with third graders comprising the largest category. The findings showed that aspects of the test language could interfere with comprehension. She concludes that "standardized reading tests do not measure the processes involved in the construction of meaning from a text nor do they evaluate an individual's ability to manage those processes" (p. 33).

279. Nicholson, Tom. "Experts and Novices: A Study of Reading in the High School Classroom." READING RESEARCH QUARTERLY XIX (Summer 1984): 436-451.

Nicholson takes us into two junior high school classrooms and gives us much fascinating dialogue between teachers and students dealing with the knowledge students need to accomplish the reading task, the strategies they are using while reading, and the confusions and problems they're encountering. The analysis of the dialogue seems particularly useful as a way of giving teachers insights into the dialogues they have with students. Nicholson suggests that "concurrent" interviewing is a way of studying student reading strategies as well as monitoring their progress.

280. Nitko, Anthony J. "Distinguishing the Many Varieties of Criterion-referenced Tests." REVIEW OF EDUCATIONAL RESEARCH

50 (Fall 1980): 461–485.

This article should be extremely useful for the reader who is looking for an in-depth discussion of criterion-referenced tests. Nitko recognizes the definitional confusions that exist because of the many varieties of criterion-referenced tests. Through detailed discussion and examples of specific tests, his goal is to order a complex topic.

281. Rogers, Douglas B.   "Assessing Study Skills." JOURNAL OF READING 27 (January 1984): 346–354.

Rogers bases his suggestions and checklist on the distinction between reading to comprehend and studying to remember what is read. His focus is on the latter. He advocates using informal procedures rather than formal tests to assess students' abilities in the using study skills. The checklist contains many of the traditional skills (such as using graphic aids, locating information in text books, and using the library). He also includes studying and organizing information. The preferred technique for assessment is observation and the author provides many specific examples of this.

282. Samuels, S. Jay. "A Cognitive Approach to Factors Influencing Reading Comprehension." JOURNAL OF EDUCATIONAL RESEARCH 76 (May/June 1983): 261–266.

Samuels views reading as "the active construction of a text's meaning, proceeding from an interaction between writer and reader" (p. 261). He presents a detailed, useful analysis of the external and internal factors that influence comprehension. The discussion of text readability is particularly useful for a content teacher. Samuels advocates using a list of inside- and outside-the-head factors as a basis for identifying sources of difficulty.

283. Samuels, S. Jay. "Diagnosing Reading Problems." TOPICS IN LEARNING AND LEARNING DISABILITIES 2 (January 1983): 1–11.

Samuels examines a comprehensive list of external and internal factors related to learning to read and to reading comprehension. He establishes a useful framework for looking at the student, the materials he is to read and the instructional setting. The discussion of internal factors is clearly cognitive, with stress placed on the student's background knowledge, knowledge of text structure, language facility and metacognitive strategies. In addition, factors such as decoding skills and motivation are also included. The inclusion of external factors is particularly useful for secondary teachers, because it alerts us to the significance of our role in the process as well as to the importance of carefully choosing the materials students use.

284. Schell, Leo M.   "Test Review: California Achievement Tests:

Reading (CAT, Forms C and D)." JOURNAL OF READING 23 (April 1980): 624-628.

On the secondary level, the California Achievement Test: Reading assesses vocabulary and reading comprehension. The vocabulary subtest examines word knowledge in three ways: opposites, synonyms, and multimeaning words in context. The reading comprehension subtest includes literal, interpretive and critical reading. Scores are reported both as norm-referenced scores and as criterion-referenced scores. Schell warns that because of statistical limitations, "educators should treat these mastery scores with extreme caution" (p. 627).

285. Schell, Leo M. "Test Review: Comprehensive Tests of Basic Skills (CTBS, Form U, Levels A-J)." JOURNAL OF READING 27 (April 1984): 586-589.

This article is interesting as much for giving the reader insights into how to analyze tests as it is for the analysis of the test itself. The format of this norm-referenced test of reading achievement is "relatively traditional in content and format" (p. 586). Problems are identified in the areas of reliability and validity, which causes the author to recommend that teachers not analyze scores on specific objectives.

286. Simpson, Michele L. "A Diagnostic Model for Use with College Students." JOURNAL OF READING 26 (November 1982): 137-143.

The author proposes a diagnostic model based on the four major variables in learning identified by Brown, Campione and Day: task characteristics, learner strategies and processes, text characteristics and learner characteristics. She advocates using questioning techniques as well as cloze procedures, observation, oral reading, written summaries and diagnostic teaching in order to identify why students are not succeeding and how they can improve. Although the article is aimed at college students, the framework provided is also useful for high school students.

287. Tullock-Rhody, Regina, and J. Estill Alexander. "A Scale for Assessing Attitudes toward Reading in Secondary Schools." JOURNAL OF READING 23 (April 1980): 609-614.

This scale for assessing attitudes toward reading is easily administered and scored. The authors present evidence of its validity and reliability. They suggest that it can be used as a pre- and posttest to demonstrate attitude change as well as a source of information in program planning. An item analysis is provided to allow of the analysis of student responses.

288. Webb, Melvin W., II. "A Scale for Evaluating Standardized Reading Tests, with Results for Nelson-Denny, Iowa, and Stanford." JOURNAL OF READING 26 (February 1983): 524-529.

Although the focus of the article is on the use of the Nelson-Denny, the Iowa Silent Reading Test, and the Stanford Diagnostic Reading Test in community colleges, the general areas covered are of use to secondary schools. The article gives criteria for rating tests on purpose, validity, reliability, standard error of measurement, normative data, item analysis data, theory, forms, manual, time and cost. Sources for the ratings are also provided.

289. Ysseldyke, James E., and Douglas Marston. "A Critical Analysis of Standardized Reading Tests." SCHOOL PSYCHOLOGICAL REVIEW 11 (Summer 1982): 257-266.

This article illustrates an analysis of reading tests based on a "bottom-up" approach to reading. Within this theoretical construct the authors analyze a variety of norm-referenced and criterion-referenced achievement, survey and diagnostic tests to determine what skills are tested and the kinds of educational decisions that can be made on the basis of the information obtained. For a critique of this and other articles in this issue which focused on reading assessment and intervention, see Henk, Readence and Mason (275).

290. Zigmond, Naomi, and Rita Silverman. "Informal Assessment for Program Planning and Evaluation in Special Education." EDUCATIONAL PSYCHOLOGIST 19 (Summer 1984): 163-171.

Zigmond and Silverman advocate the use of informal tests because formal tests provide little information for instructional program planning or program evaluation, although they do have value for "predictive purposes or for gaining a normative perspective" (p. 164). The authors provide guidelines for a 12-step strategy for assessment for instruction. It includes careful decision-making and planning before testing, error analysis and hypothesis formation, probing to test the hypothesis and finally, planning for instruction. Program evaluation can be accomplished using informal tests that test what has been taught either at the end of the year or as a continuous evaluation throughout the year. The problem of reliability and validity is discussed. Suggestions are made which are designed to increase the technical adequacy of informal tests.

CHAPTER VIII

COMPUTERS AND READING

It is hard to think of an aspect of our lives that has not been touched by computers, from lottery tickets to the most sophisticated and advanced medical treatments. Yet, as Langer (307) states, "the resistance to computer technology in schools is widespread" (p. 21). Mathematics departments and science departments may be embracing computers as an integral part of the curriculum, but the same is not true of reading programs. Thompson (315) found that

> Reading development and instruction is an area of priority at all educational levels. However, the impact of computers on educational practices in teaching reading has been minimal. Although numerous examples of computer usage can be cited, possibilities and capabilities far outweigh existing practices. (p. 38)

We, as teachers concerned with reading, cannot ignore a fact of life; we cannot fail to understand and utilize a resource with the potential inherent in computers.

Recognizing Problems and Potentials

Before examining practical ways of implementing and using computer programs in secondary school reading programs, we need to look at the jobs computers can do for us, the advantages and problems associated with them, and their effectiveness in teaching reading, particularly to secondary students.

The most immediate question is: what can computers do for teachers and for students? They can help in the process of instruction and in the management of that instruction.

Computer-Assisted Instruction (CAI). Students work on the computers using three basic types of program (293, 296, 302, 315).

1. Drill and practice. This is the most common type of program and is based on the theory that reading is a set of subskills to be mastered, a bottom-up approach. According to Balajthy (295) "experience has shown that reading teachers are far more impressed by the capability of the computer to present drillwork that they are by the many other types of software available" (p. 494).

2. Tutorial. Tutorial programs model and guide learning. The more common type of tutorial is one in which the program makes the decisions about what will come next based on the student's responses to the task. In a second format the user, assuming more control, asks for more information or more examples as needed. The student and the program interact.

3. Problem-solving, games, and simulations. This format allows for manipulation by the user and provides opportunities for the user to be in control.

Computer-Managed Instruction (CMI). Computers can help manage instruction in a variety of ways including: testing, maintaining student grades and data, determining readability levels of materials, and scheduling (292, 293).

What are some advantages of using computers to teach reading skills in secondary schools? For students, computers can:

1. be patient instructors. Don't underestimate this. Think of yourself at the end of a long day, an even longer week. You have gone over something 87 times (a rough estimate, of course!) and you hear someone say "I don't get it." (293, 295, 315)

2. be motivating. This may be due to the program itself, the format, the content, the control exercised by the student in working through the program or some combination of these. Computers may focus attention and increase time-on-task. (291, 303, 307, 315)

3. provide immediate, nonthreatening feedback. (291, 293, 308)

4. provide for the active involvement of the student in the process of reading, particularly if the program is interactive. (307, 315)

5. allow for variations in the time used to complete a task. This feature can be controlled by the computer, the teacher or the student. (293, 295)

6. allow for variations and flexibility in sequencing. Everyone does not go through the task the same way. The computer can present new, advanced material, additional material on the same level, or easier material depending on the student's response to a particular task. Think about how difficult this is to do consistently in a classroom. (291, 308, 315)

7. allow the student to assume control. This is an important potential. A student works directly with the computer. He can ask the computer for help, for more information, for another example. He can change the time allowed for the task, decreasing it as he feels he is becoming more competent. (291, 307)

For teachers, computers can:

1. permit better use of time. You can efficiently manage instruction and provide instruction if you have convenient access to the hardware, appropriate software and an understanding of how to use the computer facility. (307, 315)

2. allow you to provide "strategy-based activity" (307, p. 17). You will see from the examples given later that it is possible for students to go beyond answering multiple-choice questions as an instructional activity to practicing and using strategies we have discussed in this text. (307)

3. allow you to provide guidance, while at the same time being non-directive and non-threatening. (307, 308)

4. provide you with a means of direct control over the curriculum, once you have learned some fairly simple programming. You can use classroom content materials to provide instruction and practice in skills and strategies relevant to your students and your school demands. (307)

For administrators, computers can:

1. increase the time spent by students on reading and writing tasks. (307)

2. provide more continuity between classrooms by insuring that all students are working on a core of skills and strategies. (307)

These advantages, of course, depend on the software being used.

We have looked at advantages. What are the problems associated with computers? There are four that are often cited. First, consider the problem of cost: purchase and maintenance of the hardware, purchase or development of software, and teacher time in learning to use the system (303, 308, 315). However, the question is not completely one of cost but rather one of cost-effectiveness. Is this the most effective use of the educational dollar? The answer depends on how the computer has been applied and utilized in a particular educational setting. Geoffrion and Geoffrion (291) assert that "using a computer as an expensive workbook seems a waste of money and resources" (p. 78). We agree. We also agree with Langer (307) that computer activities should not duplicate or replicate what is already easily available in the classroom. With this in mind, schools can begin to evaluate the cost effectiveness of computers.

A second problem with computers that is often mentioned is that of the quality of the software available (307). Mason, Blanchard and Daniel (292) cite the fact that

There has been an explosive growth in the quantity of instructional microcomputer software for reading. From a few programs in the late seventies, there are now over a hundred different computer programs designed for reading instruction. One would assume from such a growth that a corresponding growth in the quality of reading software had occurred. Such an assumption, however, would be exceedingly optimistic, given the current state of reading software. (p. 140)

Why this dissatisfaction with current software?

1. Programs are not based on reading theory. We have the capability of designing programs based on current reading theory, programs in which the student is actively involved in the process of reading, in which prior knowledge is an essential element, in which comprehension is the focus and connected discourse is the medium, and in which a variety of strategies are used based on the reader, the text and the purpose for reading (291, 296. 307, 315). The problem is according to Langer (307), among others (291, 292), that "at the present time there are a plethora of computer programs that provide reading practice in bottom-up tasks....Few presently available instructional programs provide activities for getting at meaning" (p. 11). Geoffrion and Geoffrion (291) document this problem on the word, the sentence and the connected discourse level. We are forced to choose "the best from the mediocre" (294, p. 5).

2. The programs use limited formats. Not only is there concern about the content but also about the format. A common view is that software programs are little more than workbook activities (291, 307) and workbooks would probably be cheaper. The full range of possibilities with the various formats has only begun to be tapped. Mason, Blanchard and Daniel (292), in 1983, assert that "few innovative instructional programs for reading have been developed since 1978" (p. 140).

3. Programs are often inappropriate for a particular student or school. Not only is the problem one of quality but it is also one of inappropriateness of software for the needs of particular teachers, students and curriculum (294).

4. Programs are designed by computer specialists not educators. Langer (307) decried this condition, stating that "instructional aspects are being permitted to happen to rather than be shaped by professional educators who know about children, schools and learning" (p. 2). The solution to this problem seems to rest, partially at least, with teachers, with teachers demanding quality software, and working with publishers to obtain this (293, 294) as well as with teachers designing software to fill their identified needs using their own materials (294, 310).

A third problem is that of resistance of teachers to using computers. In fact, Holmes (303) states that "studies have indicated that the second greatest obstacle, after cost, to the implementation of CAI is likely to be teacher acceptance" (p. 9). Part of the solution to this problem may rest with how teachers and administrators perceive the role of computers. "Any attempt at implementation of a CAI system is more likely to succeed if the system is viewed as a supplement to traditional modes of instruction" (ibid., p. 12). Teachers, like everyone else, don't want to feel threatened. In order to ease that feeling, knowledge and understanding are needed. This calls for a program of staff development (307).

A final problem remains, that of the effectivenesss of computers in reading instruction and practice. Generally, how effective have computers been in instructing and reinforcing reading skills? Thompson (315) found they were effective as a way of delivering instructional services but she cited difficulties with the research projects that had been used to evaluate the role of computers in instruction. Many of them have been "minimal, superficial, have yielded inconclusive results, or have been inadequately funded" (p. 40).

The quality and appropriateness of the software used may also have created difficulties with the research done on effectiveness as well as with the instruction provided students. Thompson (ibid.) cited the fact that much of the software used in research was created by computer programmers, not educators. Holmes (303) cited the "acknowledged fact that the lack of adequate courseware is the main reason why CAI has not been as successful as was first anticipated" (p. 12). The problem of quality software is far-reaching.

Blohm (296) reviewed research on the impact of the formats used in computer instruction and found "strong evidence" (p. 6) for the effectiveness of drill and practice software compared to a traditional skills and practice approach. He found little research on the effectiveness of games and almost none on effectiveness of tutorial programs on reading comprehension.

Schuelke and King (312) reviewed research in reading and concluded that results "do not universally show improvements in learning" (p. 3), but they found that "computers are so formidable a communication medium that they cannot be ignored" (p. 8).

A more specific question though for us concerns the effectiveness of computers in teaching reading in secondary schools. There is not, at the present time, a substantial body of information on this topic. In fact, skimming the research projects reported on by Mason, Blanchard and Daniel (292) reveals that those dealing with secondary students are in the definite minority. Singer, Dreher and Kamil (293) stated that results of computer use in elementary schools had been "extremely favorable" (p. 178) and in colleges had been "modest, but positive" (ibid.). They were forced to the conclusion that "by extrapolation, the effects in middle and secondary schools should be somewhere in between" (pp. 178-179).

A sampling of current research topics on the secondary level shows the range of skills, strategies and types of readers being studied. For example, there are studies ranging from word analysis skills and the use of context for poor readers (300) and fluency through repeated reading for poor readers (297) to study skills for advanced students (301). The results have added bits and pieces to our knowledge. Frederiksen et al. (300), in the first example, obtained positive results on the tasks taught as well as on the transfer of skill to other related reading tasks. Carver and Hoffman (297), in the second example, found an increase in fluency in the task as well as in related tasks but only partial support for a transfer to reading ability in general. Gadzella (301) demonstrated that the use of computers in teaching study skills was effective with advanced students.

The fact remains though that we do not have a comprehensive body of research documenting the effectiveness of computers in teaching reading to secondary students. We are certainly working toward this, but at the present time this is another item we can file under MacGinitie's "uncertainty" category! However, we cannot wait until we have that complete body of research before we begin to use computers in teaching reading. We, as teachers may, in fact, need to become part of the research base that documents the ways in which computers can or cannot be effective.

Using Computers in Reading

In spite of these problems, the computer is in your school or maybe even in your classroom. The students want to use it; the administration expects it will be used. There are many suggestions on how to proceed.

Becoming comfortable with computers.

Langer (307) offers a number of suggestions for developing computer literacy and gaining acceptance for computers among teachers.

1. Start in a low-key fashion. Begin by playing games on the computer in the teachers' room and gradually use reading and writing programs.

2. Become involved in the decision-making process of planning what to buy and how to use it. Don't let someone else do this for you. Just listening to others, reading catalogues, trying the programs will help.

3. It takes time to become comfortable with computers. Don't rush it.

4. Attend workshops and inservice programs. Langer warns us that this will not overcome all problems. It will get you started. The International Reading Association Computer Technology and Reading Committee (304) suggests staff development in the areas of application, evaluation, selection and integration of computers into the classroom.

5. Suggest to your principal that there be someone available, "on-call," to provide a support system to answer questions and make suggestions.

Planning computer instruction and choosing software programs

1. Choose programs that incorporate activities and formats "consistent with established reading theory and practice" (304, p. 63). The lists and suggestions given in the literature vary but only in detail not in substance. They include items which focus on the reader, the text, the skills and strategies included, and the kinds and levels of materials provided. (291, 296, 304, 307)

2. Don't choose the program and then see how it fits into your curriculum. The process should start with the curriculum and your instructional objectives. Then you determine what you want in a program. (294, 315)

3. Evaluate software using specific criteria that cover not only the characteristics of the program, but also the backup and services provided by the company. (291, 295, 304, 305)

4. Go beyond drill and practice. Consider and use other formats. (294, 295)

5. Look for programs that incorporate both reading and writing. Word processing might be a useful part of your reading program although "to date there has been only a minimal attempt to apply such software to the task of reading instruction" (292, p. 148). (291, 292, 294)

6. Review the feedback provided in the program. Does it simply tell the student whether he's right or wrong, or does it go beyond that? Alternatives might include providing contradictory information for the student to consider or asking the student to go back to the text to confirm or reject the response. Does the feedback gradually fade out, leaving the student in control? (291, 307)

7. Consider programs that incorporate the teacher in the process. It may be that the program stops after the student has written a precis or summary with the help of the program. Then the teacher critiques the product. The student goes back to the program to complete the task. (294)

8. Demand appropriate programs from publishers. Work with them to design appropriate software. They may be more receptive than you think. After all their aim is to sell software to schools. They want to develop and sell materials that teachers want and will order. (293, 294, 307)

Using computers

     The three uses for computers that can have an immediate impact on reading instruction, in a reading center or in a content classroom, probably include assessing (CMI), instructing (CAI), and establishing readability levels (CMI). Let's look at some specific possibilities here.

Assessing. The potential for computers for assessing reading levels, skills and strategies seems almost unlimited. To anyone who has corrected group reading tests or who has waited impatiently for commercially corrected ones to be returned, the computer offers an ease and immediacy which is certainly appealing. However, their potential is not limited to correcting and scoring multiple choice. Consider all possibilities.

1. Use a multiple-choice testing format, either one developed by a publisher or one developed by you or your school system. The second alternative gives you an opportunity to use your own materials. (309)

2. Consider the capabilities of the computer in designing other types of assessment instruments. These might include: adjusting the test for difficulty and item type depending on the response of the student; identifying the number and kind of hints or cues required by the student in order to obtain an appropriate response; selecting "items and alternatives to test hypotheses about specific processing strategies" (253, p. 156); and identifying lookback and search strategies. (253)

3. Choose and/or develop instructional programs that keep a record of student responses to particular tasks. This provides a way of assessing progress and areas of difficulty. (296, 316)

Instructing.

1. Examine the literature on instructional software to get a picture of the full scope of the present and potential possibilities here. Note how many of the suggestions made here are based on a process-oriented approach to reading and include problem-solving, the use of strategies and student decision-making as well as activities before, during and after reading (307). These include:

cloze procedures to teach reading comprehension. (293, 316)

an information-retrieval system of books and articles. (298)

interactive texts in which the reader can point to a word not recognized and the computer will say it. The reader can ask for help or ask for an expanded version of the text. (298)

a "dynamic book" in which the reader selects a topic from an index, the text appears on screen with key words highlighted. (291, 298)

computer-generated questions to make sure the text is understood. Changes are made in the level of difficulty of the text to correspond to student answers and to prior knowledge. (298)

innovative displays of text--with text presented in thought units, and key words highlighted--for example, text structure.

(291)

an automated dictionary in which the reader points to a word not understood, the dictionary defines it and provide examples in different contexts, with animated pictures when appropriate. (291, 298)

pre- and postreading organizers which the reader either uses or develops based on reading and prior knowledge. (296)

gloss notations which the reader may call up on the screen as needed. (296)

a speed reading program designed to reduce dependency on subvocalization and make students aware of redundancies in the text. "To date, few reading software explicitly draw a student's attention to these reading strategies, even though such software are feasible" (291, p. 125). (291)

an SQ3R program in which key parts of the text are highlighted for skimming. In the future, the program may help the student form questions. (291)

notetaking using a file format to insure consistency and completeness of notes. This also enables the student to cross-reference. (291)

2. Consider using programs not designed as reading programs. These "can, with the aid of a talented instructor, be adapted to fill a variety of educational needs. Word processing software and data based software are but two examples of this. Surely others exist" (292, p. 149). (292)

3. Develop your own programs to insure instruction that is relevant and that draws on material the student actually needs to comprehend. There are two possibilities here. You can buy templates and fill in with your own materials, or you can author your own program using a language designed for computer novices. There are guidelines available for doing this although you may want (or need) to have some help. "It is perhaps this kind of creative involvement in CAI that will best assure its success" (303, p. 12). (292, 296, 302, 303, 310)

4. Begin instructing with computers by considering this as supplementary to the classroom instruction. This is easier to implement and more likely to be acceptable to most teachers. (303)

Determining readability levels. As Geoffrion and Geoffrion (291) point out, we must recognize the limitations of the available formulas and the variables they don't take into account. (More on this in Chapter IX.) In the meantime, be aware that it is very possible to perform this time-consuming task on a computer (291, 292). You can use one formula or several. Results can be compared graphically as well as numerically.

1. Program the computer yourself using using programs in the public domain. (292, 299, 306, 311, 313, 314)

2. Review and purchase commercial software that will perform this function. (292)

Summary

Our hope is that by the time you read this chapter on computers and reading, it will be outdated. We will have the "theory-driven" (p. 156) approach to using computers that Johnston (253) calls for and that is echoed by every serious student of this topic. We hope that as you read this, software programs, whether for instruction or testing, are interactive, offering you and your students opportunities to explore strategies, not simply work on skill hierarchies. We also hope that programs can be be adjusted or adapted so that you and your students can make them fit individual and local needs. Authoring programs are flexible, easy to use, and inexpensive.

On the other hand, it may be that the conditions cited by Langer (307) have not yet been fulfilled. She stated that "it is clear that before computer technology can make a positive impact on instructional programs, the technology must 1) reflect the best professional judgements regarding what is known about students and learning, and 2) reflect knowledgeable views of schools and teaching" (p. 7).

In any event, the role the teacher plays in computers and reading is critical. Mason, Blanchard and Daniel (292) have summed it up well. "It is the teacher, not the software that is the primary determiner of the success of most computer programs" (p. 149). In addition, the teacher's role is central in the development of an overall plan for computers and reading instruction and in the development of specifics of programs and implementation strategies.

We must not only use computers, we must be part of the process of developing these uses.

BIBLIOGRAPHY

Books

291. Geoffrion, Leo D., and Olga P. Geoffrion. COMPUTERS AND
READING INSTRUCTION. Reading, Massachusetts: Addison-
Wesley, 1983.

Geoffrion and Geoffrion examine both the reality and the
potential for using computers in the teaching of reading. A
firm grounding in current reading theory and research forms
the basis for guidelines for evaluating software. Their
premise is that reading instruction must emphasize connected
discourse, focus on comprehension, develop total reading
abilities not isolated skills, be child-centered when possible
and promote active student involvement. The inclusion of
samples from various programs is very helpful in identifying
relevant features. The discussion covers topics from reading
readiness through advanced reading and looks are various ways
of using the computer. This range may prove an advantage for
the reader unfamiliar with the subject because it provides
clear, easy to understand examples of critical features of
software for the teaching of reading. The authors have also
included a useful bibliography and list of publishers and
programs. Their expectations for computers are high; their
disappointment in current software is evident.

292. Mason, George E., Jay S. Blanchard, and Danny B. Daniel.
COMPUTER APPLICATIONS IN READING. Newark, Delaware:
International Reading Assn., 1983.

Mason, Blanchard and Daniel have given us an invaluable
resource. This book covers major topics related to computers
and the teaching of reading, including computer based reading
programs developed in colleges and universities; applications
of programs in school systems; computer uses in readability
assessment, text analysis, reading programs, and research;
software; and the future of computers in reading instruction.
Examples, particularly of the programs, are provided. The
unique value of this book is the exhaustive bibliography, in
many cases annotated, provided for every topic. The reader
will discover that the majority of the references deal with
programs and software suitable for elementary schools.
Nevertheless, there is much here for the secondary school
teacher.

293. Singer, Harry, Mariam Jean Dreher, and Michael Kamil.
"Computer Literacy." SECONDARY SCHOOL READING: WHAT
RESEARCH REVEALS FOR CLASSROOM PRACTICE. Edited by Allen
Berger and H. Alan Robinson. Urbana, Illinois: ERIC
Clearinghouse on Reading and Communication Skills and The
National Conference on Research in English, 1982, pp. 173-
192.

Singer, Dreher and Kamil review the history of technological innovations beginning with the development of language to the present uses of computers. They provide a brief discussion of software and its impact on secondary school reading. A major concern of the chapter is the problem of developing computer literacy in teachers as well as students. They provide numerous descriptions of preservice and inservice programs designed to achieve this goal. The bibliography is particularly useful.

Periodicals

294. Auten, Anne, and Sally Standiford. COMPUTERS IN ENGLISH: IS THERE ANOTHER WAY? 1983. 7pp. (ED 227 514)

Auten and Standiford clearly put the teacher in charge of the computer. Don't choose programs already developed and see how you can fit them into your English or reading curriculum. Instead, determine what aspects of your program have "specific, identifiable traits that can be modeled on a computer" (p. 3). Then, choose from existing programs, demand appropriate programs from publishers, or develop your own. A number of examples are given that go beyond drill and practice and often involve both reading and writing, such as writing a precis or summary.

295. Balajthy, Ernest. "Reinforcement and Drill by Microcomputer." READING TEACHER 37 (February 1984): 490-494.

Balajthy suggests that there is a place for using computers to reinforce in order to attain accuracy and to drill in order to attain mastery of important subskills of reading. He warns teachers, though, that reading programs should include other types of computer programs in order to take "advantage of the computer's power to enhance language instruction" (p. 494). The discussion of varieties and characteristics of reinforcement and drill programs is clear and concise, providing us with a useful framework for evaluating and using these programs.

296. Blohm, Paul J. "I Use The Computer To Advance Advances In Comprehension-Strategy Research." Paper presented at the Reading Symposium on "Factors Related to Reading Performance," Milwaukee, Wisconsin, June 10-11, 1982. 24 pp. (ED 216 330)

Blohm strongly asserts that there is a need to develop instructional software based on current reading theory. He defines his premises: an interactive model of reading, schema theory, and active participation of the reader using graphic organizers before and after reading and glossing while reading. The program he developed and describes records student requests for help and responses, thus providing diagnostic information that can be used to teach reading to that student in the content areas. He provides clear examples of software he developed for a college reading course and suggests that it is possible for any "noncomputer-oriented" (p. 14) teacher to do this.

297. Carver, Ronald P., and James V. Hoffman. "The Effect of Practice Through Repeated Reading on Gain in Reading Ability Using a Computer-Based Instructional System." READING RESEARCH QUARTERLY XVI (No. 3, 1981): 374-390.

The authors describe two studies, using high school students who were poor readers, in which computer-controlled feedback was used to affect fluency of reading using "repeated reading" practice. The results indicated an increase in fluency on the material used and on similar material but only partial support for the hypothesis that gains in fluency transfer to reading ability in general.

298. Collins, Allan. LEARNING TO READ AND WRITE WITH PERSONAL COMPUTERS. (Reading Education Report No. 42.). Urbana, Illinois: Illinois University, Center for the Study of Reading, May 1983. 32pp. (ED 229 728)

Collins gives us a "wish list," describing computer programs for reading and writing that have been developed in a somewhat limited fashion but that show great potential for the future. The potential lies in meeting individual needs and interacting with students. His examples generally relate to elementary students, but the format of the programs described can also apply to secondary students. The programs include an information-retrieval system, interactive texts, an automated dictionary, a writing coach, a text editor, an editorial assistant, a message system, and a publication system. Even though these programs are not widely available, the descriptions can provide a framework for looking at and evaluating current programs.

299. Feldman, Phil, Carolyn Casteel, and Maurice Field. "Using Microcomputers to Determine Readability Levels." READING IMPROVEMENT 20 (Summer 1983): 82-86.

The authors describe a computer program developed to compare readability levels as determined by five formulas (Lorge, Flesch, Dale-Chall, Fog, SMOG). The program also provides an analysis of various characteristics of the text. It is possible to obtain a copy of the VISICALC readability template described in the article by writing to one of the authors at an address provided.

300. Frederiksen, John R., Phyllis A. Weaver, Beth M. Warren, Helen P. Gillotte, Ann S. Rosebery, Barbara Freeman, and Lorraine Goodman. A COMPONENTIAL APPROACH TO TRAINING READING SKILLS. Washington, D.C.: National Institute of Education, March 1983. 206pp. (ED 229 727)

The authors used three game-like microcomputer training systems to teach secondary school students with poor reading skills two word analysis skills as well as word meaning through context frames. The participants reached performance levels equivalent to or higher than students with high ability. In addition, the participants were able to transfer the skills learned. The authors concluded that the games provided a "focus on developing particular skill components," direct, immediate feedback, and a motivating format (p. 177). Much detail is provided on how the games progressed and what phonic elements and words were used. Sample materials are also included.

301. Gadzella, Bernadette M. "High School Students Participate In A CAI Study Skills Program." Paper presented at the Southwest Educational Research Association Meeting, Houston, Texas, January 27, 1983. 19pp. (ED 230 185)

Gadzella reports on a study conducted with advanced high school seniors in which instruction in study skills using computer-assisted instruction was compared to using a notebook on study skills. The results supported the use of the computer as a tool in teaching study skills. Not only did the experimental group score significantly higher than the control group on a study skills posttest but they also spent more time on the modules and had more insight into them.

302. Gagne, Robert M., Walter Wager, and Alicia Rojas. "Planning and Authoring Computer-Assisted Instruction Lessons." EDUCATIONAL TECHNOLOGY 21 (September 1981): 17-26.

The authors provide valuable guidelines for developing instructional lessons. They examine types of learning outcomes, events (or steps) of instruction, and types of CAI (drill and practice, simulations, and tutorial). Although the detailed examples given do not come from the field of reading, they clarify the text and suggest applications of the authors' principles. The reader might also use the guidelines for examining programs written by others.

303. Holmes, Glyn. "Computer-Assisted Instruction: A Discussion of Some of the Issues for Would-Be Implementors." EDUCATIONAL TECHNOLOGY 22 (September 1982): 7-13.

Holmes presents an overview of the advantages and problems associated with computer-assisted instruction. He identifies the fears teachers may have, the needs of students and the role of CAI in the curriculum. The heart of a successful CAI program is the software. He addresses the problem of how to obtain appropriate software, urging teachers to begin to create their own. This article is for those contemplating moving into CAI.

304. International Reading Association, Computer Technology and Reading Committee. "Guidelines for Educators on Using

Computers in the Schools." JOURNAL OF READING 28 (October 1984): 63-65 and READING RESEARCH QUARTERLY XX (FALL 1984): 120-122.

This International Reading Association committee has provided guidelines for the most effective use of computers in reading classrooms. The guidelines cover software, hardware, staff development, equity of use, research, networking, inappropriate uses and legal issues.

305. Krause, Kenneth C. "Choosing Computer Software that Works." JOURNAL OF READING 28 (October 1984): 24-27.

Krause suggests three categories of questions to ask before buying computer software. One group contains questions we might ask when spending our own money on many items. We certainly need to ask them when spending the school's money. A second group is made up of questions general to any software program, while a third group is more specific to reading programs. A list of secondary reading software programs is provided.

306. Kretschmer, Joseph C. "Computerizing and Comparing the Rix Readability Index." JOURNAL OF READING 27 (March 1984): 490-499.

According to Kretschmer, the Rix index compares favorably to other short readability indexes and also provides a sentence-by-sentence monitoring of readability level. The author provides listings for TRS-80 Color Computer and for Apple II and Apple IIe Computers.

307. Langer, Judith A. COMPUTER TECHNOLOGY AND READING INSTRUCTION: PERSPECTIVES AND DIRECTIONS. 1982. 26pp. (ED 214 131)

Langer reviews the history of computers in schools and examines current research on school use. The results are discouraging. Computers often are not being used or are not used effectively. Software is inadequate. Teachers are uncomfortable with computers. She addresses these problems and makes suggestions. Of particular interest are the suggestions for relating computer instruction in reading to what we know about the process of reading (for example, the need to activate prior information, encourage predictions, and teach metacognitive strategies). Her concern about overcoming teacher resistance with a workshop or a one-week summer program is well taken. The suggestions she makes are interesting. Put computers in the teacher's room and let teachers first explore games, then reading and writing programs. Support the efforts of math departments to put on computer fairs for teachers in a school district. Encourage teachers to become involved in the planning for and development of computer uses.

308. Mason, George E. "Advantages And Disadvantages Of The
     Computer As A Teacher Of Reading." Paper presented at the
     Annual Meeting of the National Reading Conference,
     Clearwater Beach, Florida, December 1-4, 1982. 20pp. (ED
     232 130)

     Mason's discussion of advantages of computers in the
     teaching of reading may serve to lessen the resistance of
     teachers to using computers. The author cites the interactive
     nature of the computer, the immediate response it provides and
     its nonthreatening nature along with other characteristics as
     reasons for using computers in this way. The disadvantages
     include cost, quality and physical characteristics of the
     screen.

309. McArthur, David, Steven Shaha, and Bruce Choppin. DIAGNOSTIC
     TESTING SYSTEM: A COMPLETE DIAGNOSTIC MULTIPLE-CHOICE TEST
     PACKAGE FOR THE APPLE II. Los Angeles, California:
     California University, Center for the Study of Evaluation,
     August 1982. 56pp. (ED 228 266)

     This document describes a system designed to provide
     diagnostic information on the level at which a student
     comprehends material. The system can be used by teachers,
     with limited knowledge of computers, to write and edit their
     own tests. The authors provide a good indication of how the
     program works, using content materials in the testing and
     diagnosing of problem areas.

310. Rauch, Margaret, and Elizabeth Samojeden. "Computer-Assisted
     Instruction: One Aid for Teachers of Reading." Paper
     presented at the Spring Meeting of the Minnesota Post-
     Secondary Reading Council, St. Cloud, Minnesota, April 1981.
     12pp. (ED 204 702)

     Rauch and Samojeden cite advantages of using computer-
     assisted instruction for presenting new concepts and
     reinforcing skills. Because of the difficulty of obtaining
     relevant programs, they suggest that teachers write their own
     programs. Using a study skills course as an example, the
     authors suggest areas that could be put on a computer program,
     such as test taking, note taking, and time management. They
     further show how these modules could be incorporated into the
     course. A teacher who is designing a program may well need
     help from others in programming, typing in the program, and
     evaluating and modifying it.

311. Schilkowsky, Carl, Gwendolyn Peck, Gilles Fortier, and George
     E. Mason. "Open to Suggestion: Extending Schuyler's
     Program." JOURNAL OF READING 26 (March 1983): 550-552.

     The authors have translated Schuyler's program, designed for
     the Apple Computer, for computing readability levels with nine
     formulas into a program for the TRS-80 Computer. See Schuyler
     (313, 314).

312. Schuelke, David, and D. Thomas King. "New Technology In The
     Classroom: Computers and Communication and the Future."
     Paper presented at the Annual Meeting of the American
     Educational Research Association, New York, March 19-23
     1982. 15pp. (ED 217 879)

     The authors review recent research in communication related
     areas, particularly reading comprehension and skills,
     composition, and organizational communication and information
     utilization. They conclude that although the research has not
     been consistently supportive of using computers in these
     areas, "computers are so formidable a communication medium
     that they cannot be ignored" (p. 8).

313. Schuyler, Michael R. "A Readability Formula Program for Use
     on Microcomputers." JOURNAL OF READING 25 (March 1982):
     560-591.

     Schuyler advocates computing several readability formulas
     and comparing the results in examining reading materials.
     Because of the tediousness and, in some cases, the difficulty
     of computing formulas, teachers rarely use more than one. The
     author has developed a program for computing and comparing
     readability levels using the Dale-Chall, Holmquist, Fry, Fog,
     Flesch, Flesch-Kincaid, Coleman, and Devereaux (ARI) formulas.
     The article provides a program listing for the basic program
     and two supplementary programs for the Apple computer, as well
     as the address where the program may be purchased at cost.
     See also Schilkowsky et al. (311) and Schuyler (314).

314. Schuyler, Michael R. "Open to Suggestion: Supplementary Note
     from Michael Schuyler." JOURNAL OF READING 26 (March 1983):
     552.

     Schuyler identifies changes made in his program with a view
     to making it easier for the teacher with little computer
     knowledge to use. He provides an address where he may be
     contacted for further information. See also Schilkowsky et
     al. (311) and Schuyler (313).

315. Thompson, Barbara J. "Computers in Reading: A Review of
     Applications and Implications." EDUCATIONAL TECHNOLOGY 20
     (August 1980): 38-41.

     Thompson describes computer-assisted instruction, computer-
     managed instruction and other computer applications. She
     examines associated advantages, disadvantages, potential and
     limitations on that potential. She does not view the computer
     as the solution to the problem of reading instruction but
     rather as an effective tool we can use to respond to students'
     needs.

316. Wells, Bethany J., and D. Scott Bell. "A New Approach to
     Teaching Reading Comprehension: Using Cloze and Computer-
     Assisted Instruction." EDUCATIONAL TECHNOLOGY 20 (March

1980): 49-51.

The authors describe a program developed to teach reading comprehension skills to elementary Pueblo students using culturally relevant material and utilizing the cloze procedure. It was based on meaning approach to reading and requires student participation in the reading process. The examples are useful in showing how a cloze or maze program might be developed on the computer whether for elementary or secondary students.

CHAPTER IX

PROGRAM ALTERNATIVES

This book is based on the assumption that it is the responsibility of secondary schools to provide for the reading needs of all students. This means working with a wide range of reading abilities and strategies and offering a variety of services. One way to categorize the services is by reading level--students reading below grade level (remedial and corrective) and students reading on or above grade level (developmental and advanced). Another way is to consider those services offered as separate programs (generally all of the above) and those offered as part of a total school program (reading in the content areas). We will look at these alternatives.

In any event, according to French (345), "an overall plan for organization and evaluation is crucial for reading program success" (p. 6). Unfortunately, a study reported on by French with reading specialists in Wisconsin as subjects indicated that program development and program evaluation were the most common areas of deficit in graduate programs. If reading teachers are to meet the needs of schools and students, these are areas in which they must become competent. We will examine program development in this chapter and program evaluation in the next.

Meeting the Needs of Students

Remedial and Corrective Instruction

Herber and Nelson-Herber (328) state that "the predominant configuration of secondary school reading programs has been the remedial/corrective model, that is, the creation of pull-out reading classes for limited groups of students with special needs" (p. 177). A recent study by Greenlaw and Moore (349) confirms this. Let's look at what the experts say about these classes.

1. Remedial classes consist of students who:

    are two or more years below grade level (372).

    have poor command of basic reading and study skills (340).

    are severely deficient in skills (328).

    have failed or are failing minimal competency tests (347, 350).

2. Corrective classes consist of students who:

    are a year or two below grade level (328).

    have specific skill deficits (324).

3. Instruction in these classes often seems to include:

    a diagnostic/prescriptive approach (372).

    large and small group instruction (ibid.).

    basic skill instruction (322, 324).

4. Problems identified with remedial programs include:

    a history of failure and a lack of interest on the part of the
    students (356).

    lack of transfer to content classes with resulting inability to
    meet demands of content teachers (23, 24).

    increasing sense of isolation as student falls further behind
    in content classes (24).

    a paucity of research available on long-term effectiveness of
    remedial programs (332).

    short-term skills-centered programs seem to have little
    significant effect on reading achievement (332).

5. Instruction should probably include:

    materials and skills that are relevant to the student (346).

    a focus on strengths not weaknesses (24).

    modeling the process of reading (343).

    an emphasis on strategies and techniques other than basic
    skills: thinking skills (321, 359), processing skills (372), a
    language approach (332), learning how to learn (343), learning
    to read to learn (23).

    integration with and tie in to content area instruction. This
    may be in the introduction, practice, and/or reinforcement of
    skills and strategies taught (24, 328, 332, 350, 372).

    the components of effective teaching (student involvement in
    learning, accepting environment, instruction in vocabulary and
    comprehension, free reading, well-defined methods of
    instruction) (356).

    continuous instruction, not single lessons (332, 346).

respect for students. Sims (335) suggests this as an important aspect of working with black students. It is appropriate to all remedial students (321, 335).

6. Suggestions include courses:

offering a variety of electives in the areas of study skills and reading rate, vocabulary, main idea and details and inferences. These can last for a semester or for a few sessions (351, 356).

in areas where students have identified they are deficient (351, 356).

based on television or including creative and concrete art experiences (356).

which include a Directed Listening-Language Experience approach to teach reading skills and content materials (347).

in which students learn about themselves as learners (243).

and strategies:

an interactive approach to learning how to learn from text using reading and writing (343).

processing strategies related to content texts (372).

levels of comprehension using journal articles (130).

which use thinking skills related to reading (24, 321, 359).

Developmental and Accelerated Instruction

Reading instruction can take another form. Developmental and accelerated classes, although not as common, are frequently offered in secondary schools (349).

1. Developmental classes consist of students who:

have adequate mastery of word recognition and literal level comprehension but need higher level reading skills (372).

need to develop reading rate and vocabulary (350).

need a diversity of reading experiences including recreational reading (ibid.).

may be unmotivated and reluctant (340).

2. Accelerated classes include students who:

   are college bound and need efficient ways of comprehending and retaining complex material (340, 345, 350).

   may be gifted but need to develop advanced reading skills with a wide range of subject matter and materials (361).

3. Instruction in these classes generally includes:

   high-level comprehension skills, speed reading, efficient reading, and study skills, such as outlining, notetaking, summarizing (328, 345, 350).

4. Problems identified with this instruction include:

   lack of general availability. Many students could benefit from these programs but they are either not available or students do not elect to take them (324).

   lack of automatic transfer of strategies and skills to content classrooms (23).

5. Instruction should include:

   strategies for easing the transition between structured elementary reading programs and the unstructured, complicated reading demanded in secondary schools (23).

   strategies for insuring transfer between reading class and content classes (23).

   an emphasis on the differences between expository and narrative text stressing both reading and writing (111).

   thinking skills, processing skills (321, 372).

6. Suggestions for courses and strategies:

   a nine-week developmental course covering rate, vocabulary and a variety of reading experiences required of all sophmores (350).

   "Power Reading," a semester course for 11th- and 12th-graders which includes reading and study skills for efficient reading (350).

   short intensive mini-courses designed to promote personal reading, develop interest in children's literature, improve speed or vocabulary (324, 351).

   thinking skills and processing skills (321, 372).

Content area reading

All of the alternatives discussed so far are run out of the reading center, are supplementary to the total school program and involve some selected percent of the total school population. There is a concern that this is not sufficient. Another program alternative is to have reading/study instruction in content classrooms as part of a total school program.

1. Content area reading—a program alternative?

Is instruction in reading skills to be conducted in separate reading classes, in content classrooms, or both? The question here is one that Moore, Readence and Rickelman (363) have identified as "compelling" (p. 426). It is a question of the "locus of instruction" (ibid.). Consider the following opinions.

Petrosky (25), after reviewing the findings of the NAEP, concluded that we must address the problems of teaching reading, writing and thinking and we must do it across curricular lines, involving all content teachers.

According to Nelson-Herber and Herber (24) fewer students would need corrective help if they were receiving reading instruction in content classrooms. This would facilitate the transition between elementary and secondary reading and would focus on application of thinking skills. "All students should have the benefit of reading instruction in every classroom where reading is required, and...reading strategies should be taught simultaneously with the content of the subject being taught" (p. 234).

Gambrell and Cleland (346) state that "functional reading instruction can be incorporated into varied subjects....Functional reading programs are far more effective when curriculum areas share a commitment to their development" (p. 344).

Memory (360) believes that "the issue is where the primary responsibility for survival reading should be placed. It is this writer's view that the content area classroom is the most appropriate place for instruction in that area" (p. 351).

Swenarton and White (372) identify the components of a successful secondary reading program as including remedial reading, developmental reading and reading in content areas. They view these three components as intimately related. "Teachers must not only make an active attempt to ascertain what common content-related reading skills exist and how they can be juxtaposed with content material, but teachers should also seek to mutually reinforce them. It seems logical to assume that if a systematic approach is not developed to instruct students in reading/content processing skills, then students are not going to improve their functional or critical reading skills" (pp. 6-7).

Early and Sawyer (324) propose that "beyond grade 8 greater emphasis should be given to applying strategies in content courses than to direct instruction either in English classes or in "extra" reading classes.   However...although direct instruction absorbs less time and fewer resources in the senior high it does not disappear from the curriculum" (p. 113).

There is certainly support for placing reading instruction in the content classrooms. The question no longer is should we provide instruction in the content classroom, but rather how to emphasize both the classroom and the reading center depending on the resources available and the outcomes desired. Another item to file under MacGinitie's label of uncertainty! However, it does appear that in planning instruction we must certainly consider the need for reading/study instruction in content classes.

2. Teachers' concerns.

We cannot successfully mandate that content teachers include reading/study instruction in their classrooms. Instead we need to examine teachers' concerns and begin to establish ways of helping alleviate them. Consider the following statements.

Content teachers are resistant to teaching reading. They don't want responsibility for teaching content reading; they are not prepared to do it (348, 369, 372).

Content teachers often fail to implement strategies in the classroom once they have been introduced to them (368).

There is a concern about the time involved for teachers in planning appropriate lessons and in mastering use of strategies, with a resulting reluctance to get involved (368).

Teachers need to balance reading instruction with content instruction so that both benefit and neither is neglected (363).

One way to tackle these problems efficiently and effectively is by establishing a working relationship between the reading specialist and the content teachers. The basis of this is inservice training (23, 328, 368, 369, 372).   Petrosky (25), in fact, identified "a massive inservice need" (p. 18). The implementation of instructional strategies and procedures in the content classroom can be accomplished in a variety of ways. More on these two topics in the next chapter!

Another solution to these problems might be found in establishing a common focus--that of learning from text. Readence, Baldwin and Dishner (369) state that "the tools of content area reading are perfectly compatible with the orientation of the subject matter specialist; i.e., both aim to aid students in learning from text" (p. 523).   As Singer and Donlan (27) found out, while secondary content teachers do not perceive that their job is to teach students to read text, they do perceive that their job is to teach students to learn from text.

3. Skills and strategies.

What skills and strategies should we be teaching in a content
reading program? This question is far from resolved and is one that
must be addressed in any model of content reading. The lack of a
single accepted model here adds another dimension to MacGinitie's
notion of uncertainty. One alternative is that we teach generic
skills--the thinking, reasoning, reading skills that can apply to
any discipline. Much of the discussion in this book, particularly
in Chapters IV and V, has dealt with those kinds of skills.
References have been made in the discussion on remedial,
developmental and accelerated programs to the need to teach these
kinds of skills. A second alternative is that we examine the
structure of the discipline, identify specific text or content
dependent skills and strategies, and teach those. This might
include, for example, particular content vocabulary or text
structure (chronological for history, cause/effect for science). A
third alternative is that we identify the processing (reasoning)
skills appropriate to a discipline and use those in reading/study
instruction. An example of this might be social inquiry skills in
the social sciences. A fourth alternative is that we combine two or
more of these three in some fashion. The problem is complex.

Generic skills and strategies. You can probably anticipate many
of the suggestions that are made here. The assumption is often made
that "a common set of strategies underlies all content area reading
texts and tasks but that the strategies are adjusted to handle
specific demands" (363, p. 430).

Swenarton and White (372) developed a program based on six
content processing skills: perceiving relationships between
ideas, recognizing main ideas, discovering cause/effect
relationships, perceiving comparative/contrastive
relationships, arranging information into proper sequence, and
developing problem solving techniques.

Robinson and Schatzberg (333) suggest strategies that can be
used in all content areas before, during and after instruction.
These include: developing and activating schema, predicting,
using preorganizers, brainstorming, developing and using a
structured overview, and utilizing metalinguistics before
reading; using role modeling and metacognition during reading;
and utilizing postorganizers and questioning after reading. In
addition, they advocate the use of integrating activities such
as the ConStruct Procedure, PReP, and semantic organizers such
as maps and networks.

Herber and Nelson-Herber (328) advocate teaching global
processing skills such as vocabulary acquisition and
development, prediction and anticipation of meaning, levels of
comprehension, organizational patterns, reasoning, assessment
(transferring reading skills to test-taking) and interpersonal
communication. They (24) emphasize reading-reasoning
processes, not basic skills.

Manzo   (358) emphasizes language and thinking skills and
describes three strategies: one based on oral reading by the
teacher and summarizing by the students, a second which
isolates the concept, terminology, and questions (C/T/Q), and a
third called Questions-Only in which students learn about topic
through their own questions.

Moore, Readence and Rickelman (330) state that "students are
ready to read and learn from a passage when they have acquired
adequate prior knowledge, appropriate reading strategies, and
control of that knowledge and those strategies to satisfy their
reasons for reading" (p. 2). They list "five characteristics
of students that can be addressed directly in order to prepare
them for immediate content area reading tasks....The five
characteristics are: 1) Motivation, 2) Content Knowledge, 3)
Word Knowledge, 4) Learning Strategies, and 5) Attention"
(ibid.).

Content specific skills and strategies. There is much written
addressing   the   relationship of comprehending and studying to
specific content areas.   When viewed this way, the skills and
strategies are categorized under various labels, such as "content-
specific" (363), "content-dependent" (ibid.) or "text dependent"
(367).   Authors differ in the label they use. Generally, they
include under their label the traditional reading skills which have
been adapted to the particular demands of a particular subject.
This has been an approach to content reading that has been around
for something over fifty years and, in fact, has been referred to as
a "legacy" (363, p. 430).

Some   specific   suggestions   from   current   literature   are
identified here. This list is designed to whet your appetite.   In
some cases, specific suggestions are made. In all cases, a list is
provided of sources to consult for a variety of suggestions in
addition to the specific ones.

English
Be prepared to deal with both expository and narrative text in
terms of both comprehension and appreciation (325).
Consult: 86, 99, 111, 245, 323, 326, 329, 334, 336, 337.

Social Studies
Use a series of general questions that can be applied to any
historical writing and are designed to engage the reader in the
act of comprehension (370).
Incorporate writing patterns, vocabulary and study skills into
social studies (373).
Consult: 86, 319, 326, 329, 334, 336, 337.

Mathematics
Recognize the particular characteristics of mathematics texts:
few verbal cues and lack of redundancy, density of concepts and
information, particular vocabulary and symbols and the variety
of eye movements required to read diagrams (331).
Develop and use a taxomony of mathematical terms as a way of

developing math vocabulary (354).
Teach reading/thinking skills as a way to solve math word
problems, modeling the process for students (355).
Use techniques such as an IRI, an interview or a cloze
procedure to identify reading level in mathematics and
readability of material (364).
Consult: 86, 326, 329, 334, 336, 337.

Science
Recognize the particular characteristics of written material
that may be a source of difficulty for the secondary reader:
the terseness of language, the lack of redundancy, the
particular precise vocabulary, the frequent emphasis on
cause/effect patterns (338).
Consult: 86, 326, 329, 334, 336, 337.

Foreign Languages
Recognize the complexity of the demands in this area: students
have processing and language skills of adolescents, may or may
not have the appropriate background information for the text,
and may be reading text written on a level different from their
regular reading (320).
Consult: 329, 335, 337.

Physical Education and Health
Capitalize on the inherent motivation and interest in this
subject by including a variety of critical reading and study
skills in the curriculum (327).
Consult: 318, 329, 334, 337.

Art and Music
Consult: 317, 329, 334, 337.

Vocational Ed., Home Ec., Industrial Arts, Business Ed., Driver
Ed., Career Ed.
Consult: 329, 334, 337.

Some authors present illustrations of applications in all
content areas of generic and/or specific skills. Authors who do
this quite consistently include: McNeil; Moore, Readence, and
Rickelman; Readence, Bean and Baldwin; Santeusanio; and Vacca.

Discipline-related skills and strategies. A third point of
view on this topic, expressed by Peters (367), is that content
reading requires both text dependent and text related skills. Text
dependent skills are those in which "the focus is primarily on
comprehending the material in the text. For all practical purposes,
text dependent operations have been what has constituted the
traditional approach to content reading" (p. 7). In addition, and
certainly equally important, are text related skills, which are used
once the material has been comprehended "to cognitively restructure
the original text so that it is consistent with the cognitive
operations that underlie the desired conceptual approach, i.e.,
social inquiry, moral education, or values clarification" (ibid.).

Peters provides an example in social studies, in which the reader would read about government between 1763 and 1789 and comprehend its structure and function as stated in the text using text dependent skills, such as "interrelating concepts, distinguishing between major and minor ideas, and comparing major ideas" (p. 11). Then, the reader would apply the text related skills for this particular discipline of social inquiry in order to organize the information and determine what the major problem with the Articles of Confederation was. The reader "would employ such text related skills as developing a tentative answer to the problem, testing the tentative answer, drawing a conclusion based upon the tentative answer, and applying the conclusion beyond the context of the text" (ibid.). Peters calls this a Content Processing Model.

Peters's model has evoked considerable discussion. Steinley (371), in reviewing and extending Peters's model, asserts that we will need to develop a model of reading that incorporates both "specific processing demands of different approaches and content areas" and "significant skills of the reading process" (p. 244). There is a need for both reading teachers and content teachers to work together to develop an appropriate model. Conley and Savage (342) wonder if Peters's stress on text related skills is essentially different from the applied level of reading comprehension or from the processing skills of stating a problem, generating hypotheses, and drawing conclusions. This issue is far from resolved and a comprehensive model of content area reading is still in process. In the meantime, the discussion is certainly useful in helping us examine the issues in content area reading.

The question for us as teachers is, What do I do tomorrow? The strategies advocated here are not new to you. They, and others like them, have been discussed throughout this book. Content teachers are trained in a discipline. Reading teachers understand process. Our job is to merge the two perspectives to plan comprehensive programs for students.

The Role of the School Administration

One notion that appears consistently and is often stated with fervor is that the school administration must understand and actively support whatever reading program a school adopts (23, 25, 324, 372, 374). This can take the form of budget support, guidelines for communication and staff development, attendance and participation in workshops, and sustained public relations efforts. "Administration" refers to both the principal (372, 374) and to the superintendent (23, 324).

Meeting the Needs of Special Students

It is a truism to say that every student has special needs. Accepting that, we need to address the problems of particular groups of students with identifiable special needs--speakers of other dialects and languages, such as blacks and Hispanics, learning disabled students and gifted students. None of these groups, of course, is mutually exclusive. Each group is worthy of study on its own; we can only introduce the topic and draw some tentative conclusions. In reviewing the literature, you find relatively few references to the problems of teaching reading to secondary students who are members of these special groups. Most of the emphasis in both research and practice is on elementary students.

There are special needs within the general category of special education that we will not address. Not that these needs are not pressing, both for students and for teachers. They are. The needs of the mentally retarded, the slow learner, the low verbal, the language impaired, the severely emotionally disturbed, to name a few major groups, are unique and are beyond the scope of this book.

Reading Achievement

What can we say about the reading achievement of blacks, Hispanics, the learning disabled? First, blacks. The National Assessment of Educational Progress (34) identified blacks as one group which "continued to perform below the national level" (p. XIX) in all age groups although they have "narrowed the gap between themselves and the nation" (ibid.), particularly those "students who attend schools in advantaged-urban communities" (p. XX). This finding is confirmed by others. Sims (335), for example, cites blacks' "relatively poor performance" (p. 226) on reading achievement tests.

The NAEP (366) also examined the reading achievement level of Hispanic students, the one non-native speaking group identified. Their performance was below the national level, but as a group they did make some gains. "The general trend was positive, even though not all of the advances were statistically significant" (p. 3). Students from urban areas in the 13- and 17-year-old group showed some improvement, the former in literal comprehension and the latter in inferential comprehension. There were some problems with the sample used, but we are left with somewhat the same impression as we had about black students. There is a gap; it seems to be closing; there are areas of improvement. Representatives of these two groups need help with reading skills and strategies.

What about the learning disabled? Deshler, Schumaker, Alley, Warner, and Clark (344) caution that information on the academic achievement of learning disabled adolescents "remains extremely limited" (p. 2), but in their research they found that "LD adolescents exhibit low levels of basic skill development compared to their age peers including other low achieving (LA) adolescents" (ibid.). In many schools, often because of state requirements, these students will work with special education teachers, not reading teachers (324). The problem is twofold: special education teachers often are not trained to teach reading and reading instruction is not always required for LD students (365).

Needs of Students

What specific needs do these groups of students have?

Remember, in discussing groups, we have to be very cautious about assigning all qualities and characteristics to every member of the group. Deshler et al. (344) identify the learning disabled as a heterogeneous group. Keen (352) asserts that "since ESL [English as a Second Language] populations are characterized by their diversity of needs, results from ESL research can rarely be generalized to all ESL students" (p. 140). Not everyone would go that far, but the point is well taken.

1. Background information.

Tonjes and Zintz (379) identify this as a possible source of problems.

> Students who have a cultural background different from the main culture of the school may have problems with text material. They may not have the experiential background needed to deal with the concepts, or it may well be that there is a cultural conflict between what they have experienced and what they are reading. (p. 262)

Andersson and Barnitz (339), in reviewing cross-cultural studies of both adults and children, concluded that there were several areas where differences in background information could be sources of potential difficulty for comprehension including, for example, text structure, story grammar, inferences.

This problem is not unique to blacks and speakers of other languages. We have already identified this as a potential problem for many students. The problem of lack of or inappropriate background information is not unique to particular groups. It may not be a difference of kind but more one of degree.

2. Linguistic competencies.

Consider these two statements. They identify one of the major issues in teaching black students.

> Students of linguistically different backgrounds often have more difficulty mastering "standard" English. Since mastery of written language is built on the student's oral language, it is not hard to see why those with a variant dialect ("I be here") will have more trouble making the transfer. (379, p.262)

> It is the premise of this paper that speaking black dialect (or any dialect of American English) does not, in and of itself, interfere with learning to read (i.e., comprehend) written American English. (335, p. 222)

The first point of view advocates such strategies as using non-standard English primers for beginning readers and teaching the use of generative grammar and context to adolescents (353). The suggestions for adolescents are certainly not new ones. Linguistically different students are not the only students who may need this kind of instruction. The second point of view suggests that non-standard English speakers need the same good reading instruction, with the same emphasis on language and meaning, taught with the same respect for the student as any student needs (335).

Instructional strategies

There is an identified need for more research in the area of instruction for all of these secondary students as well as more instruction based on research (341, 344, 353). The suggestions given here are limited, representing only the tip of the iceberg. If you are interested in the topic or have many students from these groups, consider this as your introduction.

1. Students need quality reading instruction. This appears in the literature dealing with all of our groups (335, 341, 344). This is not a new proposal. Every student needs quality reading instruction.

2. Instruction should be designed to meet the needs of content areas and school demands (335, 344). This is the heart of secondary reading for all students.

3. In working with linguistically different students, an eclectic approach before, during and after reading seems useful. Keen (352) found that an emphasis on discourse analysis and text cohesion enables students to read different kinds of text. Andersson and Barnitz (339) in looking at culturally different students also suggest strategies before, during and after reading which particularly stress vocabulary development and activating and building prior information. These are certainly similar to suggestions made for other students.

4. In speaking of learning disabled students Deshler et al. (344) stated that "our data would suggest, or at least fail to contradict, the proposition that similar interventions would be appropriate for both school-defined LD students and low-achieving students" (p. 4). At or above 4th-grade-level-skill students need to learn how to learn, including such skills as problem solving, comprehension monitoring, and self-questioning. Does this sound familiar? Below 4th grade level, students need a combination of by-passing skill deficits (using tapes for example) and intensive basic skill instruction.

5. Gifted students need a range of subject matter and materials in order to apply advanced reading skills (357, 361). Also true of non-gifted! Bates (341) suggests building on the characteristics of the gifted, such as their internal locus of control, their ability to handle ambiguity, and their preference for discussion rather than lectures by using strategies such as student construction of study guides and the ReQuest procedure. The aim of secondary reading programs must be to enable students to reach toward these goals and to use these strategies as they are able, gifted or not.

The bias of this book is that these students, although they fall into specific groups that we identify in schools as having special needs, really have the same wide diversity of problems, needs, and strengths as the "average" student does. In presenting guidelines for instruction for culturally different students, Andersson and Barnitz (339) remind us that "these guidelines are also relevant to teaching content materials to any students" (pp. 105-106). All students require the same kind of quality, effective reading instruction using content materials and emphasizing skills and strategies needed to meet the demands of secondary schools.

This instruction can be provided in a variety of settings. Some students will probably require individual or small group remedial instruction, at least for some period of time. This might be decoding help or assistance in acquiring basic language skills. The reading teacher can work with other specialists, such as the ESL teacher or the LD teacher, to insure there is quality reading instruction. Other students can have their needs met in the content classroom which incorporates reading instruction, possibly with some supplementary help. Perhaps there is an identified need for a mini-course. Be prepared to offer it. The key here is flexibility with a focus on reading as a meaning-gathering activity, on expanding and extending all students' skills and on the use of thinking/processing/learning strategies for all students.

Summary

We have come full cycle. We began this book by discussing reading theory, then we looked at specific strategies for different units of written text. Finally, we have looked at programs. The common elements in all of this have been concept development, thinking, interacting actively with the text. By now, you can add many items to this list. It appears that in order to provide everything that is needed, secondary schools must look to a comprehensive reading program for all students.

BIBLIOGRAPHY

Books

317. Badiali, Bernard J. "Reading in the Content Area of Music."
      READING IN THE CONTENT AREAS: RESEARCH FOR TEACHERS. Edited
      by Mary M. Dupuis. Newark, Delaware: International Reading
      Assn., 1984, pp. 42-47.

      Badiali cites the "comparative scarcity of research linking
      reading music" (p. 42) and concludes that although there is a
      difference of opinion about the impact of linking the two
      areas, he supports the notion that "one can facilitate the
      other" (p. 45). He provides an analysis of how some music
      abilities   can help reading abilities and discusses a few
      strategies teachers can use.

318. Badiali, Bernard J. "Reading in the Content Area of Physical
      Education and Health." READING IN THE CONTENT AREAS: RESEARCH
      FOR TEACHERS.   Edited by Mary M. Dupuis. Newark, Delaware:
      International Reading Assn., 1984, pp. 48-53.

      Citing the fact that there has not been a great deal of
      research in this area, the author recognizes the motivational
      value of using these areas in the teaching of reading skills.
      Suggestions are made for relevant skills and strategies for
      teaching them.

319. Berryhill, Philip. "Reading in the Content Area of Social
      Studies."   READING IN THE CONTENT AREAS: RESEARCH FOR
      TEACHERS. Edited by Mary M. Dupuis.   Newark, Delaware:
      International Reading Assn., 1984, pp. 66-81.

      Berryhill recognizes the importance and complexity of
      reading in social studies. He reviews relevant research and
      gives suggestions and specifics for skills and strategies for
      teaching those skills. He outlines ways reading and content
      teachers can cooperate in the task of incorporating reading
      into social studies classrooms. The bibliography includes a
      variety of sources both from the field of reading and from the
      field of social studies.

320. Carlson, John E.   "Reading in the Content Area of Foreign
      Language." READING IN THE CONTENT AREAS: RESEARCH FOR
      TEACHERS.   Edited by Mary M. Dupuis. Newark, Delaware:
      International Reading Assn., 1984, pp. 21-27.

      Carlson identifies difficulties students have in making the
      transition from learning to read to reading to learn in a
      foreign language. He advocates, among other things, that
      readers read for global meaning, and that reading assume its
      place in a total language program. Specific suggestions are
      made and a relevant bibliography is included.

321. Cleary, Donna McKee. THINKING THURSDAYS: LANGUAGE ARTS IN THE READING LAB. Newark, Delaware: International Reading Assn., 1978.

Cleary describes how she started a reading lab and engaged students in its activities. The particular contribution of this book is the wealth of practical activities with detailed descriptions and student reactions all centered on "what reading and learning is really all about: THINKING" (p. 5). The book is written with a teacher's point of view and with a teacher's eye to what is practical, moves quickly, and is skill and strategy oriented. Often, the tie-in to content materials is implied not stated. The experienced reader will usually be able to make the transfer.

322. Early, Margaret, and Diane J. Sawyer. "Remedial Reading and Other 'Special Help.'" READING TO LEARN IN GRADES 5 TO 12. New York: Harcourt Brace Jovanovich, 1984, pp. 212-240.

The authors address the problems of the seriously disabled secondary reader in terms of possible settings, attitudes toward these students, and skills to be taught and materials to use. The suggestions are made within a framework of a content area reading program.

323. Early, Margaret, and Diane J. Sawyer. "Responding to Imaginative Writing." READING TO LEARN IN GRADES 5 TO 12. New York: Harcourt Brace Jovanovich, 1984, pp. 436-464.

Early and Sawyer examine the differences between literature and expository text and conclude that these differences require some different approaches on the part of the teacher and the student. The discussion is useful and informative, including such topics as inferencing, questioning, using and developing study guides, and written responses to literature.

324. Early, Margaret, and Diane J. Sawyer. "The School Setting." READING TO LEARN IN GRADES 5 TO 12. New York: Harcourt Brace Jovanovich, 1984, pp. 105-136.

Early and Sawyer provide a comprehensive overview of reading program that provides for all students--remedial, corrective, developmental and content reading. Staff functions and responsibilities are identified; course offerings are suggested; needed staff development is outlined.

325. Fishel, Carol T. "Reading in the Content Area of English." READING IN THE CONTENT AREAS: RESEARCH FOR TEACHERS. Edited by Mary M. Dupuis. Newark, Delaware: International Reading Assn., 1984, pp. 5-20.

Fishel examines the broad range of reading demands in expository and narrative materials in the area of English, discusses related research, and identifies skills and strategies needed by students. She includes a particularly useful bibliography.

326. Friedman, Myles I., and Michael D. Rowls. "Desired Learning Outcomes in the Content Areas." "Problems in Reading Content Materials." "The Organization of Content in the Content Areas." TEACHING READING AND THINKING SKILLS. New York: Longman, 1980, pp. 407-427, 452-512.

Friedman and Rowls examine four major content areas (English, social studies, science and mathematics) from the perspective of curriculum objectives, particular reading demands and problems of each area, strategies for teaching and making assignments and the organization of content and of textbooks with related thinking skills. They look at content-specific skills and strategies as well as some generic ones.

327. Gentile, Lance M. USING SPORTS AND PHYSICAL EDUCATION TO STRENGTHEN READING SKILLS. Newark, Delaware: International Reading Assn., 1980.

This book contains a wealth of practical suggestions for incorporating reading into an area that is usually considered as having little to do with reading. The focus of the book is on reading skills, but many of the activities can be adapted to include strategies. Gentile clearly recognizes the motivation inherent in sports and physical education and capitalizes on that in developing suggestions for reading activities.

328. Herber, Harold L., and Joan Nelson-Herber. "Planning the Reading Program." BECOMING READERS IN A COMPLEX SOCIETY. Eighty-third Yearbook of the National Society for the Study of Education, Part 1. Edited by Alan C. Purves and Olive Niles. Chicago, Illinois: The University of Chicago Press, 1984, pp. 174-208.

The authors acknowledge the need for remedial, corrective and developmental reading programs but only in the larger context of a content-area reading program. Global processes, which might include vocabulary strategies, prediction and anticipation of meaning, and organizational patterns, should be emphasized in all classes with special classes backing up the content classrooms and filling in gaps for some students. Herber and Nelson-Herber recognize the political and financial constraints on reading programs but suggest that eventually fewer students would need special help. They propose a program of inservice training to involve the teachers, based on volunteerism, continuity in training and materials used, and professional interaction with teachers eventually training teachers.

329. Lamberg, Walter J., and Charles E. Lamb. "Teaching Reading in the Content Areas." READING INSTRUCTION IN THE CONTENT AREAS. Chicago: Rand McNally, 1980, pp. 199-294.

In this section of their book, Lamberg and Lamb examine the special reading demands of each of the curriculum areas found in secondary schools. They present alternative strategies and sample lessons for content teachers.

330. Moore, David W., John E. Readence, and Robert J. Rickelman. "Readiness to Read in Content Areas." PREREADING ACTIVITIES FOR CONTENT AREA READING AND LEARNING. Newark, Delaware: International Reading Assn., 1982, pp. 1-12.

Moore, Readence and Rickelman have identified readiness for content reading as including "adequate prior knowledge, appropriate reading strategies, and control of that knowledge and those strategies to satisfy their reasons for reading" (p. 2). They discuss in some detail the characteristics of students that must be taken into account in planning lessons. These include: motivation, content knowledge, word knowledge, learning strategies, and attention. The framework is applicable to any content area.

331. Nolan, James F. "Reading in the Content Area of Mathematics." READING IN THE CONTENT AREAS: RESEARCH FOR TEACHERS. Edited by Mary M. Dupuis. Newark, Delaware: International Reading Assn., 1984, pp. 28-41.

Nolan discusses the difficulties of mathematics texts, reviews research and offers useful suggestions and guidance in relevant skills and strategies. In addition, he looks at assessing readability of materials and matching text to student. A number of useful sources are included in the bibliography.

332. Palmer, Barbara C., and Virginia M. Brannock. "Specialized Services." SECONDARY SCHOOL READING: WHAT RESEARCH REVEALS FOR CLASSROOM PRACTICE. Edited by Alan Berger and H. Alan Robinson. Urbana, Illinois: ERIC Clearinghouse on Reading and Communication Skills and the National Conference on Research in English, 1982, pp. 159-171.

Palmer and Brannock review the limited research available on the short-term and long-term effects of secondary remedial programs and draw some tentative conclusions about what makes programs successful. Short-term, skills-centered approaches do not appear to make a difference in reading achievement. Instead, the focus needs to be on a holistic language approach which is based in the content areas and involves parents and the community.

333. Robinson, H. Alan, and Kathleen Schatsberg. "The Development of Effective Teaching." BECOMING READERS IN A COMPLEX SOCIETY. Eighty-third Yearbook of the National Society for the Study of Education, Part 1. Edited by Alan C. Purves and Olive Niles. Chicago, Illinois: The University of Chicago Press, 1984, pp. 233-270.

Robinson and Schatsberg review a wide variety of reading strategies that are appropriate for all content areas and that can be used before, during and after reading. These include strategies such as: developing and activating schema, prediction, SQ3R, brainstorming, structured overviews, metalinguistics, role modeling, metacognition, postorganizers, and questioning. In addition, they propose the use of integrating activities such as the ConStruct procedure and PReP as well as semantic organizers such as maps and networks.

334. Roe, Betty D., Barbara D. Stoodt, and Paul C. Burns. "The Demands and Common Elements of Content Reading." "Reading in the Content Areas: Part 1." "Reading in the Content Areas: Part 2." SECONDARY SCHOOL READING INSTRUCTION: THE CONTENT AREAS. Boston: Houghton Mifflin, 1983, pp. 157-270.

In the first of these three chapters, the authors compare expository and narrative writing and examine the demands made on the reader by content text. In the latter two chapters, Roe, Stoodt and Burns examine the specific reading and content demands of eleven subjects commonly taught in high schools. They also look at general reading skills related to content teaching. The authors present study guides, process guides and concept guides for each area. Particular emphasis is placed on organization patterns. Ample illustrations are given, making it easy to transfer ideas to content classrooms.

335. Sims, Rudine. "Dialect and Reading: Toward Redefining the Issues." READER MEETS AUTHOR/BRIDGING THE GAP. Edited by Judith A. Langer and M. Trika Smith-Burke. Newark, Delaware: International Reading Assn., 1982, pp. 222-236.

Sims states her position clearly at the beginning of the chapter: "It is the premise of this paper that speaking black dialect (or any dialect of American English) does not, in and of itself, interfere with learning to read (i.e., comprehend) written American English" (p. 222). She reviews research, generally done with young students, and finds that although the research is not conclusive, it gives evidence that the students failed to learn to read from some cause other than the difference in dialect. Her suggestions to teachers deal with recognizing and appreciating the differences in dialect, respecting students, and providing quality reading instruction to all students.

336. Singer, Harry, and Dan Donlan. "English." "Social Studies." "Science." "Mathematics." READING AND LEARNING FROM TEXT. Boston: Little, Brown, 1980, pp. 259-380.

In each of these chapters, the authors look at the content curriculum and the specific demands each makes on the reader. Particular emphasis is placed on the processes involved in each discipline. Instructional strategies are provided that move from teacher directed to student directed. A useful feature is the discussion of both single-text and multiple-text strategies. Many detailed suggestions and examples are provided.

337. Tonjes, Marian J., and Miles V. Zintz. "Identifying Writing Patterns and Content-Specific Skills." TEACHING READING/THINKING/STUDY SKILLS IN CONTENT CLASSROOMS. Dubuque, Iowa: Wm. C. Brown, 1981, pp. 335-355.

The authors examine writing patterns in ten content areas, giving specific examples and suggestions. They also identify reading/thinking/study skills for each area.

338. Weidler, Sarah D. "Reading in the Content Area of Science." READING IN THE CONTENT AREAS: RESEARCH FOR TEACHERS. Edited by Mary M. Dupuis. Newark, Delaware: International Reading Assn., 1984, pp. 54-65.

Weidler describes the scarcity and the diverse focuses of research relating reading and science. She reviews strategies that can be used in science/reading such as advanced organizers, vocabulary development, study guides and process guides. The bibliography is useful for providing specific resources.

Periodicals

339. Andersson, Billie V., and John G. Barnitz. "Cross-Cultural Schemata and Reading Comprehension Instruction." JOURNAL OF READING 28 (November 1984): 102-108.

Andersson and Barnitz review the role of background knowledge in reading in general and then examine research on the effects of cross-cultural schemata in adults and children on reading such as recall, speed, inferences, elaborations, and distortions. A number of suggestions are made to develop reading comprehension in these students by developing relevant background knowledge and vocabulary, and encouraging active thinking and reading. The authors make an important point. The guidelines provided for these students "are also relevant to teaching content area materials to any students" (p. 106). In addition, some culturally different students may need language instruction.

340. Auten, Anne. "High School Reading Labs." JOURNAL OF READING 24 (April 1981): 634-636.

Auten reviews a number of articles describing the organization and evaluation of high school reading labs. This overview does not present details but does give some useful sources for further information.

341. Bates, Gary W. "Developing Reading Strategies for the Gifted: A Research-Based Approach." JOURNAL OF READING 27 (April 1984): 590-593.

Bates reviews studies which identify characteristics of the
gifted student and relates these to reading strategies,
identifying strategies which fit the characteristics and ones
which do not. Characteristics include traits such as:
independence, fluency, tolerance for ambiguity, preference for
independent not group projects, and discussion not lectures,
to name a few. Based on these traits, for example, he does
not advocate the Guided Reading Procedure but rather the
ReQuest Procedure. Other examples are provided.

342. Conley, Mark W., and Peter F. Savage. "What's Really New in
Models of Content Reading?" JOURNAL OF READING 28 (January
1985): 336-341.

Conley and Savage review Peters's Content Processing Model
which emphasizes text dependent skills (traditional reading
skills) and text related skills (in social studies, inquiry
skills such as stating the problem, formulating hypotheses and
developing conclusions). They conclude that other models have
also included text related skills, perhaps using a different
label. Teachers need to develop flexibility in adapting
various models and instructional approaches to their
classrooms. See also Peters (367) and Steinley (371).

343. Crismore, Avon. "An Interactive Model for Secondary Remedial
Reading Classrooms: Turning Reading Labs into Learning
Labs." Paper presented at the Annual Meeting of the Indiana
State Council of the International Reading Assn.
Indianapolis, Indiana, March 26-28, 1981. 39pp. (ED 203
279)

Crismore describes, in some detail, two remedial reading
courses developed for high school students, based on a number
of important assumptions: high-risk students have more
potential than is generally predicted; reading is a meaning-
centered activity involving risk-taking; reading and writing
are related; students learn from direct teaching, modeling and
assuming control; cognitive psychology contributes much to
secondary reading particularly in the form of schema theory,
problem-solving and metacognition. The discussion of
strategies and techniques used is interesting and could
certainly be adapted to a number of situations.

344. Deshler, Donald D., Jean B. Schumaker, Gordon R. Alley,
Michael M. Warner, and Frances L. Clark. "Learning
Disabilities in Adolescent and Young Adult Populations:
Research Implications." FOCUS ON EXCEPTIONAL CHILDREN 15
(September 1982): 1-12.

The authors review the results of research conducted over a
four year period and discuss related educational implications.
They found that LD adolescents are similar to other low
achievers and that both groups can benefit from similar
educational programs. They do not recommend basic skill
instruction for students above a fourth-grade level but rather

suggest a program of learning strategies, including "word identification, paraphrasing, visual imagery, self-questioning, multipass (a strategy for attacking textbook chapters), sentence writing, paragraph organization, error monitoring, and listening and note taking" (p. 9).

345. French, Michael P. "Organizing and Evaluating Secondary Reading Programs." Paper presented at the Annual Meeting of the Wisconsin State Reading Association Spring Conference, Oconomowoc, Wisconsin, March 19-21, 1981. 15pp. (ED 208 347)

French advocates a "balanced" reading program in secondary schools including skill development, recreational and applied reading, and reading to gain information through content. He makes brief suggestions for ways to include these three strands in a program and identifies formal and informal evaluation strategies. His discussion of the function and role of a reading committee in a high school provides some useful insights into a group not found in every secondary school.

346. Gambrell, Linda B., and Craig J. Cleland. "Minimum Competency Testing: Guidelines for Functional Reading Programs." JOURNAL OF READING 25 (January 1982): 342-344.

In order to teach skills identified as deficient in minimum competency tests, schools will need to offer programs in functional reading. Gambrell and Cleland offer general guidelines for setting up a program. They include providing for varying rates of learning, assessing students individually using informal tasks, making programs and materials relevant to students, incorporating problem-solving situations, providing continuous instruction which incorporates content areas, sharing of reading materials and resources and working with parents to apply skills at home.

347. Gold, Patricia Cohen. "The Directed Listening-Language Experience Approach." JOURNAL OF READING 25 (November 1981): 138-141.

Gold gives detailed guidance in using a listening-language experience approach with remedial students. It is designed to teach both content and reading. The teacher establishes a purpose for listening and then reads content material aloud to the students. While students summarize, the teacher guides the discussion and then records their summary.

348. Grano, Vivian, and Claire Ashby-Davis. "Reading Teachers and Content Teachers: A Collaborative Program." JOURNAL OF READING 27 (December 1983): 245-247.

The authors report on a program developed in New York City in which reading teachers and social studies teachers were paired, sharing the same students and using the same materials. They also briefly describe an inservice course.

349. Greenlaw, M. Jean, and David W. Moore. "What Kinds of Reading
     Courses Are Taught in Junior and Senior High School?"
     JOURNAL OF READING 25 (March 1982): 534-536.

     Greenlaw and Moore present the results of a survey done with
     61 schools in 29 states designed to determine the kinds of
     reading courses offered in secondary schools. They found the
     reading course is offered "extensively" as a separate course
     with the majority of courses being remedial. It is
     interesting to note though that a "substantial proportion" of
     the courses were developmental and accelerated.

350. Ince, Elizabeth, and Clyde G. Colwell. "The Manhattan
     Project: Combined Resources for a Diversified Secondary
     Reading Program." Paper presented at the Annual Meeting of
     the International Reading Assn., New Orleans, Louisiana,
     April 27-May 1, 1981. 21pp. (ED 204 723)

     Ince and Colwell provide a complete description of the
     various reading courses offered in the Manhattan Project and
     of the inservice program which formed the basis of the Reading
     in the Content Areas component of the project. They also
     discuss the procedures they intend to use to evaluate the
     program both in terms of students and teachers.

351. Kapinus, Barbara A. "Miniclinics: Small Units of Reading
     Instruction Can Be a Big Help." JOURNAL OF READING 24
     (March 1981): 516-518.

     Kapinus describes miniclinics which were developed to meet
     reading needs identified by both students and content
     teachers.

352. Keen, Dennis. "The Use of Traditional Reading Approaches with
     ESL Students." JOURNAL OF READING 27 (November 1983): 139-
     144.

     Keen cites ESL research which documents the need to
     "introduce discourse analysis, separate oral skills from
     reading skills, and instruct students in the various subskills
     needed to read different types of academic material" (p. 143).
     Based on this, he analyzes Language Experience, phonics and an
     eclectic approach and concludes that the last is the most
     appropriate for advanced ESL students.

353. Knott, Gladys P. "Developing Reading Potential in Black
     Remedial High School Freshmen." READING IMPROVEMENT 16
     (Winter 1979): 262-269.

     In order to address the problem of syntactic differences
     between standard English and non-standard Black English and
     the resulting effect on reading comprehension, Knott proposes
     a program of training in generative transformational grammar

and context clues. This is based on research conducted with two classes of high school freshmen.

354. Kossack, Sharon Wall, and Nicholas Vigilante. "A Proposed Taxonomy of Mathematical Vocabulary." Paper presented at the Annual Meeting of the American Reading Forum, Sarasota, Florida, December 10-12, 1981. 13pp. (ED 219 723)

Kossack and Vigilante propose an interrelated taxonomy of mathematical terms. Words are categorized as standard (common), transitional (both common and mathematical), technical (mathematical), changeable (technical words with changeable meanings), and phrases (groups of words with specialized meanings). The taxonomy can be used for a variety of reasons: instruction, diagnosis, text selection, to name a few.

355. Kresse, Elaine Campbell. "Using Reading as a Thinking Process to Solve Math Story Problems." JOURNAL OF READING 27 (April 1984): 598-601.

Recognizing the importance of having the teacher model a process, Kresse developed a classroom strategy designed to help students read and solve math word problems. The instructional strategy is "a blend of SQ3R and inference awareness, which also relies heavily on visualization" (p. 599). The strategy is clearly presented and could be replicated fairly easily. As the author cautions, it would need to be used repeatedly throughout the year.

356. Lehr, Fran. "New Approaches to Remedial Reading Programs at the Secondary Level." JOURNAL OF READING 24 (January 1981): 350-352.

Lehr reviews four ERIC documents relating to remedial reading programs, including guidelines for developing programs and three specific programs: choosing elective minicourses, improving reading through the arts, and incorporating television into a reading program.

357. Lehr, Fran. "Reading and the Gifted Secondary School Student." JOURNAL OF READING 26 (February 1983): 456-459.

Lehr identifies the need to provide gifted students with activities "to develop their skills in critical analysis and verbal expression, as well as to provide them with an outlet for creativity" (p. 456). Within this framework, she reviews a number of projects that provide this kind of experience, including activities such as Think Boxes or courses which treat topics or authors in depth and require high level thinking skills.

358. Manzo, Anthony V. "Three 'Universal' Strategies in Content Area Reading and Languaging." JOURNAL OF READING 24 (November 1980): 146-149.

The three strategies Manzo proposes are based on three premises: that the teacher should serve as a model of effective reading, that thinking skills should be included in content and reading skills, and that teachers and students need to interact in "oral languaging." The content teacher plays a pivotal role in developing students' reading and thinking skills. The strategies are briefly but clearly explained. The Oral Reading strategy requires students to listen to the teacher read text aloud and then put it into their own words. The C/T/Q/ strategy is a reminder to teachers to identify the concepts, terminology and questions related to a unit of study before beginning. The third strategy, Questions-Only, has students use their own background as the sole source of information on a topic. In addition, Manzo also highlights potential problems with training teachers to use new techniques.

359. McGeehon, Martha B. "Strategies for Improving Textbook Comprehension." JOURNAL OF READING 25 (April 1982): 676-679.

This article describes a course for remedial high school students entitled "Thinking Skills" which McGeehon designed to improve textbook comprehension as well as scores on standardized tests. Enough detail is given to enable a teacher to use this as a starting point in developing a similar course. The course described included instruction in comparing and contrasting, using analogies and text structure, and problem solving.

360. Memory, David M. "Preparing Students in Survival Reading: The Content Area Option." THE CLEARING HOUSE 56 (April 1983): 349-353.

Because of the need for schools to teach students the skills required to pass minimum competency tests, Memory proposes that the logical place to do this is in the content classroom. Some students may still need instruction in these areas in remedial programs, but the basic responsibility lies with the classroom teachers. He provides some suggestions for implementing this proposal as well as specific ideas for instruction and materials.

361. Moller, Barbara W. "An Instructional Model for Gifted Advanced Readers." JOURNAL OF READING 27 (January 1984): 324-327.

Moller cites the need to provide gifted students with exposure "to a range of subject matter and to challenging works in different areas so they they develop and apply advanced reading skills" (p. 324) while at the same time, organizing instruction so that the teacher is not overwhelmed with planning and preparation. She provided guidance in setting such a course which incorporates small group instruction with students assuming responsibility for locating some of the materials to be read.

362. Moore, David W., and John E. Readence. "Approaches to Content
      Area Reading Instruction." JOURNAL OF READING 26 (February
      1983): 397-402.

      The authors examine four approaches to content reading:
      providing isolated skill instruction, aiming at content which
      focuses attention on important text information, guiding
      toward content which identifies both the information and the
      skills necessary to learn it, and presenting skills and
      content concurrently which teaches both the process and the
      product of learning. The discussion is detailed, particularly
      with the last alternative. Modeling a process and then fading
      the guidance given students is well described and can be
      adapted to many situations. Instead of stating that one
      approach is better than the other, the authors conclude that
      because there is no evidence to support such a conclusion, we
      must decide which approach to take based on available
      resources and outcomes desired.

363. Moore, David, W., John E. Readence, and Robert J. Rickelman.
      "An Historical Exploration of Content Area Reading
      Instruction." READING RESEARCH QUARTERLY XVIII (Summer
      1983): 419-438.

      Moore, Readence and Rickelman have given us an interesting,
      enlightening and thorough review of the history of content
      area reading and of the major issues we must address today.
      It provides an invaluable overview of the topic. Much of what
      we see today in content area reading had its roots in the
      early writing of the humanists, developmentalists and
      scientific determinists. The issues raised provide a
      framework for thinking about the topic and planning
      instruction. Who will provide the instruction? Are the
      skills in content reading content-dependent or generic? How
      do we teach study skills? What materials do we use and how do
      we use them? What age student should we include in content
      reading instruction? Research is discussed; theories are
      explored; questions are raised.

364. O'Mara, Deborah A. "The Process of Reading Mathematics."
      JOURNAL OF READING 25 (October 1981): 22-30.

      Based on a review of theoretical and research studies on the
      relationship between reading and mathematics, the author
      presents conclusions about reading ability and math
      achievement, specific reading skills, and readability of
      mathematics. O'Mara clearly identifies the need for further
      research in order to arrive at a definition of reading
      comprehension as it relates to mathematics. Specific
      suggestions are made in regard to the use of an Informal
      Reading Inventory to match reader with word problems and the
      use of the cloze procedure to determine readability of written
      math.

365. Ostertag, Bruce, and Janice M. Schnorr. SECONDARY LD READING
      PRACTICES AND PROCEDURES.   Flagstaff, Arizona: Northern
      Arizona University, 1981. 30pp. (ED 204 986)

      The authors conducted a survey of 138 secondary LD teachers
      to identify the practices and procedures being used in
      schools. They found that larger programs do not always
      provide for reading instruction as part of the LD program,
      individual instruction is common, basal readers and reading
      kits are frequently used and that comprehension is stressed.
      Diagnostic batteries commonly include the Wide Range
      Achievement Test, the Woodcock Reading Mastery Test and the
      Peabody Individual Achievement Test.

366. PERFORMANCE OF HISPANIC STUDENTS IN TWO NATIONAL ASSESSMENTS
      OF READING.   National Assessment of Educational Progress.
      Denver, Colorado: Education Commission of the States, June
      1982. 16pp. (ED 217 397)

      This report compares the performance of Hispanic students on
      the 1974-75 assessment and the 1979-80 assessment. In all age
      groups Hispanic students performed below the national average
      although 9-year-olds improved 5.3% compared to 2.6%
      improvement for all 9-year-olds and city students in the other
      two age groups showed improvement, 13-year-olds in literal
      comprehension and 17-year-olds in inferential comprehension.
      The report identifies the questions associated with the sample
      used.

367. Peters, Charles W.   "The Content Processing Model: A New
      Approach to Conceptualizing Content Reading."   RESEARCH ON
      READING IN SECONDARY SCHOOLS 12 & 13 (Fall-Spring 1984): 1-
      15.

      Peters proposes a model of content reading that includes the
      traditional reading skills and also includes skills related to
      the conceptual approach of the particular discipline.   This
      article reviews the traditional approach taken in a number of
      textbooks on content reading, identifies the specifics of his
      approach with flowcharts and a discussion of social studies
      text, and reviews relevant research. The article is thought
      provoking, particularly for secondary teachers.   See also
      Conley and Savage (342) and Steinley (371).

368. Powers, Walter L., Michael C. McKenna, and John W. Miller.
      "Content Area Reading: A Modular Approach."   READING
      HORIZONS 23 (Spring 1983): 175-178.

      The authors describe an approach designed to aid content
      teachers in developing and using content area reading
      strategies. Subject teachers work together to develop modules
      in vocabulary, comprehension and study skills to accompany the
      subject textbook.

369. Readence, John E., R. Scott Baldwin, and Ernest K. Dishner.

"Establishing Content Reading Programs in Secondary Schools." JOURNAL OF READING 23 (March 1980): 522-526.

The authors provide a framework for reading teachers to use when working with content teachers. Reading teachers must come out of the "closet" and work as resource people for content teachers in teaching reading-related skills at appropriate times in content courses. The framework includes five developmental stages: awareness of the variables involved in content reading, knowledge of specific teaching strategies, simulation of the strategies, practice using them in content classrooms and incorporation of them into daily teaching. Examples for each stage are provided. A short self-report form for the effectiveness of specific strategies is included.

370. Sandberg, Kate. "Learning to Read History Actively." JOURNAL OF READING 25 (November 1981): 158-160.

The author proposes seven questions to be used before, during and after reading historical expository material. Enough detail is provided so that the questions can be presented to students and used with many texts. The goal is to enable students to read independently. The questions also require that they read critically.

371. Steinley, Gary. "In the Works: A New Model of Content Reading?" JOURNAL OF READING 27 (December 1983): 238-244.

Steinley examines one of the major issues we must address in developing a model of content reading. Are there "specific processing demands of different approaches and content areas" (p. 244)? Are there "significant skills of the reading process" (ibid.)? Who needs to be involved in developing a model of content reading? Reading specialists? Content specialists? Both? He reviews Peters's Content Processing Model and the questions he raises are ones which must concern us all, not just the reading theorists and the researchers. See also Conley and Savage (342) and Peters (367).

372. Swenarton, Eva, and Judith White. "Project READ, Secondary Reading." Paper presented at the Annual Meeting of the Michigan Reading Association, Grand Rapids, Michigan, March 8-10, 1981. 35pp. (ED 208 344)

Swenarton and White describe a high school reading project predicated on the belief that there are common content related reading skills that can be taught and reinforced in all the content areas. These include: "(1) perceiving relationships between ideas, (2) recognizing main ideas, (3) discovering cause and effect relationships, (4) perceiving comparative and contrastive relationships, (5) arranging information in its proper sequence, and (6) developing problem solving techniques" (p. 3). They detail a three-year training program involving consultants, content teachers and reading specialists and include specific lessons illustrating comparative and contrastive relationships.

373. Tixier y Vigil, Yvonne, and James Dick.   "Problems and
     Suggestions for Improving the Reading of Textbooks: A Social
     Studies   Focus."   THE   HIGH   SCHOOL   JOURNAL   67
     (December/January 1984): 116-121.

     The authors present detailed examples on helping students
     read social studies text books by dealing with problems of
     writing patterns, vocabulary and study skills.

374. Wilhite, Robert K. "Principals' Views of Their Role in the
     High School Reading Program."   JOURNAL OF READING 27
     (January 1984): 356-358.

     This article reports on a study conducted to identify
     principals' perceptions of their role in reading programs.
     The principals reported that they were involved in
     administrative, operational and public relation aspects of
     reading programs.   They were not involved in the daily
     operation of programs or the selection of equipment and
     materials.   The authors conclude that secondary principals are
     powerful decision-makers and, if reading instruction is to be
     effective, principals must be committed to it.

CHAPTER X

THE PROFESSIONALS

Programs, defined on paper, written up and elaborated in memos and directives, and discussed at Board of Education meetings, will not by themselves result in improved reading and study skills abilities of students. Teachers play a key role in the effectiveness of programs. In fact, many would say that teachers are the crucial element in the equation. Wade (409), for example, in reviewing research dealing with reading and social studies, found that teacher attitude, ability, and involvement were the critical elements in achieving improvement. The instructional design and strategies used were not as consistently important as the teacher. With this in mind, let's look at how to make programs work and how to evaluate to make sure they did work.

Making the Programs Work

The Roles of the Reading Teacher

All of us have a vision of a secondary reading program we remember or have seen. Miss Jones is closeted in a little room next to the boiler preparing endless worksheets, organizing shelves of workbooks and exhorting students in remedial classes to "find the main idea." When she doesn't have anything else to do, she is "diagnosing" (an awe-inspiring word!) and/or filling out forms.

Actually, this vision is fairly close to reality. Recent surveys indicate that teaching reading courses and diagnosing reading problems are still the ways most reading teachers spend their time (375, 400). However, questions are being raised about the role of the reading teacher. Because this particular teacher's skills cross departmental lines, there appear to be opportunities for wider contributions to the education of students beyond working with relatively few students each day. In many schools, according to Bean and Wilson (375), there are too many students for the reading teacher to work with effectively. In order to reach more students and to insure that there is transfer of instruction to the content classroom, the reading teacher must begin to consider assuming a role with different dimensions.

219

Consider these suggestions. The reading teacher should function as:

1. a reading teacher and diagnostician. This is the traditional role and one that will undoubtedly continue. The question is not whether to eliminate this but rather what proportion of time should be spent in this aspect of the position. (328)

2. a resource person. The reading teacher's specialized training and background provide a foundation for working with content teachers on skills and strategies of comprehending and studying. This can add an important dimension to the content classroom and can help insure transfer and reinforcement of skills taught in the reading center. (328, 375, 402)

3. an inservice leader. The reading teacher can play a critical role in schools by planning, organizing, conducting and evaluating inservice programs. (328)

4. a change agent, an instructional leader. These roles go beyond talking about reading in the teachers' room and planning some workshops. They suggest that the reading teacher is a person with a broad view of the school, of students, and of curriculum, as well a professional with the commitment and skills to affect change and assume leadership. (369, 399, 402)

What qualities does the reading teacher need to fulfill these roles? Readence, Baldwin and Dishner (369) suggest "tact, perseverance, and a sound game plan" (p. 523). It's hard to argue with that. We might add, a sense of humor. Shannon uses the word "diplomat" (402, p. 57) and cites the need to demonstrate credibility as a teacher. Bean and Wilson (375) have provided a rather complete list. A reading teacher needs to understand and be able to work in an organization, have good interpersonal and communication skills, assume leadership roles and develop them in others, use appropriate decision-making processes, use self-evaluation techniques and know the legal rights of students and teachers.

We are, admittedly, looking at what are emerging possibilities, with some schools and some teachers farther along this road than others. This is an area where schools need a common set of priorities with principals and teachers agreeing on the roles of the reading teacher. Mangieri and Heimberger (400) found in their study that principals and reading teachers did not have this common set of priorities. Reading teachers put instructor and diagnostician at the bottom of a list of jobs they should be doing and put inservice leader and resource person at the top. Principals reversed the desired roles, in effect maintaining the status quo.

These are general roles. What are some of specific tasks that reading teachers need to address in working with individual students and in working with content teachers? This list is not meant to be exhaustive. It deals with the tasks that connect the reading teacher to the larger institution, rather than those tasks such as record keeping and management systems that maintain the reading center.

1. Organize a school-wide reading committee. This is useful for encouraging good working relationships between reading and content teachers. It allows for interchange of ideas and can be a vehicle for staff development and program evaluation. (203, 345, 384, 402)

2. Schedule classes in the reading center and with the content teachers. Consider a variety of alternatives, choosing the one (ones) that best serve your school. Don't settle for the same old schedule. There are a variety of possibilities here.

   All students needing remedial help are assigned to a reading class. This may be divided into blocks so students can have individual time with the reading teacher. (394, 410)

   The reading and content teachers team teach the class together or alternate classes. (404, 410)

   The reading lab and content class are offered back to back with the same group attending both classes. (410)

   The content class as a whole attends the reading lab once a week. (410)

   There is a working relationship between teachers with limited cooperation. The reading teacher teaches a strategy or a unit either in the content class or the reading class. The content teacher provides reinforcement and practice. (410)

3. Work with content teachers in developing flexibility in groups, teaching strategies and use of materials, and in developing skill in planning lessons which integrate reading into content areas. (379, 382)

4. Maintain a file of professional materials, particularly journal articles, which is available to the faculty. (350)

5. Develop competency in using paraprofessionals. Provide inservice training for them, include them in the training developed for teachers, insure that they have opportunities to interact with other educators and parents. (395)

6. Plan and coordinate teacher research. This is an area teachers feel they don't understand, haven't time for, and nobody will listen to them anyway. Take some courses. Work with someone from your local college. Read the journals for teacher-conducted research and see how various authors did it. (324)

7. Give a demonstration lesson to parents or the Board of Education involving them in the act of reading and writing. Be an advocate for your program and the school by showing others what students are doing and what is involved. You might also make a

videotape of students interacting with teachers and responding
to text. (372, 406)

Staff Development in Teaching Content Reading

The area of staff development assumes critical proportions when
you combine the lack of training most content teachers have had with
the need to incorporate some instruction in reading in content
classrooms. We will examine a number of aspects of staff
development: requirements for success, planning a program,
conducting workshops, implementation in classrooms, and measuring
success.   Staff development must result in classroom teachers'
ownership of the program (402), mastery of newly acquired skills and
strategies to the point where they are automatic (369), and transfer
of skills and strategies to the classroom (397).

Requirements for success.

1. Administrative support. Have you heard this before?   This
   requires more than lip service. It requires more than funding.
   Shanker (378) believes that "the importance of active
   participation by the school principal cannot be overemphasized"
   (p. 7). Anyone who has given or attended an inservice workshop
   and watched the reactions of teachers when the principal walks
   in, says this is really important and then walks out, knows what
   Shanker means. (378, 393)

2. Time. We can present a well-planned workshop, provide handouts
   and a reading list and leave confident that behavior will change
   and new strategies will be implemented. Right? Wrong! Joyce
   and Showers (397) assert that "to the extent that we have
   communicated this message to teachers, we have probably misled
   them" (p. 9). Estimates of the time needed for effective staff
   development programs vary. Ince and Colwell (350) based their
   program on three hours a week for 30 weeks.   Others suggest
   three to five years (328, 372, 393). In any event, we cannot
   rely on one or two workshop sessions to meet all training needs.

3. Involvement of classroom teachers in the planning, execution and
   implementation of any inservice program. Content teachers need
   to be involved in assessing needs and establishing priorities.
   You can't work on everything at once, so you need to identify
   what is important to the teachers. (393, 402, 409)

   Getting started with staff development.   There are choices
here. All programs do not start the same way, with a mandate from
the superintendent's office instructing all teachers to participate.
In planning, think about these alternatives.

1. Begin with a few teachers who have identified a need and who are
   receptive to learning about content reading. Teachers can start
   the process and demonstrate to the administration that there is
   a need. (369)

2. Gradually phase in new groups of teachers as the current

teachers become competent. If possible, use teachers to teach teachers. (328, 372)

3. Begin with volunteers even if the program is started by administrative fiat. (328, 372, 378)

4. Require that all teachers participate. The other side of the coin is that if the program is important and it is a school goal, then all teachers should be part of it. (378)

5. Consider offering an incentive to participate, such as a stipend, released time, inservice credits. (378)

6. Conduct a needs assessment to determine what the priorities are and what the faculty strengths and weaknesses are. (378, 380, 407)

   Presenting workshops. There are a number of approaches to designing the format of workshops, but they seem to differ more in detail than in substance. Most sources give suggestions for presenting a workshop within the larger framework of a staff development program. The following references can provide you with very helpful details: Gove (393), Ince and Colwell (350), Joyce and Showers (397), Readence, Baldwin and Dishner (369), Shannon (402, 403), Swenarton and White (372), and J. Vacca (380, 408). The inservice program can take a variety of formats. Offer one workshop on a specific topic. Offer a series of meetings on a broader topic (372), with teachers receiving local, inservice credit for them. Involve a local college and plan a course that teachers can use for graduate credit (348, 350, 389).

   Generally activities in workshops should cover three areas.

1. Awareness of content reading and the processes, skills and strategies involved.

2. Demonstration of the skill or strategy. This can be done by the reading teacher, an outside consultant, or a content teacher who has developed expertise in the topic. The connection to content reading should be made clear.

3. Practice. Within the framework of a single workshop this might involve teachers developing lessons related to their content areas and/or presenting lessons to small groups. These activities might also take place in a subsequent workshop. Practice can also take place within the teacher's own classroom.

   Carefully consider alternatives in deciding on presenters at the workshops. Outside "experts" can help defuse a situation when teachers may be resentful of having to attend the workshop. Someone from outside often has a special mystique--it's hard to be a prophet in your own land. Outsiders do need to understand the school and its needs and be prepared to follow-up if necessary (378). There are times though when local talent has expertise and can and should share it. You may want to combine the two, with the outsider leading off and the insider providing practice sessions or following up in the classroom.

Workshop leaders need expertise; they also need a number of other qualities.   J. Vacca (408) polled teachers and identified a number of characteristics in the areas of content delivery, personal influence, professional competence and arrangements that seemed important for effective staff development.

Topics for workshops. There is no need to rediscover the wheel here.   Many of the sources already discussed in this book will give you formats, ideas and materials for many workshop topics.

One set of topics might be concerned with skills and strategies for students and teachers. The following list will provide you with a starting point for activities but be sure to check the source for information on waiver of copyright or on how to obtain permission to use the material.

1. Understanding the reading process. (9, 45)

2. Examining the affective dimension in reading. (11)

3. Assessing yourself as a mature reader. (11)

4. Self-rating of the teacher as motivator. (229)

5. Identifying teacher attitudes toward reading instruction in content classrooms. (11, 27)

6. Comprehension tasks and their application in content classrooms. (398)

7. Comprehending at different levels and using background knowledge. (130)

8. Restructuring schemata. (136)

9. Identifying text structure. (88)

10. Summarizing. (136)

11. Developing questions. (411)

12. Varying rate and flexibility. (186)

13. Designing lessons based on a strategy or process approach. (150, 389)

14. Selecting texts. (388)

15. Using computers in reading instruction. (304, 307)

A second set of topics might be instructional techniques for teachers to use in providing reading and content instruction. This list could include:

1. Providing instruction before, during and after reading. Almost every topic has included a reference to this, but particularly review the material in Chapter IV on thinking.

2. Demonstrating. You identify a skill or strategy, explain the process and show how to use it. This involves direct instruction. For example, you might show students how to identify text structure (see Chapter III) or how to answer an inference question based on Raphael's (166) model (see Chapter IV). Much of what we do is demonstration (401).

3. Modeling. Modeling goes a step farther. You describe orally what's going on in your head while you are working through the process you are demonstrating. This has been recommended in a number of situations, such as formulating and evaluating hypotheses and understanding the process of reading. Modeling can also be done in a written form such as glossing. Chapter IV in particular includes a number of references to modeling. Also check the subject index under Modeling.

4. Providing for simulation. Moore and Readence (362) define this as giving students certain rules for learning from text. The rules for summarizing developed by Brown, Campione and Day (13) are an example of this (also see Chapter V).

5. "Fading." The goal in instruction is to enable the student to be an effective, independent learner. Fading is the process by which "teachers first present students clear guidance in studying text but then gradually diminish guidance until students assume responsibility for their own learning" (362, p. 400). The discussion of questioning strategies in Chapter IV is an example of this.

6. Encouraging students to debrief. In this procedure, Moore and Readence (362) suggest the importance of student introspection and review of processes used and difficulties encountered. Instruction in metacognition, for example, entails this (see Chapter IV).

7. Allowing for interaction. Interaction between teacher and students and between students and other students provides a way of clarifying and verifying strategies and outcomes (401). Sentence comprehension provides an example of the usefulness of interaction (see Chapter II). The Anticipation Guide for activating and using prior knowledge (see Chapter IV) is a specific example of the use of interaction.

8. Providing opportunities for students to practice in a variety of ways with a variety of materials. Consider, for example the discussions of text structure and critical reading in Chapter III, reading rate in Chapter V and motivation in Chapter VI.

9. Teaching a variety of strategies, so students can apply different ones in different situations. Reading words and understanding words both provide examples of the importance of this (see Chapter II).

10. Teaching for transfer. The importance of this has also been stressed repeatedly. See, for example, the discussion of text structure in Chapter III.

11. Developing an atmosphere that encourages risk-taking. Reading involves risk-taking. Chapter IV, in particular, highlights the importance of this for students. Also see the Subject Index.

None of these suggestions should be limited to the examples given. They all have a wide application to many of the topics discussed in this book. Obviously, the two sets of topics can be effectively combined, but the participants should be aware of this.

Implementation in classrooms. This is where staff development programs may fail. One of the problems seems to be that content teachers get back in their classrooms and aren't sure what to do or aren't sure they're doing it effectively. In fact, in trying to change behavior and add a new item to their teaching repertoire, teachers may have very legitimate problems (368, 397). There are a variety of ways to insure implementation on the part of the content teachers. Consider these possibilities.

1. Demonstration in the classroom. The workshop leader can teach one or more lessons in the classroom, interacting with students and using the required text and content. The approach is no longer removed or theoretical. It's on the firing line. (369, 393)

2. The reading teacher or workshop leader as observer. The specialist can provide "honest feedback" with discussion not evaluation as the goal, according to Lindsey and Runquist (399, p. 48). (348, 350, 399)

3. A team approach. Pair the content teacher with a reading teacher, another content teacher or an outside person, possibly from a university. Planning can be done together and teaching responsibilities for the strategies can be shared and discussed together. This approach has some similarities to the first two alternatives but goes farther. (348, 368, 372, 397, 402, 405)

4. The Reading Committee. The committee can begin to assume responsibility for implementation, putting ownership with the teachers. Each academic department might have a reading leader. (203, 345, 384, 402)

5. Reinforcement by the total school. Programs are often set up so that the total school is working on the same skills and strategies. The teachers as well as the students get reinforcement from this. Teachers see others implementing the same things and can discuss and get feedback from each other.

(372)

6. Division of labor. Another way to implement is not to have every department use every strategy. Instead, each department chooses the ones that seem most appropriate for the content and the easiest for the teachers to implement. Teachers may not be as overwhelmed by this approach. (402)

7. Shared modules or ideas for lessons for each department. Teachers may not have the time or the creativity to construct each lesson incorporating the learned skills and strategies from the beginning. Start a file that they can draw on. (368, 372)

8. Checklists of skills and strategies developed in workshops. These can remind the content teacher of possibilities and when and how to use them. (405)

<u>Measuring the effectiveness of staff development.</u>

1. Use an evaluation form immediately after a workshop for participants to identify what was helpful, what wasn't and to evaluate the presentation and any audio-visual aids used. (378, 380)

2. Teach a strategy to one class and not another. Then evaluate the ease of planning and the effectiveness of using what was learned in the staff development session. (369)

3. Develop or adapt a checklist based on items included in the staff development program in order to determine whether teachers are actually using them in the classroom. The evaluation might be a self-evaluation or one done by someone from the staff development program or the school administration. (18, 369, 403)

<u>Selecting Textbooks</u>

As we have seen in a number of different contexts, the question of the difficulty and appropriateness of textbooks for particular students is a critical one. In selecting texts we must consider the level of difficulty in order to match students and text and in order to plan appropriate instruction no matter what text is used (388). We are not advocating that students read only easy books. They need books of varying degrees of difficulty in order to understand content but also be challenged to use new and more advanced skills (391). This approach, though, places additional responsibility on teachers. As R. Vacca (381) suggests, teachers, in using varied textbooks, need to understand the demands of the book in order to prepare lessons that will not frustrate, but rather will teach students. This requires careful analysis and selection of texts. Text selection is a crucial area in which reading teacher and content teacher can work together.

A traditional way of analyzing textbooks is to use a readability formula to determine the reading level of the book. Let's consider some aspects of readability formulas. First, what do they measure?

Formulas measure "only things that can be counted" (274, p. 696). This generally means the number of words not on a list of common vocabulary and/or the number of syllables in words, and the number of words in sentences (274, 282, 381, 387, 390, 391).

The charge has been made that readability formulas "ignore or violate much of current knowledge about reading and the reading process" (387, p. 1). Since we put so much stock in the concept of readability levels, this is a serious matter. Much of the concern is centered in two areas: text comprehensibility and the characteristics of the reader.

Because of the way they are constructed, readability formulas do not take into account characteristics related to text comprehensibility (282, 387, 388, 390, 391). This includes items such as cohesion, density of ideas, sentence construction, text construction, the number and sources of inferences required, and the content load. Because of this Samuels (282) asserts that "texts having the same readability levels may vary widely in the degree to which they can be comprehended" (p. 262).

The formulas also do not take into account the characteristics of the reader (282, 387, 390). Does his background fit the requirements of the text? Does he speak a dialect that does not match that in the text? In what context is he reading the text? "You have five minutes to read the next four pages, then I'll give you a test on it which will count for one-half your grade" is a very different context from "I think you'll enjoy the next four pages. Take your time and then we'll discuss them." Is the reader motivated to read? Is he interested in the topic and the task? What is his purpose in reading? R. Vacca (381) suggests that the omission of the reader from the formula "is one of the reasons why you should approach readability formulas with a healthy skepticism" (p. 270).

A further problem that is raised concerns the statistical basis of formulas (387, 390, 391). Many of them are based on McCall-Crabbs Standard Test Lessons in Reading, yet the lessons were not designed for this function and "are dated in regard to both materials and norms" (390, p. 12). Criticisms have been made about the samples used, the validity and the predictability of formulas. Dreyer (391) states the problem clearly. "The use of the word formula carries unfounded scientific implications" (p. 335).

There is also a question about the number of text samples needed to compute the readability level. Most formulas recommend three. Yet, there can be wide variation in levels within one textbook (391, 392). In looking at the Fry formula Fitzgerald (392) concluded that "the teacher, reading researcher and publisher cannot confidently use the Fry graph with data based on samples of three" (p. 408) even though that is the number recommended for that particular formula. She advised using "readability estimates with extreme caution" (p. 410).

Based on these concerns, you will not be surprised to find Bruce, Rubin, and Starr (387) stating that "as practical tools either for matching children and texts or for providing guidelines for writers they (readability formulas) are totally inappropriate" (p.1).

We know what you're thinking. Everyone uses readability formulas to help select books. If I don't use a formula, what do I use? This reflects a common insecurity and uncertainty on the part of teachers. Teachers need to become more knowledgeable and more confident about their abilities to make judgments about text based on the characteristics of the text and of the readers (390, 391). Let's consider some ways to accomplish this.

1. Use a formula but use it as a beginning step for a gross screening in the process of selecting books. (377, 390)

2. Become familiar with some of the more widely used formulas, such as the Fry, Raygor and SMOG so you understand how they work and what they can and cannot do for you. Also, take a look at some of the less well-known, such as the Lix and the Rix. Don't forget the possibilities of using computers to apply formulas-- see Chapter VIII. (377, 381, 385)

3. Use a cloze or maze passage which measures readability based on the reader actually reading the text. Remember the discussion in Chapter VII. (381)

4. Use a checklist or a series of questions which cover many aspects of text structure and reader characteristics as a basis for evaluating textbooks. (82, 89, 381, 386, 388, 396)

5. Combine all of the techniques discussed: the readability formula, a checklist, and student response as seen in a cloze or maze passage. (377)

Making Sure the Programs are Working

In this age of accountability, we hardly need to say that program evaluation is an important element in any school program. Reading teachers have traditionally been concerned with evaluations of programs within a lab setting recognizing that "evaluating the results of setting up and operating a reading lab is essential to its effectiveness" (340, p. 635). As reading and content teachers become more involved in a total school approach to reading, they need an understanding of a larger view of program evaluation. Yet, as French (345) points out, this is an area in which reading teachers identified they were deficient.

Effective program evaluation depends on careful planning, execution, coordination, compilation, and communication of results, as well as an evaluation of the program evaluation and can be done internally or by outsiders (376). The depth required to do justice to this topic is beyond the scope of this book, but we can introduce the subject.

We have already identified some ways of evaluating staff development.   Now, let's look at total reading programs in terms of both product and process by looking at some sources of information.

1. Standardized tests. These will focus on growth in reading, i.e., the product of a program. This has already been identified as a major use of standardized reading tests and of the reading subtests of achievement tests. This can measure growth in a reading program for students in special programs. Ince and Colwell (350) believe it can also measure whether "a reading in the content areas program [can] improve students' general reading ability" (p. 15). Early and Sawyer (243) caution that "the use of standardized tests as a single measure of accountability has led to serious abuses" (p. 162) and should be used in conjunction with other approaches.   (243, 340, 345, 350, also see Chapter VII)

2. Observations and observation checklists. This approach can help evaluate process.   In looking at a program, Shannon (403) suggests that observations are a way to "rate whether or not the [effective] practices are actually being used. (244, 345, 403)

3. Surveys of teachers and students. These can provide valuable information on the producers' and the consumers' perceptions of what is actually going on in the program. You might use a survey specifically designed for this purpose, adapt a needs assessment survey, or develop your own. (244, 383, 407)

4. Attitude scales. This measure may help define a change in attitude toward reading as a result of a program by using pre- and postassessments. (350)

5. Library use. Are students using the library more?   The various usage records of the library may give some indications about students' willingness to transfer reading skills. Remember, this is only an indication. (345)

6. Elective reading course enrollments.   Enrollments may indicate that students recognize the usefulness of the content and are motivated to learn more. (345)

7. The all-school Reading Committee. This group can make some very useful contributions to program evaluation by coordinating opinions and data and putting it into a total school perspective. (345, 402)

Summary

The theme of this chapter is not new.   We have consistently pointed out the need for cooperation and collaboration between reading teachers and content teachers. Shannon (403) suggests that "greater dialogue between the content-oriented teachers and process-oriented reading specialists will be a service to researchers, practitioners, and students" (p. 133). Dialogue is important, but it is only a beginning. We need implementation of well thought-out plans on the part of all faculty in a school to insure growth in reading competencies and application of these abilities to content areas.

BIBLIOGRAPHY

Books

375. Bean, Rita M., and Robert M. Wilson.   EFFECTING CHANGE IN
      SCHOOL   READING   PROGRAMS: THE   RESOURCE   ROLE.   Newark,
      Delaware: International Reading Assn., 1981.

      Although reading teachers are currently functioning mainly
      as remedial teachers, Bean and Wilson believe a more useful
      role is that of resource teacher.   They   examine   the
      competencies needed to fulfill this role. Generally, specific
      details are provided which should enable the reader to begin
      the process of self-evaluation and growth needed to meet the
      demands of this role.

376. GUIDELINES FOR REVIEWING READING PROGRAM EVALUATIONS. Edited
      by Michael D. Beck and Mary Seifert.   Study of Reading
      Program   Evaluations   Committee.   Newark,   Delaware:
      International Reading Assn., 1984.

      Beck and Seifert summarize the process by which this IRA
      Committee arrived at guidelines for reviewing plans for an
      internal evaluation of an educational program and for judging
      the quality of external evaluation reports. The guidelines
      cover a wide range of areas in considerable detail although
      not all guidelines can be used in all evaluations.

377. Readence, John E., Thomas W. Bean, and R. Scott Baldwin.
      "Selecting and Introducing the Content Area Textbook."
      CONTENT AREA READING: AN INTEGRATED APPROACH. Dubuque,
      Iowa: Kendall/Hunt, 1981, pp. 56-72.

      Text selection should be based on two sets of factors:
      quantitative and qualitative. The Raygor Readability Estimate
      is presented in detail as an example of a valid, easily
      administered formula that measures quantitative factors.   The
      authors also suggest a checklist to be used in combination
      with this formula as well as a cloze or maze procedure to
      identify qualitative factors.   Because of the importance of
      familiarizing students with the text, detailed guidelines are
      provided for introducing the text in the beginning of the
      term.

378. Shanker, James L. GUIDELINES FOR SUCCESSFUL READING STAFF
      DEVELOPMENT. Newark, Delaware: International Reading Assn.,
      1982.

      This IRA Service Bulletin takes the reading specialist from
      the point of conducting a staff development needs assessment
      to evaluating the staff development activities after they have
      concluded. Major steps to be taken and responsibilities to be
      assumed are outlined. Some specific forms are included.

379. Tonjes, Marian J., and Miles V. Zintz. "Meeting Diverse Needs
      through   Classroom   Organization."   TEACHING
      READING/THINKING/STUDY   SKILLS   IN   CONTENT   CLASSROOMS.
      Dubuque, Iowa: Wm. C. Brown, 1981, pp. 255-274.

      The authors describe organizational alternatives for meeting
      the diverse needs of secondary students within a content
      classroom. A brief overview is provided of these needs, with
      the major focus of the chapter on how to organize groups and
      materials using various teaching formats.

380. Vacca, Jo Anne L. "Working with Content Area Teachers."
      CONTENT AREA READING. By Richard T. Vacca. Boston: Little,
      Brown, 1981, pp. 305-329.

      Vacca gives detailed guidelines for planning, executing and
      evaluating staff development programs. She has included
      forms, activities and procedures that can be used and adapted
      in a variety of situations.

381. Vacca, Richard T. "Estimating Text Difficulty." CONTENT AREA
      READING. Boston: Little, Brown, 1981, pp. 257-277.

      Vacca reviews the limitations of readability formulas,
      examines the Fry readability graph, the Raygor readability
      estimate, and the SMOG Grading as well as the cloze procedure
      and the maze technique, and suggests criteria for teacher
      evaluation of text readability.

382. Vacca, Richard T. "Organizing the Content Classroom."
      CONTENT AREA READING. Boston: Little, Brown, 1981, pp. 25-
      55.

      Vacca considers organization of instruction as an important
      key to fostering active reading by students. He makes many
      suggestions for organizing lessons and for organizing the
      classroom.

                            Periodicals

383. Alexander, Clara Franklin. "Urban Secondary School Students
      Evaluate Their Reading Program." Paper presented at the
      Annual Meeting of the New York State English Council,
      Grossinger, New York, October 18-21, 1981. 27pp. (ED 210
      625)

      Alexander presents the results of a survey done with
      remedial secondary students in New York City to determine
      their views on their reading needs and their reading programs.
      The discussion is useful in providing reading specialists with
      guidelines based on the results from this particular group as
      to skills, methodologies, materials, and activities that might
      at least be a starting point with other groups. Perhaps even
      more useful are the suggestions about conducting such a
      survey.

384. Anders, Patricia L. "Dream of a Secondary Reading Program?
      People are the Key." JOURNAL OF READING 24 (January 1981):
      316-320.

      Anders advocates the formation of a reading committee
      composed of representatives from every content area in a
      school. This group can provide a voice at the various
      department meetings, knowledge of specific content areas and
      their needs, advice on and support for new ideas, and shared
      responsibility for the development of a reading program. The
      author gives guidelines on the selection of members and their
      function and responsibilities.

385. Anderson, Jonathan. "Lix and Rix: Variations on a Little-
      Known Readability Index." JOURNAL OF READING 26 (March
      1983): 490-496.

      Anderson describes a readability index, Lix, which measures
      readability using sentence length and percentage of words of
      seven or more letters. He cites two studies to establish the
      validity of the measure. The author has simplified the
      procedure while maintaining its validity. Instructions for
      using this simplified procedure, Rix, are included.

386. Armbruster, Bonnie B., and Thomas H. Anderson. CONTENT AREA
      TEXTBOOKS. Reading Education Report No. 23. Urbana,
      Illinois: Illinois University, Center for the Study of
      Reading, July 1981. 68pp. (ED 203 298)

      Armbruster and Anderson examine four text characteristics
      which enable the reader to learn from the text. These
      include: structure, coherence, unity, and audience
      appropriateness. The authors provide many clear examples of
      each and give detailed explanations and forms to use in
      selecting and evaluating textbooks.

387. Bruce, Bertram, Andee Rubin, and Kathleen Starr.   WHY
      READABILITY FORMULAS FAIL. Reading Education Report No. 28.
      Urbana, Illinois: Illinois University, Center for the Study
      of Reading, August 1981. 17pp. (ED 205 915)

      Bruce, Rubin and Starr examine in some detail the
      deficiencies in readability formulas: they do not take into
      account current reading theory; they have a "shaky"
      statistical base; they are inappropriate for matching student
      and text and for providing guidelines to authors. The
      conclusion is that readability formulas are not useful and
      cannot "improve on intuitive estimates of the readability of a
      text" (p.11).

388. Clewell, Suzanne F., and Anne M. Cliffton. "Examining Your
      Textbook for Comprehensibility." JOURNAL OF READING 27
      (December 1983): 219-224.

      Clewell and Cliffton provide a detailed checklist to use in

selecting texts and planning instruction which includes
textual aids, content, coherence, types of discourse, and
language and style.

389. Colwell, Clyde G., Carol Adams, Mickey Bogart, Mary Jo
Harbour, Nancy Walker, Jan Wichman, Jeanne Pohlman, and
Elizabeth Ince. A READING GUIDE: ASSISTING CONTENT AREA
TEACHERS. Manhattan, Kansas: Kansas State University and
the Manhattan Unified School District, 1983. 96pp. (ED 228
633)

This guide is the product of a collaborative effort in staff
development involving a local high school and a university.
The guide presents a brief description of this joint venture
and sample lessons. The areas covered in the staff
development program included vocabulary and concepts,
listening, comprehension, informal diagnosis, questioning,
patterns of organization, prediction and curiosity arousal,
graphic aids and study skills.

390. Crismore, Avon. "Readability and the Black Box." Paper
presented at the Annual Meeting of the Indiana State Council
of the International Reading Assn., Indianapolis, Indiana,
March 26-28, 1981. 21pp. (ED 203 295)

Crismore reviews current literature concerning readability
and provides a useful overview and framework for understanding
the problems associated with readability formulas. His
conclusion is that we need more research here and a variety of
formulas to use with different readers and for different
purposes.

391. Dreyer, Lois Goodman. "Readability and Responsibility."
JOURNAL OF READING 27 (January 1984): 334-338.

Dreyer identifies the limitations of readability formulas
and suggests that because of their failure to measure many of
the variables we associate with the reading process, teachers
need to combine their own assessments of text readability with
those of the publisher. If materials appear difficult,
teachers should use strategies that enable students to
comprehend. The author provides examples such as activating
prior information, questioning, and developing technical
vocabulary.

392. Fitzgerald, Gisela G. "How Many Samples Give a Good
Readability Estimate?--The Fry Graph." JOURNAL OF READING
24 (February 1981): 404-410.

Fitzgerald addresses a problem that concerns content
teachers. Are the three samples of the text recommended by
the Fry graph sufficient to arrive at an accurate reading
level? She concludes that because of variations within a
single text, they are probably not sufficient and suggests
using readability estimates with "extreme caution" (p. 410).

393. Gove, Mary K. "Getting High School Teachers to Use Content Reading Strategies." JOURNAL OF READING 25 (November 1981): 113-116.

Gove reviews research related to effectiveness of staff development, makes suggestions based on this review, and describes an effective inservice program. Programs for staff development need administrative support, must be related to school goals, require three to five years to develop, should be the result of teacher planning and must provide choices to teachers. The author stresses the need to adapt the staff development procedures to meet individual teacher needs. A program is described which illustrates the points made in the article.

394. Haggard, Martha Rapp. "Organizing Secondary Remedial Instruction." JOURNAL OF READING 23 (October 1979): 30-32.

Haggard identifies sustained interaction between the teacher and the student as critical in remedial instruction. These students are not independent learners; they need instruction, not practice in completing workbooks. To achieve this, she proposes assigning blocks of time to individual students and suggests how this can be done.

395. International Reading Association Paraprofessionals and Reading Committee. "An Evaluative Survey of Reading/Tutoring Programs Using Paraprofessionals." JOURNAL OF READING 25 (March 1982): 554-558.

This article reports on a survey conducted by the committee of 82 schools in South Australia and 40 in the United States to determine how paraprofessionals are being used in reading programs. They identified 16 characteristics of effective reading/tutoring programs which are outlined in the article. The aim in reading programs seems to be to use the paraprofessionals as extensively as possible while giving them as much training and supervision as possible. For example, interaction of the paraprofessionals with teachers and parents and inservice training head the list of program characteristics. The survey gives an idea of the broad range of uses being made of paraprofessional help.

396. Irwin, Judith Westphal, and Carol A. Davis. "Assessing Readability: The Checklist Approach." JOURNAL OF READING 24 (November 1980): 124-130.

The authors present a detailed checklist covering a wide variety of items related to understandability and learnability of texts. Current readability formulas are judged inadequate to determine whether a text can be comprehended and remembered. Because of this, the authors suggest using the checklist to select text and to make instructional decisions.

397. Joyce, Bruce, and Beverly Showers.   "The   Coaching   of
     Teaching." EDUCATIONAL LEADERSHIP 40 (October 1982): 4-10.

     Joyce and Showers propose four essential elements for staff
     development: studying the theoretical basis for the new model,
     observing a demonstration of the process, practicing with
     peers and students, and coaching by peers to insure transfer
     of the new model into the teachers' repertoires of strategies.
     It is the last element that is examined in detail with a
     number of useful examples. The caveat that acquiring teaching
     skills takes time is an important one.

398. Kingore, Bertha W., and Ruth J. Kurth.   "A Workshop for
     Teachers in Teaching Reading Comprehension."   READING
     TEACHER 35 (November 1981): 173-179.

     Kingore and Kurth provide detailed instructions on one way
     to present a workshop to classroom teachers on comprehension
     tasks and with application to content area reading
     instruction.

399. Lindsey, James F., and Annette Dambrosio Runquist.   "Clinical
     Supervision: A Tool for the Reading Specialist." JOURNAL OF
     READING 27 (October 1983): 48-50.

     Lindsey and Runquist suggest that the reading specialist is
     the ideal person to provide leadership in effective reading
     instruction by giving the classroom teacher constructive
     feedback through nonthreatening observations. Guidelines are
     provided for pre- and postconferences.

400. Mangieri, John N., and Mary J. Heimberger.   "Perceptions of
     the Reading Consultant's Role."   JOURNAL OF READING 23
     (March 1980): 527-530.

     Mangieri and Heimberger surveyed reading specialists and
     school administrators in five states from urban, suburban and
     rural districts with students from a range of socioeconomic
     groups. The purpose was to identify what the respondents
     thought the reading consultant's role should be. Principals
     placed instructor and diagnostician at the top of the list and
     inservice leader and resource person at the bottom of the
     list. Reading consultants reversed the placement. They
     perceived that inservice leader and resource person were the
     most important role they should have. This difference of
     opinion may be a source of difficulties in some schools and
     should be addressed by both parties.

401. McNinch, George.   "DIRP: A Theory Based Instructional Strategy
     for Reading Teachers."   READING IMPROVEMENT 18 (Winter
     1981): 350-353.

     DIRP includes: demonstration, interaction, reclarification,
     and practice. McNinch relates this form of direct instruction
     to instructional theory and advocates these four stages for

most reading instruction. Details are provided which can facilitate the application of DIRP by the teacher.

402. Shannon, Albert J. "Raising Reading Consciousness: A Practical Framework for Effective Reading Resource." READING IMPROVEMENT 18 (Spring 1981): 56-58.

Shannon views the reading teacher as a change agent, responsible for alerting content teachers to necessary content reading skills, joining the process of reading with content instruction, and training content teachers in appropriate strategies. He provides a hierarchy of steps to accomplish this which depend on the active cooperation of all parties. The steps include awareness of skills, validation of their usefulness, establishment of priorities, division of labor so that all teachers do not need to teach all skills, assessment of the teacher's ability to teach the skill and the student's need to be taught, development of strategies to teach the skills, and decentralization to enable the content teachers to assume leadership and control.

403. Shannon, Albert J. "Monitor Reading Instruction in the Content Areas." JOURNAL OF READING 28 (November 1984): 128-134.

Shannon proposes the use of a rating checklist to identify effective classroom practices in reading, to allow teachers to rate their own ability to use and their actual usage of these practices, and to allow observers to determine whether the practices are actually being used in classrooms. The checklist covers assessing appropriateness of materials, preparing students to read, leading discussions and questioning, encouraging recreational reading, and understanding and supporting the concept of content area reading.

404. Smith, Christine C., Carolyn Burch, and Grace Warren. "Management Systems in Secondary Reading Classrooms." READING HORIZONS 20 (Summer 1980): 207-214.

The authors describe a management system that "reflects a wholistic (reading-language arts) approach to the teaching of reading" (p. 207) and allows reading teachers and English teachers to work cooperatively with groups of students. Information is provided on scheduling, classroom organization, reading lab organization, and record keeping.

405. Stein, Harry. "Building Bridges Between Workshops and Content Area Reading Instruction." JOURNAL OF READING 24 (March 1981): 523-527.

Stein proposes using planning charts and checklists to overcome the common problem of lack of implementation by workshop participants of newly learned skills in their content teaching. He provides two examples to be used for planning lessons which can be adapted to a variety of workshops. The author also offers a number of practical suggestions for implementing inservice training into the classroom.

406. Stopper, Raymond. "Reverse the Image: Involve the Public in Reading and Writing." ENGLISH JOURNAL 71 (October 1982): 26-30.

Suggestions are made for short sessions with parents to help them understand and appreciate the complexities of high school reading and writing tasks. The aim is to demonstrate that basic skill instruction is not sufficient. Students need and are receiving instruction on a variety of levels. Reading teachers and English teachers can take the ideas presented here and develop their own parent sessions.

407. Vacca, Jo Anne L. "Surveys: Valuable Tools for the Reading Consultant." READING HORIZONS 20 (Summer 1980): 268-275.

Surveys are more than a way to collect information; they can be valuable tools for strengthening a grant proposal. Vacca analyzes types of surveys and gives two examples. One illustrates a needs assessment prior to staff development for content teachers and the other identifies student reading skills in a content classroom.

408. Vacca, Jo Anne L. "How to Be an Effective Staff Developer for Content Teachers." JOURNAL OF READING 26 (January 1983): 293-296.

Vacca reports on a study conducted with more than 500 elementary, middle and secondary school teachers on the characteristics of effective and ineffective staff developers. She reports in some detail on the four factors that appeared significant: content delivery, personal influence, professional competence, and arrangements. Although the results were what we probably would have predicted, they serve as a reminder to staff developers of the need to provide for such things as active involvement, relevant materials, useful demonstrations, enthusiastic and organized presentations, respect for questions, and comfortable arrangements.

409. Wade, Suzanne E. "A Synthesis of the Research for Improving Reading in the Social Studies." REVIEW OF EDUCATIONAL RESEARCH 53 (Winter 1983): 461-497.

Wade reviewed a considerable body of research dealing with the effects of various kinds of reading instruction in a variety of settings for improving reading in social studies. "The foremost conclusion to be drawn from this review of research is that teacher involvement in the design of an instructional program and teachers' ability to modify it as they see fit during the implementation phase are crucial components of a successful treatment" (pp. 487-488). She suggests that one way to achieve teacher involvement is to have cooperatively planned research projects and in-service courses.

410. Webber, Elizabeth A. "Organizing and Scheduling the Secondary Reading Program." JOURNAL OF READING 27 (April 1984): 594-596.

Webber advocates involving the content teacher and allowing for changing needs in organizing and planning reading programs. She details five different plans that can be included in a secondary program. Only one of these is the traditional individual scheduling of students into a reading class. The others all require some form of cooperation with the content teachers.

411. Werdmann, Anne M., and James King. "Teaching Teachers to Question Questions." READING WORLD 23 (March 1984): 218-225.

Werdmann and King describe a training program designed to teach questioning techniques to preservice teachers and to insure transfer of the techniques to classroom instruction. Explicit detail is provided for both affective and cognitive questions. There is much here that can be adapted for inservice teachers as well.

AUTHOR INDEX

P. = Page Number(s), E. = Entry Number(s)

Adams, C., P. 223, 224, E. 389
Alexander, C.F., P. 230, E. 383
Alexander, J.E., P. 153, E. 287
Alkin, M.C., P. 30, 33, 34, E. 41, 72
Alley, G.R., P. 199, 200, 201, E. 344
Alvermann, D.E., P. 54, 105, 106, E. 95, 189
Anders, P.L., P. 221, E. 384
Anderson, J., P. 229, E. 385
Anderson, R.C., P. 4, 27, 28, 146, 148, 152, E. 1, 51
Anderson, T.H., P. 51, 54, 106, 107, 111, 112, 113, 114, 229, E. 96, 180, 386
Andersson, B.V., P. 200, 201, 202, E. 339
Annacone, D., P. 80, 83, 85, E. 148
Appleman, D., P. 51, 57, E. 83
Armbruster, B.B., P. 50, 51, 54, 87, 89, 90, 106, 107, 111, 112, 113, 114, 229, E. 82, 96, 149, 180, 386
Arnold, M.T., P. 52, 54, E. 97
Arthur, S.V., P. 25, 26, 27, E. 38
Ashby-Davis, C., P. 194, 223, 226, E. 348
Asher, S.R., P. 125, 126, 127, 128, 129, E. 211
Atwell, M.A., P. 78, 82, 224, E. 150
Auten, A., P. 130, 174, 177, 189, 191, 192, 229, 230, E. 212, 294, 340
Badiali, B.J., P. 197, E. 317, 318
Baker, L., P. 4, 87, 88, 89, 112, E. 2, 133
Balajthy, E., P. 171, 172, 177, E. 295
Baldwin, R.S., P. 2, 3, 25, 26,

27, 29, 30, 80, 83, 85, 86, 90, 106, 112, 113, 114, 141, 142, 145, 149, 150, 152, 153, 155, 194, 197, 220, 222, 223, 224, 226, 227, 229, E. 9, 42, 57, 61, 142, 183, 260, 369, 377
Barnitz, J.G., P. 200, 201, 202, E. 339
Bartlett, B.J., P. 51, 53, 54, E. 98
Bates, G.W., P. 201, E. 341
Baumann, J.V., P. 9, E. 28
Beach, R., P. 51, 57, E. 83
Bean, R.M., P. 219, 220, E. 375
Bean, T.W., P. 2, 3, 25, 26, 27, 29, 30, 80, 83, 85, 86, 90, 106, 112, 113, 114, 141, 142, 145, 149, 150, 152, 153, 155, 197, 224, 229, E. 9, 42, 57, 142, 183, 260, 377
Bell, D.S., P. 178, E. 316
Bellows, B.P., P. 30, E. 62
Berryhill, P., P. 196, E. 319
Bishop, D., P. 130, E. 205
Blair, T., P. 9, E. 21
Blake, K.M., P. 148, 149, E. 267
Blanchard, J.S., P. 172, 173, 174, 175, 177, 179, 180, E. 292
Blohm, P.J., P. 171, 174, 175, 177, 178, 179, E. 296
Bogart, M., P. 223, 224, E. 389
Borchardt, K.M., P. 112, E. 192
Bowman, M., P. 54, 196, E. 99
Brannock, V.M., P. 190, E. 332
Bransford, J.D., P. 1, E. 12
Brophy, J., P. 124, 125, 126, 128, E. 213
Brown, A.L., P. 1, 3, 4, 6, 49, 61, 77, 87, 88, 89, 90, 91, 112, 142, 145, 154, 155, 225, E. 2, 3, 12, 13, 133, 149, 163
Bruce, B., P. 228, E. 387

SUBJECT INDEX

P. = Page Number(s), E. = Entry Number(s)

Administrative support. See
Reading programs and Staff
development
Achievement tests. See
Standardized tests
Advanced organizer. See Graphic
aids
Analogies. See Vocabulary
development
Anticipation guides. See
Graphic aids
Applied level of comprehension.
See Levels of comprehension
Assessment, P. 141-170. See
also Computers, Informal tests
and Standardized tests
  choosing alternatives, P. 146-
  147, E. 51, 154, 242, 246,
  249, 253, 254, 258, 261,
  262, 273, 290
  purposes of, P. 141-142, 155-
  156, E. 154, 242, 243, 244,
  249, 254, 255, 258, 260, 290
  theory and research, P. 142-
  145, E. 47, 244, 247, 250,
  251, 252, 253, 254, 263,
  265, 266, 267, 268, 274,
  275, 278, 279, 282, 283, 286
Attitude inventories, teachers,
P. 224, E. 11, 27. See also
Content teachers
Bilingual students. See
Students with special needs,
ESL
Black students. See Students
with special needs
Cloze procedure. See also
Informal tests
  computers and, P. 178, E. 293,
  316
  instruction using, P. 54, E.
  77, 112
Comprehension monitoring, P. 87-
91. See also Metacognition

and Modeling
comprehension fostering and,
P. 88, 89, E. 14, 133, 141,
152, 163, 170, 174
coping strategies, P. 89, E.
163
fix-up strategies, P. 90, E.
30, 149, 153, 162, 164, 170,
177
instructing in, P. 90, E. 14,
30, 139, 142, 147, 152, 153,
163, 164, 168, 174, 175
knowledge of reading process
and, P. 89, 90, E. 30, 139,
142, 147, 149, 153, 162,
168, 174
levels of comprehension and,
P. 60, E. 115, 121, 122, 125
prior knowledge and, P. 80, E.
170
questions and, P. 89, E. 141,
163, 164, 170, 174
role in reading, P. 3, 4, 6,
87-89, E. 2, 3, 30, 133,
135, 143, 144, 149, 153,
164, 170, 174, 175, 177, 185
strategies for students, P.
89-90, E. 14, 30, 121, 135,
139, 141, 152, 153, 162,
163, 164, 168, 170, 171,
173, 174, 175
study skills and, P. 109-110,
112, 115, E. 13, 133, 155,
185, 189
Computers, P. 171-188. See also
Cloze, Motivation and Studying
advantages of, P. 172-173, E.
291, 292, 293, 295, 303,
307, 308, 315
assessment of reading, P. 178,
E. 253, 296, 309, 316
-assisted instruction, P. 171-
172, 178-179, E. 291, 292,
293, 295, 296, 297, 298,